BY DONOVAN CAMPBELL

Joker One
The Leader's Code

THE LEADER'S CODE

THE LEADER'S CODE

——————— ★ ———————

MISSION, CHARACTER, SERVICE,
AND GETTING THE JOB
DONE

DONOVAN CAMPBELL

RANDOM HOUSE

NEW YORK

Published in the United States by Random House,
an imprint of The Random House Publishing Group,
a division of Random House, Inc., New York.

RANDOM HOUSE and colophon are registered
trademarks of Random House, Inc.

LIBRARY OF CONGRESS CATALOGING-IN-PUBLICATION DATA
Campbell, Donovan.
The leader's code : mission, character, service,
and getting the job done / Donovan Campbell.
p. cm.
ISBN 978-0-8129-9293-9
eBook ISBN 978-0-679-64420-0
1. Leadership—United States. 2. Servant leadership—United States.
3. United States. Marine Corps—Case studies. I. Title.
HM1261.C36 2013
303.3'40973—dc23   2012035575

Printed in the United States of America on acid-free paper

www.atrandom.com

2 4 6 8 9 7 5 3 1

FIRST EDITION

Book design by Mary A. Wirth

This book is dedicated to my mother and father, who have selflessly modeled servant-leadership for my four brothers and me throughout our entire lives.

The greatest among you will be your servant. For those who exalt themselves will be humbled, and those who humble themselves will be exalted.

—Jesus Christ

CONTENTS

INTRODUCTION

America suffers from a leadership crisis. The economic downturn of the past three years has highlighted this shortcoming, but the downturn is only the symptom, not the cause, of our malaise. As the disease has deepened, institutions that define our views of ourselves and of our country, among them business and government, have lost substantial credibility. Their leaders are largely viewed as greedy, selfish, hypocritical, criminal, shortsighted, incompetent, or all of the above.

This widespread destruction of trust has left a leadership vacuum that is slowly becoming filled with despair. For the first time since modern polling began, a majority of Americans believe that their country will be worse for their children than it is for them. We trust no single leader, or class of leaders, to fix what is broken, because no one has offered up a compelling vision backed by powerful positive examples. In fact, the opposite has occurred—whether they are sports figures like Lance Armstrong, political crusaders like Eliot Spitzer, or business titans like Dick Fuld, Jon Corzine, or Bernie Madoff, many of the leaders we trusted have been revealed as cheaters, criminals, or incompetents. We have lost faith in our leaders, and when faith leaves, hope soon follows.

Much of the blame for this sad state of affairs rests in our business class. The spectacular bursting of the housing bubble caused the high tide of our economy to recede, and as the waves have rolled out they have left corruption, lies, and outright criminality in their wake. Though some players are reaping what they sowed, not all are receiving their just rewards, a fact that fuels a deep sense of unfairness across America. Making matters worse, very few, if any, leaders have admitted fault and taken responsibility for the messes they created. And all this at a time when many ordinary Americans have lost their savings, their jobs, and the roofs over their heads.

But if our trust in business is bad, our trust in politics is worse. Those we elect to write our laws often seem to have trouble obeying them, fueling a widespread perception across America that politicians hold Americans to one set of rules—the law—and themselves to another—personal/political convenience. Recent years have witnessed an IRS head who hasn't paid his own taxes, congressional tax-dodgers who propose to raise levies on their countrymen, and leaders on both sides of the aisle who publicly clamor for reform but privately block all efforts to fix whichever institutions contribute most heavily to their reelection campaigns. Hypocrisy and corruption seem the most nonpartisan qualities in evidence. Every month brings yet another story about a politician taking bribes, or "forgetting" to pay their taxes, or diverting public money to private projects, or soliciting prostitutes even as they prosecuted their johns.

Making matters worse, no political leader has emerged with a credible plan to fix our dysfunctional system. Legislators—Republicans and Democrats alike—arrive in Congress promising to clean up corruption and increase transparency, but the ethics violations, the closed-door deals, and the secret earmarks continue unabated regardless of who is in charge. And few will compromise, for most are concerned solely with vanquishing the opposition at all cost. Small wonder, then, that polling reveals that public trust in government is at its lowest measure in decades. We have witnessed two whipsaw elections in just four years, as Americans have tried one party and then the other. Both have been weighed in the balance and found wanting.

The reasons for our current mess are complicated, but one important underlying cause is that many in our leadership class have ceased to focus on building individual character. They may pursue a winning business strategy or a political victory, but they very rarely chase after virtue with the same energy with which they chase after fame and fortune. The goal is the ends, with scant regard for the means. Indeed, it often seems that sacrificing character is the price of success in one's chosen arena, and a win-at-any-cost mentality is arguably the most common trait among the ultrasuccessful. Many of our most prominent leaders are supremely talented, intelligent, driven, and visionary. Far fewer are righteous; fewer still even try.

In the same way that leaders have lost focus on virtue, so also has our leadership literature wandered. For at least the past twenty years, the vast majority of books on leadership have focused on methodology, that is, on practical steps for getting wherever it is that you want to go. A reader can pick up books on how to network their way to promotion, how to transform a small business into a large one, how to inspire others, and how to achieve personal happiness along with a large bank account and a small waistline. Many leadership books are little more than treasure maps to health and wealth, giving scant attention to the basic question of who you should become along the journey. There are few, if any, works that outline the various virtues, or character traits, necessary for a life of true significance. There are fewer still that challenge their readers to eschew material success, and perhaps even happiness (for a time), if it comes at the cost of character.

The problem with these how-to leadership books in today's climate is this: America has lost faith in its leaders precisely because those leaders have done *exactly* what the books have said to do. Our leaders have effectively pursued gain—they have run the playbooks well—but their material success has often come at the cost of their individual character. Many business and political leaders have been remarkably good at achieving their personal goals, but we do not trust them anymore, because the result of success divorced from morals has wreaked havoc on our broader society.

———

However, there is one national institution that is widely respected both for its virtue and its effectiveness. This institution teaches a strong, clear leadership model, one that is routinely put to the test under the most demanding circumstances imaginable. This institution bases its model on well-defined virtues—personal character traits—and it teaches these virtues to every one of its leaders through rigorous training that happens immediately upon entrance.

Unsurprisingly, this institution commands widespread admiration from Americans of all stripes, and its leaders are nearly universally respected. Indeed, this organization seems to be the only thing in America that Americans uniformly trust—a recent poll put its approval rating at more than 70 percent. What national institution could command such widespread admiration at a time of such widespread national disenchantment? The United States military.

Why is this? Though many have varied and opposing views about war in general and America's wars in particular, most recognize that the men and women fighting them voluntarily give of themselves in pursuit of a worthy goal. The military's stated mission is to serve America by protecting her against all enemies foreign and domestic. Its members sacrifice themselves, their families, their comfort, and their material well-being in furtherance of that mission. They are the opposite of the how-to leaders, for they do not study the pursuit of wealth, or fame, or comfort, or even something as simple as happiness.

Instead, they deploy to the most dangerous countries in the world, endure some of the harshest conditions imaginable, and occasionally give up life and limb. They leave their families behind, sacrificing time with them that they will never get back. In return, they get very little—a soldier will never be rich, and they are rarely powerful. They do what they do because they believe what they say—that protecting their country and its citizens is a more important mission than increasing their individual comfort and well-being. In a world disillusioned by leaders who say one thing and do another, the American military is one of the few places where we can find a whole class of people whose actions clearly support their words and their beliefs.

In spite of the respect that the military engenders, its values and its leadership model are widely misunderstood. Most believe that it is a hierarchical, top-down institution in which orders are unquestioningly obeyed and decisions and information flow one way. They assume that the rank structure ensures subservience and that soldiers rarely think for themselves. I've been told many times that "the way that the military leads could never work in _____." The blank is usually filled in with the unspoken words *my environment* or *the real world*. People also assume that order and discipline are the overriding, and maybe even the only, values that the military formally instills in its members. But people are wrong about this assumption and they are equally wrong about the effectiveness of the military leadership model in contexts outside the military.

So what does the military really teach about leadership? Put simply, it teaches a servant-leadership model. In simplest terms, servant-leadership teaches that a leader exists to serve a mission first, their teams second, and themselves a distant third. Leaders understand what they are doing and why they are doing it. They put the health of their organization, and the success of its mission, ahead of their personal well-being. Servant leaders take care of others before they take care of themselves. They sacrifice daily to ensure the well-being of their people. There is nothing that they ask their teams to do that they will not, and do not, do themselves. They lead by example, asking that others observe their actions rather than listen to their words.

To use an analogy, in the servant-leadership model, the leader is like the trunk of a tree and the team is like its branches. Whereas many picture the leader at the tip of a pyramid, sitting atop an organization designed to support them and enable their decision-making, in servant-leadership that picture is turned on its head. In a servant-leader world, the leader supports a team as the tree trunk supports its branches, digging deep, funneling nutrients upward so that the branches can climb ever higher and bear fruit. It is the trunk that does the dirty work, that eschews the sun, that exists so that others can succeed. It is the branches that reap the rewards of that hard work and the branches that are expected to bear fruit. If the two work together to support each other, then it is the entire organism that benefits. However, only servant-leadership can cause this transition to happen.

Servant-leadership compels leaders to bring their moral character to life every day in a way that allows others to believe in them, their mission, and their values. It is this model that inspires others to follow not because they *have* to but because they *want* to. It is this model that compels teams to risk their lives repeatedly; to do things that they know may very well get them killed. It is this model that keeps people motivated and engaged to perform necessary but hard missions, missions where there is absolutely no personal gain and every possible personal loss. Yet soldiers perform these missions, day in and day out, because they know that they serve one another, and they serve a noble calling.

From the moment I entered Marine basic officer training, the servant-leadership model was pounded into our heads. We were told that we had been entrusted with a sacred mission: the defense of our country and the defense of those who could not defend themselves. We were told that to achieve this mission we were entrusted with the most precious resource imaginable: the lives of young men and women. We were told that the mothers of America had given us these lives—their children— with the expectation that we would return them better than we found them; and that if we couldn't do that, then we had better have lost their children while pursuing something worth more than our lives.

We were told that our rank—particularly our status as officers— entitled us to one thing and one thing only: a heightened responsibility to serve. We were told that with promotion came only increased duty, not increased privilege. We were told that our job was to daily lay down our lives, literally and figuratively, for the two things that were far more important than were we: our mission and our team. We were told that our job was to make our team members the best Marines, and the best young people, that they could possibly be. We were to support and empower them, not vice versa. We were told to encourage free thought and open ideas, for with lives on the line, no one, no matter how low their rank, could be discouraged from putting forth a solution that might very well save many lives. And we were told that if we could do these things, then our team certainly would not fail.

When combat came, we tried hard to do what we were told, and we found out that the model works. It is servant-leadership that inspires nineteen-year-olds to charge a machine gun position, or to jump on a grenade, or to drag a wounded child out of withering machine gun fire. It is servant-leadership that allows a group of college-age kids to walk down the middle of an open road, every single morning, looking for bombs with their naked eyes and finding them five feet away. It is servant-leadership that keeps these teams able to keep doing the dangerous missions, day in and day out, without quitting once, for months and even years at a time. When the most certain outcome of any given course of action is wounds or death, and there is absolutely no personal gain for taking that course of action, the only thing that allows you to persevere is the bone-deep understanding that your leader knows the mission and that the mission is important; that your leader cares about you more than they do themselves; and that your leaders will be making the exact same sacrifices that they ask of you.

In the Marines, servant-leadership demands a greater degree of sacrifice from its officers—commissioned and noncommissioned—than from its foot soldiers. Servant-leadership requires that a lieutenant shout "follow me" as they run toward gunfire at the head of their men; that a captain eat only after every one of their two hundred Marines have been served (which often means not eating at all); that a sergeant major put off sleep after three days without it so that they can make certain that everyone under their charge has a place to sleep. The Marine Corps did a phenomenal job instilling a sense of mission in its members, and I contend that every leader, if they hope to be effective over the long run, must develop a strong individual mission and equally strong individual character.

Ironically, *character* is a word that is often used, maybe even overused, in today's popular culture. Talking heads pontificate about it throughout the 24/7 news cycle. Business leaders routinely cite "character and competence" as necessary ingredients for success. Sports announcers talk about the "character" of outstanding athletes as something that contributes to their tremendous feats on the field. Politicians refer to the crucial importance of national and individual "character" (or bemoan its supposedly inexorable decline). Teachers talk about instilling character in their students; parents talk about instilling it in their children. Character is widely agreed on as a universal good.

But when pressed, very few can precisely define what they mean by the term. Are there individual virtues that make up the desirable-yet-nebulous end-state we call character? Is there a specific morality that must be followed? What is it, precisely, that we want our leaders to become when we talk about people of character? People who are good at their jobs and avoid outright criminality? People who have superior talents that permit them a different moral standard? People who get through life without hurting others, by and large? Or is character something more than simply the visible absence of evil? Are there certain moral traits that we think leaders *must* possess? Is there any absolute standard that they absolutely must pursue?

Very few leaders can answer these questions, in part because character-based leadership has been largely ignored and in part because as a society we shy away from absolutes. So, when it comes time to drill down to what, exactly, constitutes "character," we usually find ourselves at a complete loss. We prefer to talk vaguely about what "character" is not rather than define precisely what "character" is. It makes us uncomfortable to try to pin down the specifics surrounding this word, for pinning down specifics takes us into the realm of the absolute, the certain, the unavoidable.

If a leader did want to nail it down, there are few, if any, places to turn for advice. Our business schools are largely technocratic institutions that focus on methodology, on teaching a particular trade well. For example, students learn how to analyze a balance sheet, how to conduct a marketing campaign, how to identify decision makers in the sales cycle, and how to consider stakeholders when making decisions. They do not study morality. Other graduate finishing schools—politics, law, education, liberal arts, and even medicine—are largely the same. They may discuss ethics as they relate to highly context-specific situations—attorney-client privilege, say, or end-of-life treatment—but they do not delve broadly into the study of right and wrong as applied to daily life and daily leadership. Schools do not see that as rightly their province.

The business world is similarly lacking. First off, promotion is largely a function of excellent individual performance or of time. It rarely occurs because someone demonstrates a specific set of desirable and well-defined moral virtues. But the skill set needed to do well as an individual contributor is very different from that needed to excel as a leader. And the pressure to simply go and do, particularly to perform financially—to meet the weekly, monthly, or quarterly numbers—rarely allows for significant time-out for training in technical leadership skills (for example, how to conduct effective meetings), let alone training in individual character building or personal reflection. Businesses also typically take the same approach to character, as do our technical finishing schools: teaching applied virtue (something very different from company policy, which is itself simply a substitute for virtue) in a holistic, systematic fashion is not their role.

In fact, though many of our social institutions value formal character training, most assume that that training will happen somewhere else. Schools assume that it will happen at home. Homes assume that it will happen at church, or at school, or perhaps through some general process of osmosis. Businesses largely assume that people already have character when they hire them because it was taught at home or at school or at church. And churches, if they are attended, usually have people for less than an hour a week.

Unsurprisingly, then, character is something that is rarely pursued with the same discipline, focus, and intensity with which we pursue most other things in life. How can it be, when there is no consensus on what constitutes character, little guidance on how to run after it, and no clear starting point to even begin? Thus, aspiring leaders have less direction, and fewer resources, on how to achieve the one thing that every institution views as a universal good than they do on how to lose weight.

But character must be pursued intentionally if it is to be attained. It does not happen as an afterthought and it does not happen by accident. In this it is like everything else at which we hope to be successful. Running a business doesn't happen without planning and hard work. Neither does winning a football game, or losing fifty pounds, or cutting down household debt, or taking an enemy stronghold in battle. Anything that we want to achieve takes clarity of mission up front and then focus, structure, and persistence in execution. We need to know where it is we want to go, how it is we need to get there, and what it is we need to do to stay fit enough to make the journey if we want to have any hope of reaching the final destination. Character is not something that we are born with but something that we develop if we can only take the time and make the effort. Good leadership is not something done by accident or happenstance; rather, it is an outflowing of character applied to life.

However, character cannot be applied in a vacuum. Any prospective leader must identify an overarching mission that complements the pursuit of virtues, a mission that orders their lives and transcends their own personal well-being. In fact, mission and character are so intertwined as to be inseparable. If we want the latter, we can only pursue it in the context of the former. Otherwise we will find ourselves playing a game wherein winning is impossible, for the rules are undefined, unidentifiable, and constantly mutable.

In the Marines, a mission and its accompanying virtues are flowed into action via a servant-leader model. The model rests on a simple proposition: a leader's role in life is to put their mission first, the welfare of their team second, and their own welfare a distant third. However, while simple in concept, servant-leadership is quite hard in execution, because it depends on consistent subordination of self in a leader. To do that well, a leader must come full circle, back to the pursuit of individual character.

Over the course of years, the military has honed this cycle of mission, character, and service into an elegant, powerful system—a Leader's Code, which governs the thoughts, words, and actions of all of its members. However, in spite of widespread admiration, the military has done a poor job explaining and exporting this code to a broader audience. That is why this book exists, to close this void and to give everyone who hopes to lead the confidence that they can do it well regardless of the context. And they can—the code is powerful in its simplicity.

The Leader's Code
Accomplish a worthy mission.
Pursue character above all else.
Serve others before serving yourself.

Perhaps most tricky of all is the concept of character—as mentioned above, there is no popular consensus on what, exactly, character means. Throughout the course of this book, "character" is defined as *an honorable individual condition gained through the intentional pursuit of virtue and maintained over the course of a lifetime.* And the military has a very clear picture of what virtue means. Indeed, the military teaches that there are specific virtues that are absolutes, which makes this institution unique in a world awash in relativism. In this way, the military goes far beyond simply creating a "culture" with four or five key pillars. It actually tells its members the type of people they need to become. It expects its leaders to faithfully execute this character throughout the entirety of their careers and under every imaginable circumstance, regardless of how demanding or harsh the conditions. The various military branches express the virtues underpinning character in different ways, but in all of their forms they can be boiled down to the following six:

1. Humility
2. Excellence
3. Kindness
4. Discipline
5. Courage
6. Wisdom

These are the virtues that we will explore throughout the course of the book.

Unlike so many recent leadership philosophies, the Leader's Code is a flexible model that can be applied to any situation, organization, or culture. It rests on six virtues useful to all people, and not on methodology relevant to only certain circumstances—say, marketing or strategy. The Code can be applied to anyone, whether they lead at work, at home, in business, in government, in their neighborhoods, or in their communities. What is more, the Code helps us to lead at the most basic of levels—the leadership of ourselves.

Throughout this book, we will use a simple framework to help us develop a way to understand and incorporate into our own lives each of the virtues that underpin the Leader's Code. This framework is intended to help us personalize what each virtue looks like (and could look like) to each of us, ascertain (with some precision) where we currently stand in pursuing each virtue, and guide us (with some urgency) to take action to incorporate each virtue into our own lives. The framework that we will be using to guide us is fairly straightforward:

1. Reflect
2. Analyze
3. Act

The first piece of the framework—reflection—is included at the end of each chapter and is designed to prompt immediate and deep thought. We should walk away from each reflection exercise with some idea of how we currently think—or do not think—about each of the virtues and with some initial understanding of how we currently pursue and implement—or do not pursue and implement—the virtues in our day-to-day living. These reflection exercises are not intended to give us precise understanding of the virtues as they relate to us; rather, they are intended to prompt us to begin thinking more deliberately about ourselves and our character and leadership as they currently stand.

Once the thinking has begun, we need to gather data, and that is what the analysis section is intended to do. It is very easy for us to misunderstand, misinterpret, or just plain miss the way in which we currently go about implementing each virtue in our own lives. The analysis exercises will help us gather some facts without being overly cumbersome. After all, the more that we observe what we actually do and the less we rely upon what we think we do, the closer we will get to the truth. All of the analysis exercises are combined together, in the Appendix, so that we can view them as a whole and tackle them as a whole should we so choose.

Of course, thinking and data gathering are useless without action. If we do not *do* something in our own lives to make ourselves better leaders and better people, then everything—including this book—is for naught. Again, with the exception of Chapter 1, each of the action steps is included in the Appendix. And nothing within the framework is exhaustive. This book has included suggestions, but the more that we can come up with on our own, the better off we will be. Nor is every suggestion in this book prescriptive. They are all simply tools, to be used in different ways in different lives.

I have been out of the military for some time now, and I have realized that the servant-leader model and the character qualities underpinning it are powerful and relevant no matter who you are leading or where you are leading them. The same combination that allowed me to lead Marines in combat has allowed me to lead teams in business. It has made me a better husband, father, friend, and community member, when I hewed to it, and a worse human being when I did not. I believe with all of my heart that in a world starving for leadership, the servant-leader model can help strengthen families, neighborhoods, business, politics, and, ultimately, the broader global community.

Though I no longer wear the uniform, I am passionate about serving. The world is in a dangerous place, and too many people have lost faith and hope because leaders in all institutions have behaved so poorly. Too many of us believe that tomorrow will be worse than today. We watch in despair as so many of our leaders seem unable to rise above their own narrow self-interest to solve the most important problems of our time. We wonder about the future: What will we see in our lifetime, and what will be the legacy we leave to our children? Will it be better or worse than the one left to us?

I believe that it can be better, but we must make it so. No one else will do it for us. We had a saying in the Marines that helped sum up our mind-sets before a particularly dangerous mission: *If not me, who? If not now, when?* Well, it is our time now, and times are hard. Nevertheless, there are many good people out there, people who are trying every day to restore faith and hope, to demonstrate that good leaders exist, to make a positive impact in their own spheres, no matter how large or small. There are many committed leaders who want to make life better for their fellow man, who want to be significant, who want to leave a legacy behind that is far more than an inheritance. If you are one such person, then I hope and I pray that this simple Leader's Code may be of some service to you. And I hope and I pray that together we can lead well and hand to our children a future brighter than the one handed to us.

THE LEADER'S CODE

CHAPTER 1

MISSION

My first major firefight occurred on April 6, 2004. At the time, the forty-man infantry platoon I led was garrisoned in a city called Ramadi, the capital of Iraq's Anbar Province. Anbar was soon to be the epicenter of the insurgency that blossomed across Iraq in 2004, and Ramadi was the heart of that dangerous province. With close to four hundred thousand people packed into less than ten square miles, Ramadi had one of the highest population densities on earth. To police them, we had 160 infantry Marines, 90 percent of whom were between the ages of seventeen and twenty-two.

Its buildings were equally close-packed. Throughout most of the city, two-story walled compounds joined together to form three-hundred-yard-long urban canyons, with the only breaks between them being street intersections. In the commercial district downtown, on the city's western side, several buildings rose ten stories or higher, and the walled compounds here housed small shops. In some places, the streets were wide enough to drive two Humvees side by side. In others, the streets were so narrow that it was difficult for two men to walk side by side. And everywhere the people thronged, at least until the serious fighting started.

The night before the battle had been a long one for my platoon—call sign Joker One—and me. We had spent the entire evening, from sundown to sunup, out of our base, lying awake in fighting positions on the roof of Ramadi's government center or conducting patrols in its immediate area. Shortly after first light broke, we patrolled on foot back to our base, sweeping Ramadi's main thoroughfare for bombs as we went. We found one.

When we got back into our rudimentary base, we debriefed, then turned in to catch a bit of rest. Since we were a designated quick-reaction force that day, I slept with my boots on. And a good thing it was that I did so, since barely an hour after I had fallen asleep, I was woken up again and ordered to assemble my platoon and launch them into the city. A fellow platoon had been ambushed by hundreds of attackers and separated into three disparate houses. The casualties were high—several wounded, at least one dead—and the attackers were pressing their advantage. Fragmented reports indicated that the insurgents had penetrated the compounds of several of the houses and were firing at the Marines through the windows. In other places, Marines and insurgents stood on opposite sides of the same wall, lobbing grenades back and forth.

Our friends were running low on ammunition, and the casualties were mounting. Someone needed to relieve them, and quickly. Several minutes after waking up, Joker One and I headed into the city, driving as far as we could and then dismounting. We didn't know exactly where our friends were, so we ran to the sounds of the gunfire and to the black smoke that floated up above the middle of the city. We took into the fight only what we could carry on our backs.

Several blocks later, we hit withering machine gun fire. From that point on, we fought house by house and block by block until we rescued our comrades. Machine guns tore up the walls all around us. Rocket-propelled grenades (RPGs) detonated all over the city. At one point in time, an enemy grenade landed less than five feet from me and four of my men. Had it gone off, Joker One would have immediately suffered 10 percent dead.

After we relieved the pressure on Third Platoon and evacuated their wounded, we fought for the rest of the day, clearing the city of the thousands of attackers that had besieged us. Shortly before nightfall, we made it back into the base, filthy, covered with dirt and gunpowder and, in some cases, blood. I was walking side by side into the base with Jon Hesener, leader of Third Platoon and my compatriot, when he calmly informed me that halfway through the day he had been knocked completely unconscious (for about five minutes) by a bullet to his Kevlar helmet. His men had started dragging his limp body away, thinking him dead, until he suddenly came to and started swearing robustly.

Jon and I headed into the command post and debriefed with our leadership for about thirty minutes. Then we headed back out, to check on our men and try to get some rest. I was walking through the hangar bay that housed our command post, headed to the small compound that housed my platoon. I didn't make it there, though. Halfway through the bay, I saw Joe Mahardy, my best radio operator, leaning up against the wall, with his gear off, smoking a cigarette.

Joe was all of nineteen years old, and he looked it. With his gear off, he stood a skinny six feet tall, weighing maybe 150 pounds. He came from a tight-knit family of five from New York, and he'd left Syracuse University, where he was on the dean's list, to join the Marines in the wake of the terrorist attacks of September 11, 2001. He was sharp as a tack and mouthy, which is why we'd made him the platoon's radio operator. He knew what I would ask before I did, which saved me a lot of time in the middle of a firefight. As I walked by Joe this time, though, he looked contemplative, and he didn't say anything as I passed. He just smoked his cigarette and stared off into the distance.

I walked past Joe, wanting to get over to the platoon's house and check on the bulk of my men. But I stopped. A quiet Joe was unusual. I asked him how he was doing. It was, after all, our first daylong house-to-house firefight.

Joe thought for a minute. "I'm fine, sir."

Then he said something that amazed me. "Hey, sir, do you think we fought well today? I mean, do you think that all the Marines who fought at Iwo Jima and Okinawa would have been proud of us? Did we live up to them, sir? Did we do our part?"

I didn't know what to say. My skinny, nineteen-year-old lance corporal had just been through what was arguably the most difficult day of his young life to date. He had helped carry his wounded and dead friends into the backs of medevac ambulances. He had radioed into headquarters that his comrade, Hallal, was lying dead in the street with his throat cut. He had taken cover as machine gun fire cut up the wall next to him. He had fought for twelve straight hours on almost no sleep, carrying all of his gear plus twenty extra pounds of radio. By all rights, he should have been worried about what tomorrow would hold—would he have to fight again, would he see such death, would he return to base, and if he did would he still have all of his limbs? But he wasn't worried about these things. Mahardy wondered only one thing: Had he kept the faith with the men who preceded him? Had he upheld the honor of the United States Marine Corps?

What is it that makes a nineteen-year-old more concerned with his service than his life? Why was Nelson Mandela able to spend more than a decade in prison for daring to believe that all men are created equal and then emerge to plead to his nation to forgive those who had imprisoned him? Why was Mohandas Gandhi able to steadfastly refuse the call to violence in the face of increasingly violent oppression? Why did Mother Teresa pour out her life in the slums of Calcutta? Why is it that the most respected people, and the most respected leaders, can endure hardship, pain, and even the prospect of their certain death and still persevere without bitterness and self-pity?

In Mahardy's case, it was because he was more concerned with the honor of the Corps—and how he upheld it—than he was with his own death. Mahardy was not an unusual Marine. He was not particularly more dedicated than his peers, and he was not a uniquely created human being, born with the ability to transcend his own well-being for the greater good. He was simply a normal nineteen-year-old who knew exactly what his mission in life was. The day he graduated from boot camp, Mahardy had sworn an oath to protect and defend the Constitution of the United States of America against all enemies, foreign and domestic. Ever since that day, he had submitted his whole self—and dedicated his entire life—to the pursuit of that mission, and he considered that mission more important than his own life. All of my Marines felt the same way, which was why all of them performed amazing acts of heroism: sprinting into fire to rescue wounded children, waving their arms in the air to distract an enemy machine gunner—to make him fire at them rather than their wounded comrade—running straight toward the sounds of the gunfire to help pinned-down units. The average age of my Marines was nineteen years old.

THE END IN MIND

I believe that all truly great leaders know their overarching mission in life with the same clarity with which Mahardy and my men knew their over-arching mission in Iraq. Nelson Mandela, Mohandas Gandhi, and Mother Teresa, to name a few of the twentieth century's finest, made a lasting impact on the world because 1) they had a cause and 2) they committed to it regardless of the consequences. They had determined that their reason for being was something greater than they were, something that mattered far more than did their own comfort, happiness, or well-being. But how did they develop such clarity of mission? What makes a leader capable of such self-sacrifice? How can a person keep the faith and persevere through the worst of times, for decades if necessary?

First off, I believe that great leaders have an intuitive understanding of the simple fact that our time on earth is limited, and that understanding sharpens their vision of what is truly important. Accepting the idea that we have a defined window to make an impact on this earth and integrating this acceptance into our lives helps to put our lives into a different perspective. The day-to-day, just-get-through-the-day mentality is more easily overcome once you have accepted that today may be our last chance to make an impact. If we can focus on making the most of the time at hand, it becomes easier to focus on what really matters, too.

I learned this lesson the hard way, at twenty-four, as an infantry officer leading forty young men in heavy combat in Ramadi. It took me a while to understand my own mortality, and even longer to embrace it, because even though we had simulated casualties during training, nothing can prepare you for the experience of watching one of your nineteen-year-old Marines hop to shelter on one leg—and then collapse—because he's just been shot through both his shinbones. Until something like that happens, and then happens again, and again, and again you think that you and everyone you lead are immortal. After all, you're only twenty-four years old, and they're even younger: nineteen on average.

But as combat intensified, and as the days like April 6 piled up, those endless days where we fought for hours and returned fewer than went out, every one of us on the front lines began to encounter the weekly deaths of our comrades. It was strange, your friends and co-workers dying while going about their daily business. One morning, you'd trade jokes with your buddy, and then you'd leave and go your separate ways on patrol, and the morning would pass, and the afternoon would come, and you'd come back in to the base to learn that your friend wasn't there anymore. His lower half had disappeared in an explosion two hours ago, and no one thought he'd live through the flight to Germany he was now on. And you'd learn in a few days that, sure enough, he did not make it. As the days went on, these horrible discoveries began happening more frequently.

So, I began to dwell on my own death—specifically, on how I might avoid it. For no logical reason, I absolutely rejected the idea that death could happen to me, even as I feared tremendously that it might. I spent a great deal of time terrified for my safety. My life's goal became preventing my life from ending. I played out countless scenarios in my head, trying to guess at what the near future held, hoping it wouldn't be as bad as the recent past and that if it was, then at least I could plan for the evil and mitigate its consequences. With enough skill and foresight and discipline, I believed, that which had happened to so many around me would never happen to me.

Ironically, the more I fixated on preserving my life, the less effective I became at living it. My refusal to accept the inevitable led to selfishness, which crowded out my duty to my men and our mission. Human beings have a finite supply of energy, and they can have only one first love. I chose to expend my best energy, and my first love, on myself. Thus I spent my time after missions lying in bed, sleepless, when I should have been debriefing my men, or checking on them as they stood post on the walls. I spent the time before missions scared, thinking about all of the possible ways I could be wounded, with comparatively little thought spared for what might happen to my men. I did not lead well, and my Marines suffered for it.

One day, though, I jettisoned my preoccupation with the avoidance of death. I'll never forget it—I was lying in bed, sleepless as usual, imagining everything that might happen and how I might miss the worst of it, when suddenly I stopped and told myself in my head that I wouldn't live through the deployment. I told myself that I would certainly die within the next four months, and that that was acceptable.

It was almost like flipping a switch, and it never switched back. It freed me. Since I now understood that I would die, and that I would likely die sometime in the near future, my goal was no longer to keep myself safe and comfortable. My goal was to use my time to take care of my men and protect the people of Iraq from the random violence that was engulfing us. I became a much better leader, because I finally understood my mission.

I've talked with a number of frontline leaders, and most of them can remember the moment when they accepted that they would die in the coming weeks or months. They, too, describe how freeing that acceptance was for them. I think that we discovered young and through much pain one of life's great paradoxes: The more we lose our lives, the more we find them again. The less we live for ourselves, the more we truly gain. We never arrive at happiness if happiness is all we seek. Indeed, we can hope to find it only as a fortuitous by-product of a life spent pursuing something that is worth a life's pursuit, or a life itself, if necessary.

Paul of Tarsus, the famous first-century Christian evangelist, was shipwrecked, stoned, flogged, and ultimately killed for his belief system. He expressed the peace he found in a life lived for more than himself in the following way: "I consider nothing else in life as excellent as the knowledge of Christ Jesus my Lord, for whom I have lost all things and count them as rubbish, that I may gain Christ." Writing from prison, on his way to an almost certain death, Paul used the word "joy" no fewer than sixteen times in one letter. This first-century Jew, born in a backwater of the Roman Empire, suffered greatly as he changed the course of history, but he considered his privations a small price to pay for what he gained in return. He had found the fullness of life outside of himself. He was able to find peace in any situation, even prison.

Nelson Mandela suffered as well—twenty years in prison—before he led his people to freedom with a dignity that set the standard for the rest of the world. He expressed Paul's same sentiments a bit differently: "After climbing a great hill, one only finds that there are many more hills to climb. I have taken a moment here to rest, to steal a view of the glorious vista that surrounds me, to look back on the distance I have come. But I can rest only for a moment, for with freedom come responsibilities, and I dare not linger, for my long walk is not yet ended." He, too, had found a mission that gave meaning to suffering.

DEVELOPING A MISSION

I think that both of these men, very early in their lives, were made to understand in no uncertain terms that their lives were not their own and that they had limited time on earth to make a difference. I believe that most great leaders, whether consciously or unconsciously, begin their leadership journey by internalizing man's mortality. Understanding that our days are finite makes each day an infinite gift. A limited number of actions means that every action counts. No day is irrelevant, no action is insignificant, no choice is inconsequential.

Mortality also redefines success. Nothing accumulated in this life can be carried over into the next. True achievement must lie elsewhere, apart from the material realm, apart from all of the things that can and will be taken from us in the blink of an eye. No one will write our bank account balance on our tombstones. Nor will they write the square footage of our houses, or the type of car we drove at the time of our demise, or the names on the various labels on our various clothes.

Instead, if we are lucky, people will write: "Faithful husband and father"; "Beloved wife and mother"; "Loving son" or "Loving daughter." Susan B. Anthony led the charge for female suffrage in America; her tombstone reads "Liberty. Humanity. Justice. Equality" — her life's purpose summed up in four words. Since 2001, many of our soldiers' tombstones have read thus: "He gave his life for his country." There was no question about their mission, the cause for which they gave the last full measure of devotion, to paraphrase Lincoln. When the dead are buried, the living want to know: what was the meaning of the life of the departed?

Meditating on our own limited time on earth is the starting point for a sense of mission, which is the guiding force behind character-based leadership. Without an overarching purpose in life, the pursuit of character is unsustainable, for patiently acquiring virtue requires the consistent submission of our own daily desires. And denying these immediate desires is no small thing. It is far easier simply to live day to day, satisfying our own impulses and egos to the extent that our circumstances will allow us. It is also easier to pursue the resources we need to gratify ourselves than it is to pursue the virtues we need to put our resources in the service of others. Without an overarching, all-encompassing mission that focuses us away from ourselves, we have no compelling reason to serve anything other than ourselves.

But if we hope to lead with significance, then we need such a mission. And accepting that man is mortal is the first step we need to take if we want to understand what constitutes a worthy cause or have any hope of dedicating ourselves to one. Otherwise we will procrastinate. We will be likely to think that we will serve others at some point in the future, perhaps when we retire or perhaps when we become comfortable enough to be content. This is highly unlikely. John D. Rockefeller Sr., the richest man in the world at the time, was once asked, "How much money is enough?" His reply: "Just a little bit more."

Acknowledging that we may have limited time on earth helps us make the time to understand where we are at versus where we want to be. It helps us choose our missions carefully and intentionally, which is how we should choose anything of importance. A worthy mission could be many things, and we are likely to have different missions in different contexts—work, home, community—and at different times in our lives. As circumstances change, so might our mission change over. George Washington spent his twenties and thirties pursuing military careerism, political advancement, and wealth in the form of vast landholdings. In May 1775, though, all of that changed as the American colonies began to contemplate independence from Britain. In that month, Washington wrote his brother Jack that "it is my full intention to devote my life and fortune to the cause [independence] we are now engaged in." He then put everything he had accumulated in life, including his life itself, at risk to lead a semi-extant army, many of whose members had no shoes, in mortal combat against a global superpower. In fact, Washington volunteered to serve without pay (although he did ask for expense reimbursement). He left his wife and his home behind for eight straight years. He feared that the most likely outcome of his decision would be financial ruin, dishonor, and ultimately death. Indeed, one of Washington's first acts upon assuming command of the Continental Army was to arrange for a new will to be drafted. But he forged ahead anyway, in spite of the risk and in spite of the sacrifice. Clearly, this leader had changed his mission with the circumstances.

In our lives, we will have different missions across the span of our activities. In the working world, our mission could be to build a business founded on integrity, an institution whose positive contributions will live on long after the leader is gone. It could be to invent a technology that facilitates financial flexibility, or connects people in new and wholly different ways. It could be to help the less fortunate in society through innovative microlending. Or it could be as simple as conducting ourselves with honor and ethics every day, never sacrificing the right thing to do on the altar of the bottom line.

At home, our mission could be to teach values to the next generation, to model righteousness and virtue. When our children are young, we could invest ourselves in discerning their natural talents and inclinations and then maximizing those gifts to the extent that we can. We could try to provide our children an example of the kind of marriage that we hope they will have one day. We could try to treat our spouses the way we would like to be treated, try to bring the best out of our better halves. When our children are grown and have moved out, we could dedicate ourselves to our spouse and/or our circle of friends. For those of us with siblings, we could attempt to build and maintain positive, nurturing relationships that stand the test of time. Or we could try to rebuild relationships that time and circumstances have sundered.

In our communities, our mission could be something as simple as getting to know our neighbors or being generous with our time when our friends are in need. It could be to regularly give of our time to help those less fortunate than us. We could decide to become members of a local religious body or a neighborhood association. We could make a serious effort to educate ourselves on issues facing our communities and those elected to handle those issues in local and national government. We could determine that we will always vote intelligently, and vote our consciences.

Our lives have different contexts and different seasons, and our missions may vary across each. One thing, however, is certain: if we do not know what our mission is, we will definitely fail to achieve it. And there is one constant that helps us test whether a mission is worth achieving: our cause must be more important than our comfort or well-being. Indeed, our mission must be something for which we would be willing to sacrifice those two. As we think about the various options in front of us, the different missions that we think we are or could be pursuing, there is a simple thought experiment that can help us determine whether we've hit upon one for which we think we could sacrifice. I've heard this experiment called a lot of things, but I like "the Tombstone Test" the best. It's quite straightforward. Look in the mirror and ask yourself: "If I died tomorrow, would I want whatever it is that I am pursuing today engraved on my tombstone as my epitaph?"

In 1859 a young Swedish chemist named Alfred moved from St. Petersburg, Russia, back to his country of origin after his father's Russian business venture went belly-up. A student of explosives, the chemist de-

voted himself to discovering a way to safely manufacture and employ nitroglycerine, a powerful but highly unstable compound that held huge
promise if it could only be commercialized. In 1864 a shed used to prepare nitroglycerine exploded, killing five people. Among them was Alfred's younger brother, Emil. Alfred persevered, however, and three years
later he invented a stable and powerful explosive that came to be called
dynamite. Over the next twenty years, Alfred would issue more than 350
international patents and amass huge riches in the armaments industry,
building more than ninety factories despite his deeply held belief in paci-
fism.

In 1888 Alfred's brother Ludwig died while visiting Cannes. A French
newspaper erroneously published Alfred's obituary, leading with the pro-
vocative headline: *Le marchand de la mort est mort*—The merchant of
death is dead. The paper continued to inveigh against the chemist in the
body of the article—Alfred, "who became rich by finding ways to kill
more people faster than ever before, died yesterday." Many historians believe that reading his own obituary caused the famous Swede to profoundly reconsider his life and legacy—so profoundly, in fact, that he
eventually donated the bulk of his fortune to establish a series of international prizes for science, literature, and peace. These prizes were given
the chemist's last name, Nobel, and to this day these Nobel Prizes remain
some of the most prestigious awards in the world. And all of this happened because a Swedish chemist changed his mission after reading his
own obituary.

George Washington also clearly changed his life's pursuit in light of
what he hoped to have written after his death. If Washington before war
was an example of a man who had found a mission more important than
his own life, then Winston Churchill between wars is an example of a man
who had found a mission more important than his own livelihood. He did
not lay his life on the line, but he did give up his career, which, up until
then, had been exceptionally distinguished.

As a young man, Winston Churchill served simultaneously as a war
correspondent and an army officer. After serving in—and reporting
from—Cuba, India, Egypt, and Sudan, Churchill arranged a commission

as a war correspondent in South Africa in 1899. The Second Boer War had just broken out, and he sought adventure and distinction, having just lost his first-ever election for a seat in Parliament. After a few weeks in-country, Churchill was captured during an ambush on a British armored train. He and his fellows were imprisoned in Pretoria. Churchill, however, broke out of the prison camp and traveled three hundred miles cross-country to safety. His escape made him a minor national hero back in Britain.

Churchill, however, did not return home. Instead he rejoined the army, eventually becoming one of the first British back into Pretoria. He stood again for reelection in 1900 and won this time. Thereafter, Churchill's political rise was meteoric. He served as undersecretary of state, home secretary, First Lord of the Admiralty, secretary of state for war and air, and chancellor of the exchequer—virtually every important post save that of prime minister. In 1929, though, he became a back-bencher, a politician without any leadership portfolio. Churchill had chances to rejoin the government, and assume preeminence again, but he did not take them. Churchill had a new mission, one more important than political fortune. It was his task to alert Britain to the dangers of an increasingly militant Germany. Throughout the next decade, Churchill would be one of the only British voices in stern opposition to Germany's, and Hitler's, rise.

The stance would cost him politically. No one wanted to fight again after living through the horrors of the First World War. For his anti-Germany rhetoric, Churchill was browbeaten as a warmonger while Neville Chamberlain was lauded for having achieved "peace in our time." Despite the taunts, the isolation, and the career suicide, Churchill persevered. He understood his mission: alert Europe, and the world, to the twin dangers of national socialism and Adolf Hitler. In pursuit of that mission, Churchill sacrificed nearly a decade of political leadership. And ten years of crying in the wilderness left him isolated but not mute. On August 31, 1939, Churchill's prophecies proved correct, but one wonders: Without his single-minded devotion to his mission, would he have been willing to make the same sacrifice over the same extended time period? And if he had not, then would Great Britain have had its finest hour? Would the Nazis have completed their conquest of Europe? Would Jews, Gypsies, the mentally handicapped, and other "undesirables" still be persecuted, or killed, across large swaths of the world?

A MISSION'S EFFECTS

I believe that any leader can achieve remarkable, and worthwhile, results if they can develop a sense of mission similar to Washington's or Churchill's. Why is this? First off, a worthy mission gives a leader an ending point for their journey, a guiding force for their actions, and a foundation upon which to build. Anyone who has spent any time navigating a wilderness will tell you that it is impossible to complete a trek—or to even plan for it—if you do not begin by knowing where your path ends. You must start with your goal firmly fixed, and then plot a course toward it, taking into account all of the twists and turns and the obstacles along the way. You plan left and right limits that will help you know if you've strayed too far off course. Once you are in the wilderness, you use a compass that points to true north to help you get out. A compass that points straight back at you—like a life mission that is only about serving yourself—is a useless tool that will take you precisely nowhere. Leadership over time is far more difficult than orienteering or even vacationing, yet we often approach it with less forethought than we do a week at the beach.

Beginning a leadership journey with the end—a worthy mission—in mind allows us to plan our course with the same deliberation with which we plan anything else important in life—how we get in shape, how we do our work, how we raise our children, and so on. Once we know where to go, then we can plot a course for how to get there. And once we have a destination and directions, others can actually follow us. If we know where we are going, if we have a true north that does not change with time and circumstance, then others feel confident that they have made the right choice to follow us. No matter what the twists and turns in life, a mission allows those of us who hope to lead to persevere and find our way again after even the worst setbacks. Without a concrete mission, though, it is unreasonable to expect others to follow. Would you follow a guide who seems lost and confused from the outset? Would you feel confident on a trek if your leader could not easily distinguish south from north? Would you charge a hill if your leader has fallen and refuses to get back up?

A clear mission also helps a leader serve their team. Service to others is no easy thing—it has to be practiced if it is to be maintained. If a leader has a mission to which we submit ourselves, then we are constantly practicing such service, which makes it much easier for us to apply it in other areas of our lives. When I joined the Marine Corps, I swore an oath to serve my country and my men. I had my mission. After that, I submitted wholly to the dictates of the Corps. I wore what I was told to, every day. I cut my hair according to regulations. I woke when they told me, slept when they allowed me, and practiced what they told me in nearly every waking moment of my life. If I failed to show up on time, or if I quit before I was allowed to, or if I disobeyed the strict guidance of the Uniform Code of Military Justice, then I would go to jail. My life was no longer my own.

Eventually, I deployed to combat as the leader of forty young men, my infantry platoon. I had a solemn charge to keep the peace and keep my Marines alive, if I could. Because I had passed the training, and proven that I could submit, I was now allowed great freedom. As a twenty-four-year-old, I had the power of life and death over not only my men but also nearly everyone with whom we came in contact. However, if I had any hope of completing the tour with honor, I had to subordinate my freedom to the well-being of my men and those whom we tried to keep safe. So, while my Marines slept, I planned missions. When we fought, I tried to position myself at the point of greatest danger, or to run through fire as most everyone else took cover so that I could make decisions that would keep my men alive. And when my men were wounded horribly, or killed, I pushed back my anger, and my desire for revenge, and told myself and my Marines that no matter what we felt, we would always act with honor. Our mission was more important than gratifying our own feelings. In retrospect, I wished I had served my Marines more—in spite of my best efforts, I was still all too often a selfish leader who put his own best interests ahead of his teams'. Still, I did far better than I would have without the practice of submitting myself to a higher calling from day one after enlisting. Taking care of my team first, even when that meant doing something directly contrary to my own survival, was possible only because I had practiced serving my mission before I practiced leading my men.

A good mission also allows a leader to push through adversity. Too often we judge the worth of a course of action by the difficulty we encounter pursuing it. The job is worth doing until the job gets hard, at which point in time we often switch jobs. But the worth of our cause cannot be determined by the price we pay to achieve it. The inherent value to what we are doing must lie outside time and circumstance—in other words, we must know that we pursue an objective good. A valid mission is the pursuit of something that has a worth, that does not alter as the circumstances become difficult. If a leader has identified what that something is, they are far less likely to deviate from their true north when life's headwinds blow hard. Washington persevered through Valley Forge, Churchill through the winter of his own career. As I write this, nineteen-year-old corporals in Afghanistan are enduring months without showers, electricity, or running water; months shivering at night, lying next to each other for warmth as the temperature drops to thirty degrees below zero. Months without talking to their families and friends. Months spent fighting, day in and day out. The corporals will not quit, for they serve a clearly articulated, overarching mission. And every day they create their own new missions to serve their constant one.

Finally, a clear, well-known, and well-defined mission allows a leader to guard against complacency and amorality, two things that weaken us slowly and almost imperceptibly. If we tell others our cause, it helps hold us accountable to a professed set of beliefs. Very few people on earth are capable of continued self-improvement without external pressure and constructive criticism from others. A publicized mission gives a basis for that criticism; it makes the ultimate end state of a leader—and a leader's progress toward that end state—visible to all who care. And a clear, widely known mission helps others understand exactly what a leader believes is important. When poor behavior, bad judgment, or outright evil in pursuit of short-term gains manifest themselves, a leader's mission gives others the ability and the right to call them to account. A mission allows others to judge us against our own stated standard.

THE PILLARS OF MISSION: SERVICE, ETHICS, AND ACTION

So, if we hope to lead well, and build character over time, we must have a mission. But what exactly constitutes a mission? Furthermore, if we think that we have one, how can we know that it is truly worthy of our time and energy? How can we know that it is a good mission? To answer these questions, it is worth starting with the definition of the word. *Merriam-Webster's Collegiate Dictionary* defines "mission" in several ways, among them:

1. A ministry commissioned by a religious organization to propagate its faith or carry on humanitarian work.
2. A body of persons sent to perform a service or carry on an activity.
3. A specific task with which a person or group is charged.
4. A pre-established and often self-imposed objective or purpose.
5. A calling or vocation.

The one constant running through these disparate definitions is the idea of service—to a faith, to a country, to an organization, to an obligation, or to a higher calling or profession. A mission *cannot* be centered on our own happiness or the pursuit thereof. A mission cannot revolve around making ourselves more comfortable, or wealthy, or well liked, or well connected. It must be about achieving something that does not change with our personal circumstances, something that matters no matter how much we stand to gain or lose in the course of attaining it. It must be a task worth doing regardless of who is doing it. Mother Teresa described hers as a call within a call: "I was to leave the convent and work with the poor, living among them . . . to be God's Love in action to the poorest of the poor." Often, a willingness to make consistent sacrifices is the surest sign that a leader has a true mission—from Martin Luther King Jr. to Nelson Mandela to Aung San Suu Kyi, our most respected leaders have always highlighted the nobility of their cause by the magnitude of the privations they incur in service of it.

However, sacrifice alone does not a true mission make. Hitler endured a year in prison in support of national socialism, but his cause tossed right and wrong by the wayside along with hundreds of thousands of innocent lives. Cult leader Jim Jones chose exile in Guyana over reform of his beliefs. He later forced children to drink cyanide. A true mission must conform with ethics, with generally accepted right and wrong, and these ethics must play themselves out in action as the mission is pursued. No matter how noble the ends, they never justify the means if the means abandon morality. For this reason, we respect Gandhi and revile Lenin, about whom Churchill is rumored to have said, "His goal: to save the world. His method: to blow it up." A good mission must be not only noble in theory but also ethical in being carried out.

A good mission must be ethical, but also actionable. It must be something that can reasonably be put into practice. This allows others to hold a leader accountable to achieve tangible results, results that can be measured. If a mission is not actionable, if it is so pie-in-the sky that it could never possibly be achieved, then a leader is essentially off the hook. They are free to claim whatever they would like as their mission, knowing full well that they will never be asked to match deeds with words, never be forced to measure up. A good mission passes the test of action. It allows a leader to demonstrate with their time, talent, and treasure that they are pursuing their mission by making a tangible difference.

William Wilberforce was a nineteenth-century British politician who set for himself two goals: the abolition of slavery and the "reformation of manners." Both were lofty, but only the first was actionable—if nearly impossible. It is hard for those of us in the twenty-first-century

Western world to understand the prevalence and social acceptance of slavery that characterized Great Britain's understanding of the subject in the nineteenth century. Indeed, for the entirety of human history, the enslavement of human beings by their fellow men was a commonly accepted, if abhorrent, societal condition. Those who conquered enslaved and sold the defeated. It was a simple fact of life.

By the time Wilberforce began his ascent in Parliament, Britain ruled the waves and the slave trade. British ships dominated the "triangular trade," wherein British ships transported British goods to Africa, exchanged them for human chattel, and then made the perilous journey back across the Atlantic to supply Dutch, French, British, Spanish, and Portuguese colonies with a ready supply of workers in exchange for finished goods. This trade represented around 80 percent of Britain's foreign income at the time, and in a particularly good year British ships would transport around forty thousand slaves per year across the Atlantic. The crossing was brutal, however. Roughly one out of every ten slaves died during the voyage.

So when Wilberforce and his supporters took on the mission of ending slavery, they were not only challenging a condition that had existed since the dawn of human history, but also striking at one of the economic engines of the British Empire. But their cause was actionable; their goal was tangible; and their progress could be measured. For twenty-six years Wilberforce set himself to the task in Parliament. In the interim, he lost his fortune and his health. His will never flagged, however, and just three days before his death in July 1833, Wilberforce learned that the British government had abolished the institution of slavery throughout its empire, which encompassed upwards of 60 percent of the entire world. This was a true paradigm shift, and the world would never be the same.

Yet the man who managed to fundamentally alter history and society by ending one of its most prevalent institutions never achieved his second mission: that of the "reform of manners." He lent, to some extent, his character to the Victorian era, but he never truly changed the morality of society's elite. Wilberforce's failure cannot be explained by a lack of will or talent; otherwise, how would such a man have managed to accomplish the first mission? But Wilberforce's second mission was very difficult to measure in reality. What do "reformed manners" look like? How would one measure progress toward the goal? When would an impartial judge deem that the task had been accomplished—what event would occur that would prove that, once and for all, manners have been reformed? The abolition of slavery was a lofty, maybe even ludicrous, goal at the time, but at least it was actionable. One could know exactly whether it had been done or not.

Should we choose unactionable missions, ones wherein no one can ever know with certainty whether they have been achieved, we will certainly suffer the same fate as did the great reformer. A leader's mission, then, must be one that can be reasonably put into practice. A leader's team should be able to know when they have accomplished the mission and be able to measure their progress toward their goal. Observers should be able to understand the mission and hold the team responsible for carrying it out. If a chosen mission cannot pass the test of action, then no matter how noble the goal, we are best advised to choose a new one.

FINDING OUR OWN MISSIONS

While we put off choosing our mission, and while we fail to decide, our daily choices may be at best incoherent and at worst contradictory. No matter what we would like to believe in theory, in day-to-day reality we will almost certainly be pursuing one thing—the default choice, comfort. And no matter what we would like others to think about us, they will infer our missions from what they observe of our lives—from where we spend our time, our talent, and our treasure. One of my commanders, a Navy SEAL and a sniper, summed up this reality perfectly: "Show me a man's checkbook and his calendar, and I will tell you his values."

If we hope to lead well, then we must take the time to understand the missions that we are currently pursuing *and* to define those missions that we would like to pursue. In some cases, we may be fully aware of the missions we are on. In others, we may be pursuing these missions completely unintentionally. To help us craft our own mission—and to help us understand the missions that we are on (knowingly or not), we need to begin with the first step outlined in the introduction—reflection.

We need to define what we want to achieve with any mission by asking ourselves some important questions about what really matters in life. Before we set off crafting what it is that we hope to accomplish, we need to do some hard thinking about where we want to go, why we want to go there, and why we want to dedicate time and energy to the journey.

Reflection Questions

1. Where would I hope that I am putting my most valuable resources?
2. Do I make consistent sacrifices for anything right now?
3. What do I want written on my tombstone?

The Appendix provides a useful framework to help us analyze the missions that we currently pursue—whether knowingly or unknowingly. However, whether we do the analysis or not, we need to think about what we would like our missions to be—the why that informs each of our whats. The following three simple steps can help us.

Action Steps for Mission Crafting

1. Write your own obituary.
2. For a month, write down on a note card one thing you did well each day and one thing you would like to redo. Keep in mind that you will never get the day back.
3. Make a list of the three to five areas in which you might need distinct mission statements.

Before I go any further, I would like to state my mission, so that anyone who reads this book may have the ability to observe me and hold me accountable to match deeds with words (a possibility that truly scares me, but which will hopefully help me maintain my integrity). My mission is founded on a simple belief: that all men are created equal and endowed by their Creator with certain inalienable rights; that all men are infinitely worthy because God chose to sacrifice Himself for them.

Given this belief, my life's mission is twofold: 1) love the Lord my God with all of my heart, soul, and mind; 2) love my neighbor as myself. I have failed at this mission more times than I can count, but failure does not mean that I will stop pursuing it. My only hope is that with each passing day, I can get just a little bit better and that every day, no matter how hard the circumstances, I will shoulder my load and take at least a few small steps forward. My prayer is that when I die, on my tombstone someone will write: "He fought the good fight. He finished the race. He kept the faith."

If we hope to lead, we must know where we are going. But if we hope to lead well, we need more than a well-defined end-of-the-road. We need the ability to navigate the journey well. We need the discernment to choose the right direction when the road forks and the willingness to change course quickly when our current path proves misdirected. We need the fortitude to persevere through life's valleys and humility to keep learning through life's peaks. We need the endurance to keep our foot on the gas when all we want is to coast, and we need the ability to roll down the windows and enjoy the outside when the days are beautiful. And we need to be able to take others with us, to inspire them to join our journey or to strike out on their own.

None of these things happens by accident. No matter how excellent our missions and how high our passions, if we do not have the character to back them, then we will ultimately fail. It is character that fuels us, guides us, and sustains us. And to build our character, we must pursue specific virtues with intentionality, knowing that if we attain them, then we will achieve our missions. What is more, we will live lives of significance. We will make a difference, and the world will be a better place for the fact that we are in it.

SUMMARY

- To lead effectively, we must know and understand our ultimate mission in any given context.
- Understanding our own mortality helps us craft missions that survive the test of time and carry on beyond ourselves.
- A good mission helps a leader plan their course, serve their teams, persevere through hardship, and guard against complacency.
- A worthy mission has the following characteristics: 1) service to something beyond personal welfare; 2) clear, measurable goals; 3) high ethical standards.

———— ★ ————

CHAPTER 2

HUMILITY

Abraham Lincoln was no one's first choice for president—not his party's, and definitely not his country's. In fact, when Lincoln's delegates went to Chicago in May 1860 to try to secure his nomination as the newly formed Republican Party's candidate for the presidency, their strategy was to position Lincoln as the best second choice in the event that a suitable first choice could not be found. After all, the Republican field was stacked with candidates far more accomplished and better known than the circuit lawyer from a rough-and-tumble frontier state. Salmon P. Chase was the governor of Ohio, the first Republican governor of any major state. Edward Bates had served as a state legislator and a U.S. congressman. William H. Seward—the favorite for the Republican nomination—was known as one of the brightest lights in the party, for he had considerable political experience both as New York's governor and as one of its United States senators. From among this field of luminaries, Lincoln, the undistinguished one-term congressman and country lawyer, was somehow selected as the presidential nominee.

Once elected, Lincoln did something extraordinary: he formed his cabinet from those same Republicans who had previously been his rivals for the nomination. Typically, cabinet members would come from a tight-knit circle of advisers who had proved their worth and trustworthiness over a long, hard campaign slog alongside their candidate. New presidents rewarded loyalty, not rivalry. With a shaky claim to the presidential mantle to begin with (and half of his country threatening to secede), Lincoln was hardly leading from a position of strength. If there was anyone who should have stacked his bench with cronies, it was Lincoln. Making matters worse, none of his cabinet members initially liked, or fully accepted, their positions subordinate to a man they considered their inferior. One of the most important posts, that of secretary of war, went to one of Lincoln's most arrogant rivals, a prominent Republican politician, Edwin M. Stanton. His previous position had been attorney general of the United States.

Interestingly enough, this was not Lincoln's first close encounter with Stanton. Lincoln had worked with his future war secretary six years earlier, as a fellow lawyer on a joint case in Ohio. Upon meeting the already famous and accomplished Stanton and his companion in Cincinnati, Lincoln had suggested that they all accompany one another to court. Stanton liked neither the Illinoisan's look nor his reputation, so he rebuffed Lincoln's offer and proceeded to the court alone, later commenting to a friend that Lincoln looked like a "d—ned long armed ape." For the duration of their time together on the case, Stanton never invited Lincoln to anything, not even a single meal. But once Lincoln became president, he overlooked all of this when it came time for him to hand out one of his most important staff assignments.

Initially, this magnanimity looked shortsighted and naïve. Stanton himself started off just as condescending as he did six years previously. As the staff formed and the new president confronted arguably the most difficult period in America's history, the secretary of war worked busily at cross-purposes with his president. When he thought Lincoln incompetent, shortsighted, or stupid, Stanton disobeyed him. One day, a congressman arrived at Lincoln's office, reporting that the secretary of war had not only countermanded a direct order from Lincoln but also called the president a damned fool for issuing it. "Did Stanton say I was a damned fool?" asked Lincoln. "He did sir, and repeated it," replied the congressman.

This accusation was no small thing. If true, it meant that a prominent cabinet member—the secretary of war, no less—had just ignored his commander in chief's direct order and then compounded his offense by insulting the president of the United States in the presence of a sitting congressman. By any military standard, Secretary Stanton was guilty of out-and-out mutiny. Lincoln's response reveals volumes about the man's character:

> If Stanton said I was a damned fool, then I must be one, for he is nearly always right, and generally says what he means. I will step over and see him.

There are very few leaders in Lincoln's situation—brand-new, confronting a national existential crisis with a disloyal team of prima donnas and former rivals—who would have responded similarly. Most, insecure in their position to begin with, would have felt their authority questioned (by someone who had publicly snubbed them just six years ago, no less). They would have sought to crush the offender and assert their primacy. They would have made him a lesson to the rest of the shaky team, hoping that fear might compensate for loyalty where title and authority had failed. They would have felt their legitimacy crumbling, and would have punished rather than listened. And they would have had every legal right to do so.

However, Lincoln was known for a singular quality: humility. This virtue allowed him to build one of the most talented cabinets in America's history during what was arguably the country's most difficult period, a time when talent was needed more than ever. Lincoln had no need to prove his superiority or to be right all of the time. Rather, he evinced a remarkable ability to set aside his own feelings, insecurities, and anything else that got in the way of understanding the situation confronting his country and using the best resources to make the best decisions. His humility allowed him to make the best use of the best people, and eventually, Lincoln would earn the steadfast loyalty of his team. Even his mutinous secretary of war would come to consider Lincoln as "the best of us," in

Stanton's own words. In fact, Stanton became closer to Lincoln than anyone else outside of his own family. A century and a half has passed since
then, and time has proven Lincoln to be one of America's best leaders.

DELIBERATE CRITICISM

The Marines also place a premium on humility in a leader. The emphasis
begins at the very beginning of training, either at boot camp or at Officer
Candidate School. These two institutions have one overarching mission:
to teach incoming civilians that they must humble themselves and submit
to the rules, processes, and procedures of the military establishment if
they are to succeed. They are no longer in the civilian world, subject to
civilian authorities. They are in the military, subject to military authorities and an entirely different legal system known as the Uniform Code of
Military Justice. The code is far stricter, and far less forgiving, than its
civilian counterpart.

The reason for the military-civilian distinction is straightforward:
the Marines have been entrusted to save and take lives. As part of that
trust, America has granted them a license to kill. There is little room for
error. Unlike all other professions, military mistakes are measured in the
number of young men wounded or dead. Over the course of two hundred
years, certain principles have evolved that work, principles that are right
regardless of time and circumstance. Because the stakes are so high, these
principles do not change with the come-and-go cultural trends. There is
no room for philosophical debate. The Corps does not modify them to
accommodate individual personalities, tastes, needs, or even physiolo-
gies. Anything that is prejudicial to good order and discipline goes by the
wayside no matter how popular.

Things like small unit discipline, the buddy system, the history of the
Corps, and equipment uniformity are drilled home. A soldier no longer
gets to decide whether they want to clean their weapon daily, or whether
camouflage or blue jeans suit them in battle, or whether they feel like saluting a superior officer. United States Marines are humbled from day

one—told that they know very little about what works in combat, forced
to obey the dictates that have proven themselves true over time. If any
one person fails to do so, they are summarily drummed out of the service.
The arrogant individualism that says, "My way is right, and my wants take
priority" has no place in the military. That arrogance is expunged from
the get-go.

However, even as the military spends a great deal of time humbling
others, it is itself a humble institution. As it breaks down and rebuilds incoming civilians at the individual level, so also the overarching body of
the military routinely deconstructs itself through a culture of self-
criticism and self-improvement. Again, the stakes are so high—human
lives—that institutional mistakes or blindness must be corrected as
quickly as possible. While certain principles remain immovable—things
like honor, courage, commitment—the way these principles are applied
over time must be modified to fit circumstances as they change. At one
point in time, it was considered honorable to keep women away from
frontline combat roles for a whole host of reasons (some valid, some not).
However, small unit experiences in combat in Iraq and Afghanistan,
where it is an absolute cultural taboo for a male to search a female, have
proven that principle invalid in certain contexts. So females have been
integrated into frontline units, and that integration has in no way con-
flicted with the overarching principle of honor. The system itself cannot
be arrogant, or else people die through systemic mistakes. And far more
people die through systemic mistakes than through individual ones.

Thus the military has constructed its own recurring self-criticism
process and pushed it down to all levels. This process, called the "after-
action report," takes place after every major battlefield engagement. Typically, a small unit leader, say, a forty-man-platoon commander or a
twelve-man-squad leader, will gather their troops around them once they
have reached safety after a firefight. Then the leader begins asking questions. The first questions are informational. What really happened, when,
how, and why? Who saw what? When and where?

War is unimaginably chaotic, but war in heavily urban areas (the hallmark of much of modern-day fighting—think Somalia, Fallujah, Ramadi)

is even more so. Civilians mix with enemies and the fire comes from all angles. You never know which member of a thousand-person crowd in a teeming marketplace is about to place a cell phone call that will detonate your unit. You never know which of the thousands of windows in your field of vision houses the sniper that just shot someone through the stomach. During heavy fighting a leader is hard-pressed to know where all of his own men are at any given point in time, let alone where all of the fire is coming from, what equipment the enemies are using, what tactics have their hallmark, etc.

Different individuals at different points of the battle can have widely different experiences and different data points to share about what really happened. It is therefore imperative that everyone from the lowest private to the leader himself has an opportunity to tell their story. No one has a lock on the truth no matter how high their rank. You never know when someone who would not have spoken had you not asked them will reveal a lifesaving piece of information. I have had my life saved more than once by sharp thinking from an eighteen-year-old private first class—the most junior of all of my men.

Once the situation has been pieced together, as best as possible, the second part of the after-action begins: the evaluation. First, a leader needs to know what they and their team did well. It is extremely important to understand what worked, to identify and pass along best practices, to know what to reinforce and focus on going forward. Second, a leader and team need to know what they did poorly, starting with the leader, moving to the team, and ending with the system. What decisions that were made were bad? Who froze under fire? Who can't shoot straight? What forms of communication did not work? What training was irrelevant? What processes were cumbersome? What pieces of planning were overlooked? What needs to be fixed, tweaked, or discarded altogether going forward? In the after-action, the leader is expected to do just that—to lead, especially in the criticism bit. Often, the best way to spark constructive criticism is to criticize yourself, to begin by saying, "I know I could have done better. Here is a mistake that I made."

I will never forget my first post-firefight after-action report. I had been in Iraq for only a few weeks. It was March 2004, and I was leading only my fourth or fifth urban patrol deep into the heart of a known anti-American hotbed. We were to check on a police chief rumored to be taking home quite a bit more than his fair share of pay. Halfway through the walk to the police station, I lost contact with the first of my three squads. After ten minutes of unsuccessful radioing, and no gunfire, I assumed that they had executed the lost-communication plan and returned to base. The mission to the police station continued.

An hour later, the police chief had been put on notice and my remaining two squads and I were walking back through the dense city center, headed back to base. The unbroken compound walls that make up Iraq's city blocks stretched alongside us for hundreds of yards. It created a claustrophobic feeling that we were not yet used to. After an uneventful forty-five minutes, my lead squad popped out of the housing compounds and made it back into base. My last squad and I were still two blocks away when word came back from headquarters that my first squad, the one we had not heard from in more than an hour, was still missing. My third squad and I headed back to find them.

Not ten minutes later, the "missing" first squad was found—safely back in base. Frustrated, we turned around and began the short walk back to safety. Nearly twenty minutes passed, and I finally saw the gates of our compound. I started to relax. Then two booms in quick succession ran out—the telltale signs of an RPG launch. At the head of my patrol, I whipped my head around to check out the area behind me where I had heard the explosions. What I saw horrified me: my last four men had disappeared entirely. In their place was only a cloud of smoke.

A few moments later, the missing men appeared, running through the smoke with their eyes wide. I had little time for relief, though, because at about the same time that I realized my men were alive, someone else started shooting at us with machine guns. I couldn't see our attackers, so I and the rest of the Marines at the head of the platoon turned around and began running to the sound of the guns. Before we could sort out the situation, though, the fire stopped. I never saw our attackers, and I assumed the same was true with the rest of my men. After all, all our assailants had to do was simply drop their weapons and step around the corner of one of the blocks. We would never have been able to distinguish them from the rest of the city's denizens.

Once we made it back to base safely, we dropped our gear and began the after-action process. After all, it was our very first firefight. We pieced the story together, and once we understood what had happened, I mused aloud that it had been unfortunate that we had never seen our attackers. One of my privates spoke up and informed me that he had, in fact, seen the enemy machine gunners. I knew that none of us had fired a shot, so I was furious. Why hadn't he done his job? Why hadn't he helped stop the fire? It was pure luck that none of us had been hit—no thanks to him, in my mind. I demanded an explanation.

And I got one. Head hung low, eighteen-year-old Private Dotson explained to me that he had considered firing, but he had refrained.

"Sir, I wanted to shoot, but I was worried that if I did, I would hit the kids. They were at least a hundred meters away. I don't have any special sights. Just my iron sights. I thought that was the right decision. I thought that was what you wanted, sir."

Dotson had chosen not to shoot and to put himself, and the rest of us, at risk so that he could be absolutely sure he would not injure a child. Hearing him, I was immediately ashamed of my anger. I had one more thing to add to my lengthening list of what to do better. In front of my Marines, I had to criticize myself for my earlier unjustified anger at Dotson. He was a better man than I, and I knew it. It was not the last time an after-action process would humble me. And every time, I was a better man for it.

The after-action process is a great tool to instill humility, but it is a by-product, not the root cause, of institutional humility. In the Corps, the twin pillars of humility are, rather, the belief that tried-and-true principles are more important than individual preferences and an unyielding faith that all Marines are equally worthy—a faith that says that once a civilian has proven themselves willing to submit, then they become part of an institution that values its members equally. This second belief is so ingrained that it constitutes a cultural assumption. Marines are proud to be Marines, period. No job is beneath anyone—"Every Marine is a rifle-man" is the service's motto. Officers are expected to humbly serve their enlisted men, to give up comfort and privilege so that others might have them. "The least of these"—the buck privates—are no less important than the highest-ranking general.

In my first tour in Iraq, shortly after the invasion, when everything was in mass chaos, none of the super-bases—little mini-Americas with Subways and Pizza Huts—had been built. We used whatever we could find for shelter. The First Marine Division took over one of Saddam Hussein's palace complexes, and there was not enough room for everyone to be housed inside. So the highest-ranking officers slept in un-air-conditioned tents set up on the grass and sand behind the palace. Temperatures at night remained above 100 degrees Fahrenheit. The junior Marines got the comfort of air-conditioning and the safety of accommodations inside the palace itself.

WHAT HUMILITY IS NOT

Humility like Lincoln's, and the military's, underpins every successful leader and serves as a necessary complement to a driving sense of mission. To many, this statement is counterintuitive—doesn't humility make a leader look weak, and isn't weakness the opposite of leadership? Many books have been written to help leaders look stronger, to help them learn to radiate confidence and charisma. Seminar after seminar teaches the same thing. The aim is not to recover from failure, or to take responsibility for it. The point is to teach you how to avoid it. Very few motivational speakers talk about the importance of accepting responsibility and blame for mistakes. Very few courses teach that leaders must criticize themselves, seek criticism from others, and try to learn something from everyone they encounter no matter what their station in life. And very few businesses promote people who openly acknowledge their shortcomings and failures.

Popular culture exacerbates the tendency to shun humility and flaunt self-confidence. In its ceaseless clamor for our attention, news and enter-tainment outlets fixate on certain leaders and make them out to be larger-than-life. Movies revolve around characters with superhuman abilities who go it alone as they daringly achieve great things. Our heroes are often a modern-day combination of the Lone Ranger and Rambo. They need nothing and no one; their own strength is sufficient for any situation. However, those of us who have actually lived do-or-die professionally know that, in the real world, the only thing the Lone Ranger gets is dead.

The twenty-four-hour news cycle is just as bad. Every day brings an-other larger-than-life entertainment figure busy self-promoting in a spectacular and titillating fashion. The same is true in business, where business publications lionize chief executives as if they possessed para-normal abilities—super-intelligence, infallible strategic vision, magical oratory, and so on. Before he was indicted for multiple felonies, Jeffrey Skilling, CEO of Enron, was described by *Worth* magazine as "hyper-smart" and "hyper-confident." A 1999 article in *Business Week* described the former junk-bond king (and white-collar criminal) Michael Milken as follows: "The man works—really works—15 hours a day, seven days a week. He seems almost too focused, lacking the little flaws and weak-nesses that make the rest of us fallible, susceptible to distraction, and in a word, human."* Similar statements are written about other corporate leaders nearly every single week. The CEO of Gree Electronics, an air-conditioning giant, summed up this philosophy of larger-than-life leadership neatly: "I never miss. I never admit mistakes and I am always correct."

It would seem that if we want to gain a place of prominence, if we want to lead, then we must be supremely confident in our superhuman abilities. Humility is perhaps seen as nice in theory, but besides the point and maybe even dangerous when it comes to the business of life But, in fact, the opposite is true. Humility in a leader is one of the few indicators of true strength and genuine confidence. A lack of humility only signifies

---

* Kathleen Morris, "The Reincarnation of Mike Milken," *Business Week*, May 10, 1999, available at http://www.businessweek.com/1999/99_19/b3628001.htm.

weakness, insecurity, and a brittleness that is unable to admit to and cope with mistakes. The nonhumble are not flawless; rather, they hide their failures and weaknesses until poor choice compounds upon poor choice and the truth can no longer remain hidden. The resulting fall from grace is as meteoric as it is tragic.

Consider the sports stars who are lionized for their godlike athletic abilities, only to be indicted for rape, murder, or animal cruelty. Consider the movie stars whose jet-setting lifestyles are the envy of all, until they check themselves into rehab, divorce their spouses (for the third time), or commit suicide. Consider the megachurch pastors who make their careers denouncing immorality while cheating on their wives, using drugs, or abusing children. Consider the politicians who trumpet their family values and their tough-on-crime reputations only to be caught using prostitutes one night and prosecuting their johns the very next day.

If we want to avoid the fate of leaders turned laughingstocks, then we must be humble. Far from needing to project a façade of omniscience and unassailable strength, we must be vulnerable, admit mistakes, and welcome ideas and opinions that challenge our own, like Lincoln welcoming Stanton's ill-phrased criticism, or a combat officer accepting correction from his lowest private. But to be humble, and to overcome our reflexive resistance to mastering this virtue in our own lives, we must first understand what it is, and how it can be applied.

So let us begin our exploration of humility by identifying what it is not. Humility is not thinking less of ourselves and downplaying our gifts and talents. It is not denying to ourselves that we are good at certain things, or that we have done good work in certain areas. It is not spending inordinate amounts of time obsessing about what we do wrong every day. However, many of us think that these things are precisely what is meant by this virtue, which gives this character trait a weak, even neurotic, overtone. In this view, if we are to achieve humility, we must live in a constant state of denial, wishing away our strengths and achievements lest we somehow fall victim to pride. And if we somehow cannot manage to keep our healthy pride regarding where we are strong and what we have done at bay, then we must immediately fixate on a weakness to overwhelm our strength. Thus humility becomes a virtue of the weak, the pathetic, or the insane.

Another equally prevalent misconception holds that while humility does not mean denying ourselves to ourselves, it does mean denying ourselves to others. In this view, it is perfectly acceptable to be internally proud of strengths and accomplishments, but the moment the internal becomes the external, the humble virtue vanishes. We have to turn away from all praise, no matter how well-meaning. We have to shun encouragement, lest we become puffed up with pride. Or, worst of all, we have to put on false modesty and lie to others, to tell them how we are not proud of who we are (when we really are) and are not pleased with what we have done (even when we recognize it to be remarkable). Humility thus becomes a virtue of the deluded or the deceitful. We say things like "Oh, this probably isn't very good" when we know that we have, in fact, produced something excellent. We tell others, "Oh, I didn't do that good a job" when we actually know that we knocked it out of the park. And if we say it enough, we may even begin to believe what we say, to the point that we can no longer recognize our own strengths and weaknesses.

If we are not trying to mislead ourselves or others, then perhaps we are trying to beat ourselves down. Many believe that humility entails a lack of confidence, the latter being a trait that some equate (wrongly) with pride. The humble do not make decisions or voice opinions and ideas. They shun responsibility and doubly shun giving direction or orders. Humility thus becomes a virtue of the frustrating and indecisive. I have also heard humility used to refer to undue deference—letting others speak for us when we do not need them to. Humility is now for the meek and the mute. It is again a negative virtue, good in theory but questionable, even terrible, in practice.

When we tag all of the above maladies with the label humility, as we often do, then our experience with those who practice this "virtue" only reinforces our negative perception of it. Most of us have met people who are truly gifted in a certain area, say art or math, but do not believe in their gift and therefore do not use it to its fullest potential. Their failure to respond to encouragement to grow and develop in their gift is not humble; it is frustrating and a waste of talent. Similarly, we have met people who tell us that they are less good than they think they are simply so they can hear the praise and affirmation that comes back their way—false modesty is a tedious game to play for those on the other side of it. It is also the furthest thing from humility.

Furthermore, most of us have dealt with leaders who struggled to make decisions because they did not believe in their own abilities or because they feared taking responsibility for the outcome. We've seen them sit silent through meetings when they should talk, or let someone else speak for them when they should not. We've waited for them to take charge and give direction, only to be disappointed by vague murmurs and noncommittal answers. At some point most of us have probably felt completely lost in a crisis, unsure of who is to do what, and when, or who is in charge of which decisions and responsible for which outcomes. Many times this failure to decide, this lack of clarity, gets passed off as humility. Thus we've been made even more lost by a "humble" leader who leaves us to flail in a sea of uncertainty.

The confused and confusing virtue of humility has become something of dubious worth in our society, which values positive self-image and high self-esteem (a trait highest in sociopaths and violent felons, by the way) above all else. No wonder, then, that many leaders do not value the virtue of humility. Not only is it misunderstood—it is often confused with vice.

TRUE HUMILITY

At its essence, humility is nothing more than a realistic and unflinching view of yourself and your relationships. Humility is not self-deceit, self-denial, or self-flagellation. A leader grounds humility in an honest assessment of strengths and weaknesses, an inventory of the good, the bad, and the ugly. If we do something well, whether through training or talent, it is important that we identify and understand what that is so that we can most effectively apply it. If we do something poorly, whether through

lack of aptitude or lack of virtue, it is equally important that we understand what that is so that we can most effectively fix it. There is nothing
novel in asserting that a leader should understand their makeup—whole
consulting industries are based on this premise. What is new, I hope, is the
premise that this self-understanding and self-reflection constitutes humility. By gaining a deeper and more realistic knowledge of ourselves, we
become more humble.

However, the virtue of humility is only partially practiced if we con-
fine it to simple self-knowledge. Humility in a leader finds its fullest expression in its relationship to a team. A humble leader has to have not
only a realistic view of themselves but also a realistic view of their team
and a realistic appraisal of how their team views them. Just as Lincoln
understood that title—even if it is that of President of the United States
of America—does not automatically confer respect and obedience, so
must a leader have the humility to clearly assess their standing apart from
their position. The nameplate on a door, the box on an organizational
chart, or the listing on a business card has little or nothing to do with how
a team approaches its leader. Just because your title says that you lead
does not automatically mean that your team thinks that they should follow. Respect is hard-earned, never freely given. The humble leader recognizes this fact and is willing to take the time to understand and accept
how their team relates to them in reality, rather than focus on how things
line up in theory.

A leader also needs to ensure that their accurate view of themselves is
passed along to their team. The humble leader openly and honestly edu-
cates those whom they lead about the leader's own strengths and weaknesses. It is good to know oneself and good to know one's team, but if we
cannot put that knowledge into practice and effectively bridge the gap
between ourselves and our teams, then that knowledge goes to waste. Humility becomes unactionable. So the humble leader must take the time to
pass along their self-assessment to his team. Painful or not, leaders have
to expose weaknesses so that their teams can help them avoid pitfalls.
Pleasant or not, leaders have to communicate their strengths to their
teams so that everyone can know who can help, and where. If the first two

pillars of humility are self and team knowledge, then the third one is com-munication.

There is a story about Oliver Cromwell, the famous seventeenth-century English general, that neatly brings to life this concept of humility as both knowledge and knowledge transmission. For the first forty years of his life, Cromwell—arguably the single most important English leader of his century—labored in complete obscurity. He was born into the lower rung of the landed gentry and thus lived a modest, if comfortable, existence as a yeoman farmer. However, at the age of thirty-two, Crom-well sold his property, moved, and took a step down in society. For the next eight years, his only distinguishing feature was an undistinguished two-year stint in Parliament, the only record of which was a poorly re-ceived speech against an Armenian bishop.

Then, at the age of forty-one, Cromwell was given another chance in Parliament. Shortly thereafter, the English Civil War broke out. Sup-porters of King Charles I went to war against supporters of the Parlia-ment, and Oliver Cromwell, a man who had no formal military training or experience, recruited a small band of cavalry to fight on the side of the parliamentarians. Over the next four years, Cromwell proved a master soldier and natural leader. In fact, he was so talented that he eventually took command of the entire parliamentary forces, dubbed the New Model Army, and overthrew the English monarchy. In four short years, the no-name farmer, undistinguished legislator, and military amateur had become the most powerful figure in all of England, at the head of one of the world's most effective fighting forces. He had also overturned centu-ries of established monarchical authority.

In 1654, this military and political prodigy sat for a picture. Knowing he was painting the most powerful living man in his country (and maybe even the most influential Englishman of the past five hundred years), the painter turned out a first draft depicting Cromwell as an idealized Roman god. It was the most popular style of the time and one fitting for the sub-ject. However, Cromwell took one look at the painting and rejected it out of hand. He was not a Roman god, and he knew it. In fact, Cromwell had notable facial blemishes that made him far from handsome.

He demanded the painting be redone, realistically, and this time he had some guidance for the painter. "You will paint me just as I am, warts and all," he said, "else I will not pay a farthing for it." Cromwell knew what he was, and he wanted others, and posterity, to know as well. In that single instance, he captured the essence of humility—accurate self-knowledge and realistic transmission—and he bequeathed to the English-speaking people a phrase that neatly sums up the concept: "Just as I am, warts and all."

A LEADERSHIP ACCELERATOR

Let's look more closely at why humility, properly understood, is so important for a leader. First, this virtue serves as a necessary counterbalance to a driving sense of mission. Few, if any, people choose to advance causes that they believe are inherently evil. Few leaders make it a goal to become increasingly more immoral with each passing day, or to make their name synonymous with all that is wrong with humanity. Even the monsters of history—Stalin, Hitler, Robespierre, Jim Jones, etc.—started with what they truly believed was a righteous cause. Winston Churchill himself believed that Vladimir Ilyich Lenin promoted communism with humanity's best interests at heart, that "his sympathies [were] cold and wide as the Arctic Ocean."

And that is precisely the problem with passionate leaders who pursue their mission without humility. They risk destroying that which they would save. They are prone to justifying any means that will bring about their noble end—even if that means goes against all commonly accepted human decency. With no one to check them, and with no desire to be checked, a little evil for a great good becomes an acceptable trade-off. Once a little evil is acceptable, then the dam is breached and a lot of evil becomes routine. Those who stand in the way, be they individuals or whole classes of people, become acceptable losses in the quest for a salvific goal that will redeem all of humanity. For example, to create a society characterized by liberty, equality, and fraternity, French revolutionary leader Robespierre beheaded thousands of reactionaries. To take from each according to his means and give to each according to his needs, Stalin starved, slaughtered, exiled, and imprisoned millions. To create an agrarian utopia, Pol Pot murdered a third of Cambodia's citizens and told them, "To keep you is no benefit, to destroy you is no loss." The more an arrogant leader seeks to bring heaven to earth, the greater the likelihood that they will create a terrestrial hell.

However, a humble leader is far less likely to take their mission to immoral, illegal, or illogical extremes, because humble leaders are far more likely to see themselves just as they are—warts and all—and convince others to see them the same way. Instead of being surrounded by sycophants who will praise their every decision no matter how evil, humble leaders are likely to surround themselves with true friends who will tell them hard truths when they need to hear them, particularly when the mission needs a serious course correction. Jack Welch, the famously successful CEO of General Electric, once quipped that a business leader would be lucky if 60 percent of their decisions were correct. Humility helps keep leaders from harming themselves and others with the other 40 percent. "Faithful are the wounds of a friend," says the book of Proverbs, "but the kisses of an enemy are deceitful." Humble leaders will not only seek out friendly wounds but also enable and encourage their friends to wound them. Humility, therefore, keeps a leader in check and their mission intact.

Humility also allows a leader to be self-reflective. I was very fortunate to have Nitin Nohria, now dean of Harvard Business School, as my leadership professor when I attended there. Over dinner one evening, Nitin told me that of all of the studies the department had done on various types of leaders—intellectual versus emotional, executional versus strategic, etc.—he and his researchers could find only one quality that the successful ones shared. That quality was reflectiveness. Nitin was initially surprised—surely there was something else, like charisma, that also predicted success. But there wasn't. No matter what they tried, Nitin and his team could find just that one common trait.

Whether because of natural personality or deliberate training, all of the successful leaders in the Harvard study reflected regularly on themselves—their successes and failures, their strengths and weaknesses. They often diagnosed their own problems before anyone else did. Without humility, though, it is impossible to be self-reflective. How can we acknowledge weaknesses and mistakes if we are not at all concerned with seeing ourselves as we truly are? Humility is the necessary virtue for all of us if we want to self-assess accurately, if we want to be the ones to change course when necessary, before circumstances force our hand.

Humility also accelerates the pace at which we learn from mistakes, which accelerates the pace of learning and thus of innovation. Everyone makes them. Leaders typically make more than most—after all, they have increased scope for decision-making—and their mistakes typically affect more people. Humility, however, allows a leader to fail in small ways rather than large ones. Spectacular mistakes and awesome blunders do not happen in a vacuum. They are usually preceded by minor failures and small misjudgments, each one building upon the next because the leader remains unchecked and their words remain unchallenged. Eventually, the mistakes get so big, and the failures so pronounced, that some external force steps in—whether friends, family, the boss, or the law—to take the reins.

The iconic design firm IDEO, responsible for products ranging from water bottles to board shorts, avoids the peril of the unrecoverable mistake by expecting, even demanding, that their employees make mistakes and make them visibly as the design process begins. IDEO has institutionalized this mindset in a mantra: "Fail early, fail often." They do not believe that their best products spring whole from the minds of lone-wolf designers. Rather, successes are the product of a team working together to test ideas from all directions. They fail at some, succeed at others, and in so doing create something that is far better, and far longer lasting, than any single individual's initial concept.

They also do it quickly—IDEO can go from concept to final design in under a week. It is their willingness to fail quickly, self-criticize, and fail yet again that allows them to iterate rapidly toward a final product. Without humility, IDEO would not be nearly as quick, nor would their products be nearly as good. IDEO would have to wait until consumers rejected their mediocre designs before they learned their flaws.

In addition to accelerating the learning process, humility allows the best ideas of an organization to bubble up to the surface. If a team feels that its leader will take input from everywhere, even if that input directly contradicts the leader's own assessments, then a team will be much more likely to float its ideas in the hopes of having them enacted. However, if a team feels that a leader will brook no contradiction, then its initiatives wither. What's the point of giving input if it's never acted upon? Better to save the effort, keep your head down, and put in the minimum work needed to just get by. An arrogant leader will always have a disconnected and disenfranchised team. A humble leader, on the other hand, will have a team that is engaged in finding solutions to problems and better ways to do things, for they will be accustomed to seeing good ideas put into practice to make a difference.

The "soft" virtue of humility, therefore, has some very "hard" practical consequences. A team will find that the rate at which it produces ideas and products is significantly accelerated. An organization with humility at its core will almost certainly be able to iterate more quickly than its competitors, which means that it will almost certainly be more innovative, too. What is more, deliberate humility is likely to increase the quality of both products and ideas. Paradoxically, the virtue that is often deliberately shunned by leaders and by leadership theory is the one virtue that can accelerate two of the very things they seek most: innovation and quality.

Humility also allows a leader to connect with her team at a human level by acknowledging openly that she, the leader, makes mistakes, regardless of what title she bears or chair she sits in. By formalizing this approach to patients, the University of Michigan Health System actually cut its rate of lawsuits in half in just five years (2001–2006) after implementing a policy under which doctors who had made mistakes met with the affected patients, humbly admitted their mistakes, and apologized. It did not matter that the doctors were under tremendous pressure, working long hours with little thanks in return. It did not matter that by admitting fault, the doctors exposed themselves to damaging lawsuits in an overly litigious health-care system. It did not matter that the doctors were highly trained MDs and their patients were not. None of the exacerbating circumstances mattered. The only thing that mattered was the mistake and how the system handled it; these humble apologies humanized the doctors, made them vulnerable, and connected them with their patients in a way that standoffish intransigence never can. The results speak for themselves.

Humility also allows a leader to adapt quickly to changing circumstances, because they are comfortable knowing that they can still lead well even if they make an incorrect decision. In our Infantry Officer Course (the closest thing the Marine Corps has to Army Ranger School), we were told a story about a group of American and Israeli officers put together for a planning exercise. Both groups were given a briefing on a tactical situation and then told they had half a day to formulate a plan to deal with it. The briefing was fairly complete, so the two teams had enough information to begin planning.

However, there was one twist to this exercise. A new piece of information would be given to the teams every half hour. The longer the group of officers waited, the more assured they could be that their plans fully incorporated the most up-to-date intelligence. The timer started, and both teams began working. The Israelis waited for thirty minutes and received their first piece of information. They briefly evaluated it, then turned in their final plan. They walked outside and, according to our instructors, the entire team lit up and began smoking.

Several hours after the Israeli group finished, the Americans still had not decided what to do. They wanted a perfect plan, so they waited to be sure they had all information possible. By the end of the drill, the Americans were receiving irrelevant information, like the enemy commander's belt size, but still they could not force themselves to turn in a plan. The difference between the two groups: the Israelis had been humbled by real-life combat, where no plan survives first contact with the enemy, so they knew that their initial decisions needn't be mistake-free in order for them to succeed; they only needed to be good enough to drive constructive action. Thus they made their decision quickly, prepared to adapt their plan as the circumstances changed.

The Americans, by contrast, had plied their trade in peacetime, where a zero-defects training mentality prevailed. Unlike the Israelis' wars, the Americans' exercises were highly scripted affairs in which commanders were led to believe that their plans could, and should, encompass all foreseeable eventualities. The Americans had not yet been humbled by war. They lacked the hard-earned experience to tell them that they could not, and should not, try to anticipate every eventuality. No one can, especially in the chaos that is war, but it takes humble leadership to admit this and to function well within changing and uncertain circumstances. The Israelis had humility learned through failure; thus they were comfortable with fluid situations and the adaptation required to deal with them. The Americans had no real combat experience, and as a result, they had the arrogance to believe that they could make perfect decisions. They were, therefore, uncomfortable with uncertainty and unable to make decisions, paralyzed by the fact that if they could just understand more—just reduce the uncertainty a bit—then they could make the perfect decision they had been trained to believe existed.

Last but not least, humility allows a leader to take responsibility for failure. This in turn frees them to make important decisions. Many people know that General Dwight Eisenhower led the British and American Allied troops in the famous D-Day invasion of continental Europe in 1944. Many people also know that by the time he commanded the famous Operation Overlord, Eisenhower had been promoted to "Supreme Allied Commander of the Allied Expeditionary Force." He was America's only five-star general, a commission granted him in perpetuity. However, fewer people know that Eisenhower was President Roosevelt's second choice to lead America's forces overseas (the president's first choice, George Marshall, was needed back at home). And fewer still know that Eisenhower, the five-star General of the Army, had spent an incredible sixteen years as a lowly major, serving on monotonous assignments such as the staff of the American Battle Monuments Commission. Today under such circumstances, most officers would exit the force. In fact, many of Eisenhower's West Point compatriots did. Promotion at that snail's pace is almost insulting, and it is typically reserved for the less-than-promising.

For whatever reason, Eisenhower persevered through the plodding between-wars military. The same man who had worked for two years to support his brother's college education and disqualified himself from the U.S. Naval Academy as a result (too old) stuck to his post in the Army. If Eisenhower had not learned humility before those years of drudgery (and by all accounts he had), he certainly would have learned it during them. That same virtue stuck with him for the rest of his life. On June 5, 1944, with the fate of Western Europe riding on his shoulders, General Dwight Eisenhower penned the following note: "Our landings in the Cherbourg-Havre area have failed to gain a satisfactory foothold and I have withdrawn the troops. . . . The troops, the air and the Navy did all that bravery and devotion to duty could do. If any blame or fault attaches to the attempt, it is mine alone."

Eisenhower's humility, cultivated over decades, prepared him to shoulder the responsibility for failure in the D-Day invasion, arguably the Western world's most important undertaking of the twentieth century. This humility, in turn, gave Eisenhower the freedom to order the invasion of Normandy under conditions that were far from ideal. The seas were choppy, the air was foggy, and the invasion date had been twice delayed due to weather. A lesser man might have hesitated, too proud to risk the opprobrium associated with a blighted effort. Eisenhower did not. The rest is history.

RUNNING COUNTER TO OUR CULTURE

Our culture—popular, business, political, etc.—does not promote humility as a virtue necessary for leadership. Quite the opposite, in fact. In some places people occasionally give humility lip service, but, for the most part, the leaders that make headlines, even the good ones, are rarely known for their modest self-effacement. After all, the humble person is not flashy. Magazines cannot hype superhuman humility (an oxymoron, really) in the same way that they can super-intelligence, super-drive, or super-egotism. Individuals cannot compliment themselves during interviews for being way more humble than their competitors. Humility flies largely under the radar of our everyday experience, and, sadly enough, the good leaders who possess this quality are the least likely to have their story told, simply because they are themselves unlikely to tell it, and the business/entertainment industry is unlikely to tell it for them.

Humility is countercultural and poorly understood (and often misunderstood, as we have seen), but it is absolutely necessary for leaders who want to make a positive impact on the world around them. At its heart, humility is nothing more than a realistic picture of ourselves and an ability to transmit that picture accurately to others. It is not weakness, hesitation, or self-doubt. In fact, humility allows leaders to increase their strength and to recover quickly from mistakes that would devastate many. And there is hope that all of us can attain this virtue if we pursue it in an intentional and disciplined fashion. True leaders are not one-in-a-million celebrities, nor are they special, gifted people on a plane apart from the rest of humanity. They are everymen and everywomen who realize their own flaws, accept correction and change behavior, and seek to learn from those around them.

If we can attain humility, then we can be assured that we have gained a character trait that will help us lead well in the long run. Just as Eisenhower, Lincoln, and Cromwell labored for years in complete obscurity, so also we may have to do our best to lead well with few public accolades. We may find that humility prevents us from making the headlines, or even the fast track, in the same way as do some of our more flashy and self-promoting compatriots. Humility, however, will never steer us wrong. Lincoln has a national memorial; Jeff Skilling has a jail cell. Those who lead well and the leaders who stand the test of time are invariably humble.

REFLECTION

Humility is not an easy virtue to cultivate, for it requires that we deliberately make ourselves vulnerable to others. Humility demands that we routinely seek out criticism and risk appearing weak or incompetent by admitting flaws and mistakes. Difficult as all of this may be, it is necessary, and we must begin at the beginning: by asking ourselves a few hard questions.

Reflection Questions

1. How do we want to relate to those whom we lead—do we want them to serve us (are we at the top of the pyramid) or do we want to serve them (is the pyramid turned on its head)?
2. How do we currently lead at work? At home? In our social lives?
3. When was the last time we said, "I was wrong," "I am sorry," or "Please forgive me"?
4. When was the last time we asked for constructive criticism?

Humility is a virtue that disappears the moment we are confident that we have achieved it. It requires constant reflection, self-assessment, transparency, and accountability, all of which can be extremely painful to do even once, let alone repeatedly. But if we want to know ourselves and build our strengths while minimizing our weaknesses, then that is precisely what we must do. If we can manage to stay the course, we will find that not only will we become better at what we do but, more important, we will get deeper insight into who we truly are. Humility thus lays the foundation for every follow-on virtue.

However, if we hope to lead ourselves and others well, humility alone is not enough.

SUMMARY

- Humility is a virtue that is imperative for a leader, and it must accompany a driving sense of mission.
- Popular culture (and much leadership literature) promotes a false and dangerous myth that humility is actually a weakness for a leader, because all successful leaders must be larger-than-life, possessed of abilities above and beyond those of ordinary human beings.
- Humility is widely misunderstood as thinking less of ourselves than we should, downplaying ourselves to others, denying our own very real gifts and talents, or failing to make decisions.
- True humility is nothing more, and nothing less, than a realistic and accurate view of ourselves and our relationships—"warts and all."
- Humility accelerates our leadership by putting guardrails around our passion and our mission, by enabling self-reflection, by helping us connect at the human level with our teams, by setting us at ease in rapidly changing circumstances, and by allowing us to take responsibility for failure.
- Humble teams and humble organizations will find themselves more innovative than others, will produce higher-quality products and ideas than others, and will be better able to persevere through changing circumstances than those who are not.
- Humility runs against the grain of the present day and age, but leaders who want to become and remain successful must pursue this virtue.

———— ★ ————

CHAPTER 3

EXCELLENCE

When the gargoyles at the cathedral in Nîmes, France, were removed for renovation, church authorities discovered something surprising: the backs of the statues, which no one would ever see, were as intricately carved as their fronts. The same thing was true of the gargoyles at the top of the building, high and hidden from view. The intricacy of the pieces was particularly strange because gargoyles at the time were not primarily ornamental. They were functional. Their main purpose was to funnel rainwater away from the stone so that the running water would not degrade the mortar that held the masonry together. Why would someone go to all of the trouble, and take all of the time, to intricately carve something that no one would ever see and something that did not even need to be ornamental to serve its purpose?

The answer is straightforward, even if somewhat hard for modern Western culture to understand. The medieval artists believed that all their work at the cathedral—seen or unseen, decorative or practical— glorified God, and they carved with that goal foremost in mind. Their overarching aim was not to please viewers or preserve stonework. Their aim was to honor their Maker, who they believed gave them their talents, by giving Him in return the best work that their talents were capable of producing. Their aim was not to just get by, to do whatever work was good enough to accomplish a cursory inspection. Rather, the artisans gave every statue their best effort, for they believed that excellence was an end in and of itself, that excellence was worth achieving even if it produced no personal advancement and even if no one else ever noticed.

Ludwig van Beethoven also believed in giving his best to pursue excellence. He proved it by producing a work so beautiful that, for a time, it was considered to be an unsurpassable pinnacle of artistic expression. But even as he created his magnum opus, Beethoven knew that he himself would never enjoy it. In 1817, the Philharmonic Society of London commissioned the renowned composer to write what would become his final symphony. Regardless of the composer's fame and talent, it was a strange choice, because at the time of the commissioning, the fifty-four-year-old Beethoven was nearly deaf. There was no guarantee that he would even be capable of producing a symphony in his condition. If he did, it would likely be of dubious quality. How can someone who cannot hear check his own work? Would we trust a blind painter to produce a near-photographic still life? A poor or mediocre work would certainly set back the composer's hard-earned reputation when he could least afford it, at the very twilight of his career.

Even if Beethoven could produce a completed work, he knew with certainty that he would never enjoy the fruits of his own labor. If the best case happened, and he debuted his symphony to standing ovations and widespread acclaim, the master himself would never hear that which he composed for others. He would never eat of the fruit of his own labors or take in the beauty of that which he created. He would make some money, yes, by delivering a complete work to the philharmonic, but there was no reason to deliver his absolute best work to the society. His reputation was solidified already, and a work that was just good enough would have sufficed for a payday. So, by all rights, the famous composer in the twilight of his career should have churned out something of just-passing acceptability, especially knowing that his deafness would have been an acceptable excuse for mediocrity.

However, Beethoven took a different tack. He accepted the task and poured his heart and soul into it. He gave it his absolute best effort, believing that his work brought glory to his mission (his faith) and that it therefore demanded everything that his talent was capable of producing, regardless of whether that extra effort ever produced any personal gain for the master composer. After seven years of work, Beethoven unveiled his Ninth Symphony, conducting it himself at the Kaerntnertortheater in Vienna. When the music ended, the now entirely deaf composer was still furiously conducting (he was several measures behind the musicians). Beethoven had to be turned around to accept the audience's furious applause—five standing ovations' worth, the most the concert hall had ever seen. The symphony was a work of such excellence that for some time afterward contemporaneous composers stopped writing symphonies, believing that it would be impossible to improve upon the famous Ninth. To this day, it remains possibly the best-known classical work in the entire world. And Beethoven himself never heard it.

My comrade-in-arms Michael Kurz never produced a masterpiece, but he, like Beethoven, understood the value of striving for excellence. I got to know Kurz at Marine Infantry Officer Course, the intense, three-month school that prepares entry-level Marine officers to lead troops on the front lines. Though it is little known to the broader civilian world (and this is by design), Infantry Officer Course (IOC) is one of the most physically and mentally challenging schools in the military. The Marines spend most of their time at IOC in the field, patrolling through thick, jungle-like terrain, slogging through some of America's most challenging deserts, or hiking eighty-pound machine gun systems up and down mountains. The infantry hopefuls get little more than two to four hours of sleep a night, often going for days at a time without any sleep at all. If they are lucky, they will get one meal a day. They spend most of their time in a constant state of uncertainty, never knowing what exhausting mission will come next. Almost nothing stops the training—during a record cold several years ago, all Marine schools in Quantico, Virginia, were shut down, that is, all except IOC. While the others were let out for safety reasons, the IOC lieutenants spent the week crunching through knee-deep snow, carrying mortars during the day, and sleeping in tents huddled together for warmth at night. Some of the most senior officers in the Corps were so worried that they called the instructors daily to check on the welfare of the lieutenants.

I and thirty other Marines in my class had no choice but to attend the school, as we had been given an infantry specialty and would soon become infantry platoon commanders. However, Mike Kurz did have a choice. He was a pilot, and he did not need the school to progress in his career. In fact, he had actually put his career at risk by joining us—several pilots in the past had had twigs jammed into their eyes during night patrols through heavy brush, ruining their eyesight and their dreams of flying. Most pilots chose to avoid the grueling exercise in Quantico in favor of the pleasant weather at flight school in Pensacola, Florida. Kurz, though, wanted to be a Marine fighter pilot, which meant that his primary mission in the air would be to drop bombs for the troops on the ground. And if that were to be his primary mission, Kurz reasoned, then he needed to understand what the men on the ground were going through. And so he volunteered to put himself through the twelve weeks of starvation, sleeplessness, exhaustion, and career risk. For that reason, Kurz had my respect from the get-go.

As the weeks passed, my admiration for Kurz only grew. He wasn't the strongest or fittest officer. He didn't shoot as well as some others. His tactics, mission planning, and snap decision-making in the field were just slightly above average. We had at least five other officers in our class who were all-around more talented than Kurz. But Kurz did one thing that no one else in the class did: he gave every day, and every task, his absolute best.

If you needed someone to carry the heavy machine gun, Kurz would volunteer. If you needed someone to hike the twenty-pound radio and its spare batteries, Kurz was on it. If you had to ask someone to stand the worst watch of the night, the one from 3 to 4 a.m., you could ask Kurz and he would never turn you down. Every patrol would find him carrying extra weight. Every off shift would find him doing a little bit more preparation. And he never, ever complained. No matter how miserable the weather when we were on patrol, no matter how grueling the march, no matter how irritating his sleep-deprived classmates, Kurz never commented. He simply shrugged, shouldered whatever load was his to carry, and moved on. Day in and day out, never ceasing, never complaining, Kurz brought his A-game, and his consistency put us all to shame. He would never be in the infantry, but he gave every training day his best effort so that he could learn to be the best infantry officer he could possibly be, never mind the fact that he was slated to be a pilot. None of us pursued pure excellence with the same single-mindedness as did Kurz. By the time the twelve weeks ended, even the most talented officers in our class considered Kurz to be the finest man among us.

So the students of Infantry Officer Course 1-02 voted Mike Kurz as number-one officer in the class, the best of all of us. It was the first time in living memory that a pilot had earned the infantry school's most prestigious award. Kurz earned it solely by gaining the respect of his infantry peers—there were no instructor evaluations, or field grades, or performance metrics taken into account. It was straight voting, and in the final round, the votes were unanimous. To this day, I have never forgotten Lieutenant Mike Kurz and the lessons I learned from him. He gave his best at everything he set his hand to, and he never complained while doing it. He was a better man, and a better leader, than I.

OUR BEST EFFORTS EVERY DAY

If we hope to be the best leaders we can be, the ones who are effective over the long run, then we have got to be the Mike Kurzes of the world. We must give our best, every single day. We must understand the responsibility that each of those days brings. We must believe that time is a precious and undeserved gift that must be stewarded well. We must cultivate an attitude of thankfulness—not entitlement—for every morning that we are granted and resolve to make the most of those mornings out of respect for all of those who no longer have the gift of time. And the best way to demonstrate that respect is to seek excellence, to pursue it as an end in itself with no regard for whether our material well-being is enhanced as a result. To do any less, and to demand anything less from our teams, is to waste what we have been given.

Not every day will go well and not every job will turn out right. Van Gogh painted plenty of pictures that no one would buy in his lifetime. Thomas Edison produced thousands of nonworking inventions, and even the great Steve Jobs was once expelled from the company he founded. If each of these masters regularly produced less than perfect work, then we also must expect to produce less than perfect work. It is important, therefore, to understand what true excellence is and what it is not. For the purposes of leadership, excellence means applying our best efforts, every day, to the tasks we choose to take on, regardless of the personal benefits we may accrue or the costs we may incur. Excellence does not mean consistently producing masterworks of unsurpassable quality, and it does not imply that we must succeed at every job we undertake.

In fact, excellence is not defined by the outcome so much as it is by the input. We do not need to produce a work of incomparable beauty, like Beethoven's Ninth Symphony, to lay claim to the virtue of excellence. We do not necessarily need to make better decisions than our peers, nor do we need to do better or faster jobs than they.

Intent matters as well. Rewards are nice, and we should certainly hope that just rewards will be justly granted for work well done, but anticipated rewards cannot dictate the level of effort we put forth. We must not give our best only when we anticipate being rewarded for doing so. This type of conditioned behavior is more appropriate for lab rats than leaders. And any time we give less than our best, the person we cheat most is ourselves—we waste our talent and our time, and we can never take time back once it is gone. My first Marine gunnery sergeant used to hammer this point home every day by making us chant the following before we went to bed at night:

"Today I have given everything that I have. That which I have kept, I have lost forever."

So, excellence can be viewed, first and foremost, as our right response to the gift of time. I learned this lesson the hard way in combat, by watching so many of my comrades leave the base and never return whole, or at all. Prior to those bloody days, prior to seeing people just like me, people I loved and served with and led, return home in flag-draped caskets, I assumed that I would always have another day. I viewed tomorrow as assured and each day as a given. And because I viewed each day as a given, I took each day for granted, just like I did everything else in life I viewed as a given. Rather than feeling grateful, I felt entitled. It wasn't until I saw days gruesomely ripped away from people to my right and to my left that I began to question my arrogant assumption that time on earth was a given.

As time passed, I came to realize that there was no guarantee that I had any life left beyond the next day's fighting. The fighting was fierce, and I was always in it, and the law of averages was working against me. I survived the deployment. Once I returned home from combat, I continued to realize how fragile, and how fleeting, life is. Friends were diagnosed with cancer. Healthy relatives died unexpectedly. Accidents and tragedies happened, and I realized that life is no more guaranteed out of combat than it is in it.

This realization hit me hard on the first mass memorial service I attended stateside. Seeing all the rows of white crosses, with upside-down rifles, and boots and helmets stacked on top of them, made me realize that I had something that everyone buried in that field did not. I had time. Seeing the families sitting in the front rows of the folded chairs, dressed in black and receiving flags, made me realize something else: my gift of time was something that the wives, mothers, sons, and daughters of all of my departed comrades desperately hoped for but would never get.

Seeing all the small children beside the widows wearing black, I was conscious of the fact that the gift I had returned with was truly and completely undeserved. I wasn't a better or more proficient man than the men we were burying. Combat and the law of averages do not spare the skillful and the moral. The bad guys sometimes win and the best men sometimes die. I now know that each day I am granted has nothing to do with my talent and everything to do with unmerited grace and blessing. I know now that with that gift comes a responsibility, a calling to be excellent. I owe it to all of the dead—and their families—who would love what I have not to squander what I have been given; after all, it could have been given to them. The pursuit of excellence is my only acceptable response, and I submit that it is the only acceptable response for any leader to the days they have been given.

PERSEVERANCE, HOPE, AND INSPIRATION

The conscious quest for excellence must be layered on top of mission and humility. If our mission gives us drive, and humility helps refine and restrain that drive, then excellence helps sustain it. As leaders, we may be moved by passion, but no matter how lofty our ideals, eventually they, and we, get brought down to earth by the day-to-day grind of reality. What we want to achieve may take years, even decades, to bear fruit. In the meantime, we will encounter countless setbacks and outright failures. We will have to undertake tasks that we find boring or menial. We will find ourselves working just to make ends meet, feeding our families at the expense of our own enjoyment. We will get frustrated trying to coach and teach the uncoachable and unteachable. We will be betrayed by those whom we trusted. We will get worn down when our best efforts just are not good enough. We will be frustrated by events beyond our control, and we may despair as expectation after expectation remains unmet.

In the early 1930s, Dwight Eisenhower became a member of General Douglas MacArthur's staff. Though MacArthur valued Eisenhower's talents, day in and day out the general treated the major as a mindless drudge. What is more, Eisenhower had significant conflicts with his boss on everything from how to treat unemployed World War I veterans to how to build a Philippine defense force. "I always resented the years I spent as a slave in the War Department," he later said. However, there was one thing that helped the future Supreme Commander persevere through nearly a decade of drudgery and mistreatment in those brutal interwar years: giving his absolute best to produce excellence. In the future president's own words, "My ambition in the Army was to make everybody I worked for regretful when I was ordered to other duty."

If we pursue excellence, we have an achievable mission each and every day. If we walk into each day determined to do our very best, no matter what the outcome and no matter what the circumstances, then we can walk out of each day confident that we accomplished what we set out to do. Some days our best may be less, and some days it may be more, but each day it is achievable. The pursuit of excellence gives us something meaningful to chase after on those days—and during those seasons—where our overarching mission seems impossible or hopelessly out of reach.

Thus excellence produces perseverance, and perseverance, in turn, produces hope. It is when we stop trying that we stop hoping. The loss of hope is a terrible thing for anyone, but it is an especially terrible thing for a leader. Like it or not, the entire team keys off the attitude of the leader, and when a leader loses hope, then so does their team. If we do not have an achievable mission every single day, eventually we will stop trying to achieve it. Soon thereafter, we stop hoping, because our days seem pointless.

However, if we know that today we can give our all, and we do just that today, and then we do it again tomorrow, we realize that we can continue. Once we realize that we can continue, then we have hope that we can eventually produce something of meaning and worth, that we can achieve a life well lived. Furthermore, we have hope that we can get better, and that our circumstances may get better. One of my drill instructors loved to tell us: "Candidates, today is the worst that you will ever be. You will give your best today, so that tomorrow you will be better, because the Corps cannot afford for you to remain the same." As with most drill instructor sayings, I appreciate this one much more in retrospect, and I have come to see how true it is. If I can pursue excellence, then I can be better no matter what life throws at me, and if I know that I can be better, then I can keep going. And if I can keep going, then I can keep hoping.

The quest for excellence also promotes a stewardship, rather than an ownership, ideal in a leader. Stewardship begins with the idea that each day is a gift. Once we understand and embrace this concept, then we can take it one step further—not only are our days undeserved gifts, to be held in trust for those who no longer have them, but also our talents are undeserved gifts, to be held in trust for those who have fewer than we. It is the same with our circumstances—chances are that if you are reading this book, then your life's circumstances, no matter how difficult, are better off than a good majority of the rest of the world. Having spent years in some of the poorest and most violent areas of the globe, I now know that most anyone born in the developed world, no matter how difficult their circumstances, has a blessing that far exceeds that of many, many others. The average life span in Afghanistan is forty-two: by the time someone there hits twenty-one, they are already middle-aged.

Gifts stewarded well cannot fail to inspire others. Persistent best effort—irrespective of the circumstance and outcome—allows a leader to remain steadfast throughout life's ups and downs. And the pursuit of excellence allows a leader to set steady, achievable goals that don't vary with varied circumstances. Over the course of time, it is the plodding, steady tortoises, the Mike Kurzes of the world, who come to be respected by their team. It is those who can keep on keeping on no matter how much hardship is thrown at them who succeed in the end. This type of persistence is rare. Flash-in-the-pan talent, however, is common, and a team can stay inspired by that talent for just as long as it takes that leader to make a mistake, or to get distracted by the next big idea, or to set unachievable goals that they don't even pursue themselves. Leaders who last, leaders who give their all every day, are few and far between, but they are the ones who inspire others and give them hope.

Consider the story of Dick Hoyt, an ordinary, overweight middle-aged man who one day decided to commit himself to give his best effort in the service of someone else. The story begins in 1962, when Dick's first son,

Rick, was born with his umbilical cord wrapped around his neck. The cord cut off the flow of blood to the brain, leaving Rick so brain-damaged that he was unable to control any of his limbs or to speak. Dick and his wife, Judy, were encouraged to put their son in an institution, but instead they kept him at home. Dick worked two or three jobs at a time to pay for Rick's medical care. Judy taught her disabled son the alphabet. More than one specialist told the two parents that their son had minimal, if any, brain activity, that he was a complete vegetable.

However, eleven years after Rick's birth, biomedical engineers at Tufts University created a device that allowed Rick to tap out short sentences on a computer by moving his head. The "vegetable's" first sentence? "Go Bruins!" Though he had been unable to communicate for eleven years, Rick understood every word that everybody said. As it turned out, he loved jokes, especially those that came at his own expense. The boy whom the specialists had written off was a thinking, caring, sensitive human being who at the age of eleven—for the first time in his life—could share his feelings with others.

Four years later, a high school classmate of Rick's was paralyzed in an accident, and the school organized a five-mile charity run for him. The day before the run, Rick informed his father that he, too, would like to participate in the race to show his paralyzed friend that life goes on after tragedy and to show his two younger brothers—both all-state athletes—that he, too, was a competitor. At the time, Dick was a thirty-seven-year-old, flabby former Air National Guard captain who hadn't run more than a mile since boot camp. He had no idea how he would manage to run five miles, let alone run five miles while pushing a wheelchair. He was assigned the number 00, and his two youngest sons joked that the number represented Dick and Rick's chances of finishing the race.

Nevertheless, the next morning the father and his disabled son lined up at the starting line. They finished next to last, but they finished. When they got back home, Dick collapsed on the floor. His body was wasted, and he soon discovered something extremely disconcerting: he was urinating blood. For an hour Dick lay there, convinced that his short, unhappy racing career was over. But during that hour, Rick had typed out a message with his head. It had taken him the entire hour to do so.

Dad, when I am running, I don't even feel like I am handicapped.

So Dick decided not to quit after all. It took him nearly two years to find someone to make a racing wheelchair, but he eventually succeeded. During those years, he trained with Rick, getting up before dawn to take his paralyzed son to the bathroom, shave him, shower him, dry him, and push food past his reversed tongue—and that was before the running took place. Their first official road race together was a 10K in Springfield, Massachusetts, and it did not begin well. The registration officials didn't know in which category to place the father and his disabled son. The other racers stared at Rick, slumped in his wheelchair like a sack of potatoes. Whispers ran through the three-hundred-runner field.

Dick and Rick took their places at the starting line and took off with the other racers. When they completed the ten kilometers thirty-eight minutes and thirty seconds later, Dick and Rick had beaten half the field. A few months later, they tried to enter the Boston Marathon, but their application was rejected on the grounds that they did not fit either the able-bodied runners category or the wheelchair category. So, in April 1981, Dick and Rick ran the race as unofficial bandits. They clocked an incredible time of 3:18, but still the Boston Marathon denied them entrance. So they ran as bandits again the next year, reeling off an amazing 2:59—a time considered world-class for any nonhandicapped runner.

With this time, the administrators of the marathon had no choice but to give them a chance, so they allowed the Dick-and-Rick team a shot at officially qualifying. However, there was a catch: the two would have to qualify not in Dick's age group, 40–44, but in Rick's, 18–34. The time disparity between the two qualifying times was significant—the official decision was obviously an attempt to keep Dick and Rick out of the race at all costs. Undeterred, the two chose the Marine Corps Marathon as their qualifying race, and they finished in an amazing two hours, forty-eight minutes. To this day, veterans of the event consider that time one of the most amazing feats in the history of the race. The Boston Marathon finally let in the strange duo, and throughout the entire 26.2 miles, the forty-year-old father and his quadriplegic son were cheered by crowds three-deep.

Since that time, Dick and Rick Hoyt have competed in more than three hundred endurance races, including four Ironman triathlons, multiple ultramarathons, and twenty-eight Boston Marathons. Indeed, they have become the face of the race that tried to deny them. And the flabby, middle-aged father of three's selfless example of service has multiplied a thousandfold. There are now hundreds of volunteers pushing the physically handicapped on road races across America. The Team Hoyt charity has collected hundreds of thousands of dollars for communication devices for the disabled, dogs for the blind, and running chairs for the paralyzed. Their story has been told worldwide and has inspired tens of thousands to change their lives for the better.

War veterans who have been told that they would never walk again have run triathlons after hearing of the Hoyts. Families with disabled children fly to Boston just to see them run. They receive two hundred emails a day from people with various afflictions, people who tell them that they are making amazing, positive life changes after being inspired by Dick and Rick. Billboards all over the country have the picture—almost an icon, now—of Dick pushing Rick. The subtitle reads simply, "Devotion." And all of this because Dick made the choice to be a steward of his gifts, to hold them in trust for the son who can never have those gifts. To use Dick's words, *"It's like I'm his arms and legs, but he's the one running. I have no desire to do this on my own. He drives me."*

THE IMPORTANCE OF BALANCE

Excellence is an amazing thing. It allows seemingly ordinary people to achieve impossible feats and to inspire millions. It gives us a reason to wake up in the morning, a goal that we know we can hit each and every day. It allows us to rest easy at night, secure in the knowledge that we have maximized the precious day we have been given. However, like any other good thing, excellence can be misused, even abused, and we run the risk of abusing this character trait when we pursue it in an unbalanced manner, when we seek excellence in only one area of our life, leaving the dregs of our time and energy for everything else. Dick Hoyt's quest has inspired anonymous millions, but it cost him something much closer to home: his wife, Judy, who eventually became tired of constantly coming in second in the race for her husband's heart.

So it is not enough that we strive for excellence in only one or two select arenas. We must pursue excellence in a balanced manner across all major categories of our life, which I believe are the following four: our families, our friendships, our communities, and our professions. Too often as leaders we put our best effort into just one of these areas (usually profession), because we have only so much time and energy, and we typically take our non-excellent areas for granted. For example, we often assume that our families will grow and develop, or at least hang together, with little planning, discipline, or sustained effort on our part. So we put far less time into scheduling our "date nights," say, than we do into rolling out the next change initiative at work. We put far less planning into teaching our children specific virtues than we do into crafting the next major presentation to our bosses. We put far less energy into keeping up our friendships than we do into keeping up our spreadsheets. And yet, somehow, we expect that our work and our families and our friends and our communities will all turn out equally well.

Because we take some of the most important aspects of our lives for granted, we often live unbalanced lives. Ironically, the result of this unbalance is not necessarily overperformance in our chosen area. Rather, we often hasten spectacular failure in the one area where we want to excel by homing in on it to the exclusion of all else. It is hard to focus at work when your family is falling apart, for example. It is hard to provide for your family when you give the bare minimum at work. You cannot be a good friend or neighbor if you're never home. It becomes increasingly hard to perform to your potential in one area when the pressure of performing poorly everywhere else builds and builds. Over the long run, it becomes increasingly difficult to be excellent and unbalanced.

So our quest for excellence has to start at home, for home is the one area in which we alone are qualified to do the job. There are many people who can perhaps do what we do at work, but only we are uniquely qualified to parent our own children. The nuclear family has been a stable platform for all societies across all cultures since time immemorial, and if we as leaders let that aspect of our lives slide, we risk not just our families. We risk the very thread that knits our broader communities together. Furthermore, typically only we can perform our role in the home. For example, there are many business leaders in the world, but there is only one man in the entire world who can be a father to my three daughters. There are many authors in the world, but there is only one man who can be a husband to my wife. It would, therefore, be infinitely foolish of me to focus exclusively on a job that many others can do if it comes at the cost of the role that only I can fill. Before we look to be excellent anywhere else, we must first be excellent in our homes.

Next, we must focus on our friends. Like our families, we often assume that they will simply be there for us when we need them, genie-like when we rub the lamp, with little effort expended on our part to maintain them in the interim. But like our families, our friendships have to be nourished consistently over time, or else they will wither and eventually die. We will turn to our friends when we need them, only to find that they are now regretfully declining to sacrifice their own time and effort on our behalf—they have something else pressing; they cannot be bothered just now. They will apologize halfheartedly.

Our broader communities will also wither without our engagement. In a modern, transient society it is easy to forget that those all around us have needs and that if we do not help meet those needs, it's possible no one else will, either. It is equally easy to assume that we can ignore our neighbors because our neighbors can take care of themselves. People forget, though, that in a crisis those who are physically close but emotionally distant can be better than those who are emotionally close but physically distant. An old proverb wisely states, "Better is a friend nearby than a brother far away."

Finally, it is easy to view our jobs as places where we give the minimum effort for the maximum return. It is easy to think of our professions as unpleasant but necessary interruptions to the real business of life, which in an ideal world would consist of pursuing leisure activities with no financial constraints. But many of us spend more time at work per week than we do anywhere else. How much better would it be, then, if we found purpose and meaning there every day, no matter how monotonous the circumstances or how unexciting the outcome?

THE FRUIT OF EXCELLENCE

The character quality of excellence is a leadership imperative, and if pursued intentionally, it will bear fruit. The first of those fruits is contentment, best defined as *a peace with our current circumstances that frees us from daily dissatisfaction.* Contentment does not mean that we avoid making our circumstances better if they are intolerable—it simply means that we make the best of where we find ourselves no matter where we find ourselves. Contentment is an outcome that we often seek but rarely find. The reason for this paradox is simple: we too often equate contentment with a destination rather than a journey. We believe that once we have reached a certain position at work or society, or once we have achieved a certain income level, or degree of prosperity, or once we have acquired that thing which we so desired to possess, we will finally rest and be content. The problem with this mindset is twofold: 1) there is always another position to achieve, level to reach, or thing to buy, and 2) circumstances outside of our control often have a vote (usually an unanticipated one) in the outcome of our lives.

If we pin our hopes for contentment on desired end-states, then we set ourselves up for disappointment. But if we seek excellence and are satisfied with that alone—if we give each day our best in all the areas that really matter—then we guarantee ourselves an achievable goal. We are therefore much more likely to maintain our composure when our lives upend or when we find ourselves in places we never dreamed of being. We are much more likely to radiate optimism when things do not go our way, and we are much more likely to keep control of our overall attitude, if our overall attitude depends on that which we control. And our teams will find themselves comfortable following us in all situations because they follow a leader whose attitude and optimism remain constant regardless of results and circumstances.

Our teams will also find that we are steadfast, that we remain constant in pursuit of what matters. First off, we will have systematically identified what matters to us, which is more than many can say. Thoughtfully identifying our goals up front allows us to be much more focused as we move through life and much less distractible when the next big thing—the equivalent of a new, shiny object for leaders—comes along. When we do not have a clear picture of what matters, though, we are far more likely to change our goals as often as we change our socks. We will chase the latest management theories, discarding each old one as it falls out of fashion. We will vacillate from one popular opinion to another, leaving our teams confused, distracted, and dispirited because we constantly move the goalposts on them.

But if an end is worth pursuing, people must watch us persevere in our pursuit. When we change our desired ends regularly, we tell our teams (whether intentionally or not) that it is pointless to invest fully in whatever the new target is, since we do not really care about it. After all, if the going gets tough, we will just choose another road as soon as it becomes convenient. But a leader who pursues excellence can persevere through failure and defeat and remain focused on what truly matters. Every team admires a person who every day sets their shoulder to the wheel and pushes with everything they have. Every team admires a leader who faces each day determined to give that day their all, no matter what the circumstances and no matter what the outcome. The world is full of smart, talented people who pursue things other than daily excellence, who quit as soon as the going gets tough. There are very few who, like Eisenhower, remain constant in giving their best.

Focus and steadfastness, in turn, allow us to maintain our integrity—the unity between beliefs, words, and deeds. We often associate loss of integrity with moral failures like lying, cheating, or stealing, but there are less dramatic, and equally powerful, ways to lose it. One of the easiest is simply to change our goals routinely. Changing our goals is not a moral failure, but if we do it too often then we open up a gap between what we say and what we do. One month we are telling our teams, our families, or our friends that we believe that a few things are supremely important. One month later, that supremely important thing—the one we were all going to rally around and pursue to the best of our ability—has been replaced with something else, raising the question of whether it was really important in the first place and if it was not, then why did we say that it was? Why did we ask people to spend their time and energy on something that we knew was not worthwhile, something that we knew was going to change in just a few days, weeks, or months?

If, however, we are steadfast in pursuit of what matters, and if we tell our teams that no matter what the end-state, the thing we care most about is the process and their best effort, then we can deliver them a message, and give them a goal, that does not change over time. We can pursue the same thing in our own lives, demonstrating consistency across beliefs, words, and actions. We can keep our integrity.

We will also make consistent choices and trade-offs over time, something that is imperative if we want to successfully implement a strategy. Too often we identify what we want to do, and what we want to pursue, with little regard for what we do *not* want to do and what we do *not* want to pursue. But every choice to do something implies another choice not to do other things—we cannot, for example, read two books, or play two instruments, at the exact same time. Choosing to read one book means choosing not to read all other available books that we could have read in the same time period. Because choosing to do something usually means taking action, it is far easier to know what you want to do at any given point in time than what you do not want to do, because what you do not want to do is defined solely by inaction. Inaction is hard to pinpoint and hard to quantify.

Furthermore, saying yes to every good thing that comes our way is easy. Saying no to good things (even if they jeopardize our stated long-term goal) is much harder, and we usually do not do so explicitly. So we say yes to as many things as possible until our time and our energy are consumed, or until we become tired or discouraged. Then we start saying no, or we start making haphazard choices based on whatever leftover time and energy we have available when it is time to make the choice. So over the course of time, we choose to do things that are not in line with our stated goals and we choose not to do things that are perfectly in line with the same. Our trade-offs are inconsistent, which means that either our goals will not be accomplished or that our teams will cease to believe that they matter (or possibly both).

And if it is hard for us to identify consistent trade-offs, it is even harder for us to identify them for our teams. We usually fail to do it. Too often we ask our teams to do certain things for us with little regard on our part for everything else on their plates, much of which we ourselves asked them to do at some point in time or another. If they have no guidance from their leaders on what is not important or on what can be sacrificed to take on something new, then they will make their own choices. With only twenty-four hours in any given day, there comes a point where something has to go to make room for something else. Usually the thing that gets chosen is the thing that is the most urgent, or the area in which a team feels the most pressure from their leaders regardless of whether that thing is the most important in the long run, or the most necessary to achieve stated long-term goals.

However, if we pursue excellence and remain steadfast, then we are able to stay focused on what matters, to choose the things that enable it and to say no to the things that do not. We are able to make consistent choices over time because we have a goal that does not change over time. Our teams are able to achieve what we need them to, and, what is more important, our teams will believe that we mean what we say.

The pursuit of excellence also enables competence (though it does not guarantee it). If we are determined to give our best at a task every single day, then chances are that we will become good at that task eventually, even if it is not squarely within our natural skill set. If, however, we choose to be mediocre at our daily tasks, for whatever reason—we find them unimportant, we believe that a better job is just around the corner, we think that our circumstances are about to change, etc.—then chances are high that our skill sets will remain mediocre.

What is worse, we will develop a habit of mediocrity. Giving just enough effort to get by trains us, daily, to do the bare minimum. If we are giving less now, then we are teaching ourselves to give less always. We are increasing the likelihood that our basic competence will at best remain unchanged and at worst be degraded. But if we give our all now—even in circumstances where our all is not necessary and mediocrity will suffice—then we train ourselves to give our all in the future, when it really might matter. We build our capabilities, if only through sheer effort, and we improve constantly so that when crunch time comes along, we are ready. We had a saying in the Marines: "The more you sweat in peace, the less you bleed in war." Having fought and bled, I can attest to this truth—it was a lesson I learned the hard way. Pursuing excellence, daily, makes us better at the day-to-day and prepares us for crisis.

Excellence also prepares us for increased responsibility. Those who are faithful with a little are likely to be faithful with a lot. Those who can be trusted to give their best no matter how menial the task or how unpleasant the circumstances can usually be trusted to give their best in high-profile assignments and in high-pressure circumstances. When we are choosing whom to promote, for example, what qualities do we normally look for? Do we look for those who always do a good job, no matter what the job, or do we look for those who only give their best when they feel like it—when the job interests them, or when they are in the mood, for example? Even if their best is very, very good, there's always a question that remains: do we go with demonstrated competence, or do we play competence roulette and bet on potential? Over the long run, consistency wins hands down.

Pursuing excellence trains us to do well at whatever it is that we choose to do whenever we choose to do it. That training, in turn, develops us and allows us to deploy our skills consistently over time. So, as we discipline ourselves to give our best, we prepare ourselves to take on greater leadership and more responsibility, when the stakes are higher and the consequences of laziness and failure greater. By contrast, if we give our best efforts only in certain situations now, there is no guarantee that, when we have increased duties and responsibilities, we will give our best when it really matters then. If we have not built up a default routine, then there is no way that we can be certain of where it is that we will default to when the pressure has ratcheted up. Practicing excellence, though, can make us certain and get us ready to move to the next level.

One of the best illustrations of the principle of increased responsibility through demonstrated excellence—regardless of circumstance—is found in the Hebrew scriptures, in the book of Genesis. It is the story of Joseph, the eleventh son of a Jewish patriarch. At the age of seventeen, Joseph had clearly become his father's favorite despite the fact that in the ancient Semitic culture, elder brothers were customarily accorded greater respect and greater responsibility than their younger brethren. In fact, Joseph's father so delighted in his youngest son that he made him a multi-colored coat, an expensive luxury and a visible symbol of favoritism.

Showing low self-awareness and high arrogance, Joseph not only wore this coat around his older brothers (all half brothers, really, as they were sons of a different wife) but also told them of his dreams, dreams in which the entire family bowed down to him. Apparently the brothers could stomach the first vision, but after Joseph regaled them with yet another dream of grandeur (likely while wearing his coat), they conspired to kill him. They had plenty of opportunity to do so. Like many Semitic tribes, the ancient Hebrews were nomadic herders. One of the primary responsibilities of sons was to watch over the flocks of grazing sheep and cattle—visible symbols of a family's wealth—and to find new pastures for them. Joseph's older ten brothers happened to be doing just this, and their father instructed his youngest son to check on them. It was likely a several-day journey from the father's camp to the brothers' pastures, and Joseph had to ask for directions along the way. When his brothers saw him coming across the plains, they threw him down a well, a way of killing him without shedding his blood directly.

Shortly thereafter, the brothers encountered a caravan of slave traders. Seizing the opportunity to rid themselves of their disrespectful and
delusionary half brother and make some money at the same time, the ten
hauled Joseph out of the well and sold him to the slave traders for twenty
pieces of silver. When they returned home, they handed their father Joseph's distinctive coat—dipped in blood—and claimed that they never
saw him. The implication was obvious: the boy was dead, killed by a wild
animal.

So, at the age of seventeen, Joseph fell from favored son to slave, betrayed by those closest to him, the ones who should have protected him.
After some time, the slavers sold Joseph to an Egyptian officer, a captain
in the imperial guard. Joseph had officially become an indentured servant
in the employ of a foreign army. The Hebrew could have responded in a
few ways. He could have despaired and moped, refusing to accept his new
circumstances and pining for his old ones. He could have actively sabo-
taged his employer—they were a conquering army, after all. He could
have done as little as necessary to get by. Slaves had nothing to gain by
going over and above expectations. Or he could have accepted his new lot
and given it his all. Surprisingly, Joseph chose the latter. He gave his best
effort regardless of the sudden and unexpected degradation in circumstances.

Joseph's area of responsibility prospered as a result, and soon Joseph
was promoted to master of the entire household. Over time, Joseph
proved himself so trustworthy that his master left total control of his es-
tate and its workings to his foreign slave. Joseph's excellence was rewarded
with total trust and near-total freedom. However, it was not to last.
Falsely accused of rape by his master's wife, Joseph was thrown into
prison. (Incidentally, the woman used a coat that she ripped off Joseph as
he fled her presence as evidence of his perfidy—it was the second time in
Joseph's life that his coat had been used to deceive others.) Yet again, Joseph went from master of a household to the lowest of society's elements.
But he remained true to form and did every task that was handed to him
to the best of his ability. Some time after his incarceration, the warden
turned over responsibility for all of the prisoners to Joseph. Just like the

foreign army officer, the foreign prison warden came to trust Joseph so completely that "the keeper of the prison looked not to anything that was under [Joseph's] hand." The Hebrew slave did such a good job that he was given control of even the high-profile prisoners, two of whom included Pharaoh's personal chef and personal cupbearer (a position that was a combination of sommelier and poison-taster).

Joseph performed a favor for the cupbearer, who was soon released and reinstated, due at least in part to Joseph's work on his behalf. The Jewish warden's only request: recommend him to Pharaoh upon release. The cupbearer, however, forgot all about Joseph. We do not know exactly how long Joseph remained in prison, but it is likely that it was no fewer than five years, and perhaps as many as ten or fifteen. Suddenly Egypt's Pharaoh had need of a man with Joseph's qualities. Finally remembering his fellow prisoner, the cupbearer recommended Joseph to the Pharaoh, and shortly thereafter the Hebrew prisoner had an audience with Egypt's most powerful man. Joseph so impressed the Pharaoh that the latter immediately installed Joseph as grand vizier over the entire empire, second only to Pharaoh himself. Before he turned thirty years old, the favored son turned slave found himself in charge of an empire. Thirteen years after he was thrown into a well and left to die, Joseph emerged from a foreign hellhole to become the right-hand man of the most powerful ruler in the Levant.

By doing his best in his smaller responsibilities—household and prison leadership—Joseph was now prepared for much greater things. Through years of plenty and years of famine, Joseph managed the Egyptian empire so ably that even Pharaoh himself saw his wealth and status increase. Ultimately, Joseph was able to save the brothers that abandoned him when they fled their homelands for Egypt to beg for food at the one place in the entire Near East that was rumored to have it, the best-managed place in the Levant.

There is absolutely no way that Joseph could have predicted his journey from attempted murder to slavery to prison to kingdom leadership. Paradoxically, if Joseph had never been thrown in the well, if he had remained a favored son in the house of Israel, then he would never have risen to the level of prominence that he ultimately did. He would never have been able to save his family and his nation. However, there was no way Joseph could have known that fact in advance. There was no way that he could have known, thirteen years beforehand, that his being thrown down a well and left for dead was the best thing that could have happened to him and his people. As a nomadic Hebrew sheepherder, Joseph had likely never even heard of Egypt—his worldview wasn't big enough to allow him even to dream of the position he would later hold. Joseph literally did not know that the position existed.

But because he pursued excellence in all circumstances, the Jewish wanderer eventually rose to heights that neither he nor his family could have envisioned. Throughout everything that happened to him, Joseph gave his best in spite of the fact that his future was bleak and his circumstances were often horrific. Indeed, every time that Joseph began to experience some of the fruits of his labors, his entire world got upended, and he found himself at a new low. But he never gave anything less than all he was capable of, and, as a result, each experience trained him to be something more than he was. The nomad, slave, and prisoner became one of the most powerful men in the ancient world. Joseph's commitment to excellence paid off in ways that he could never have imagined.

REFLECTION

There are four main areas in which we need to seek excellence—family, friends, work, and our broader community. A large part of being excellent involves applying time in each of these areas, but time alone is not enough. In addition to spending the right hours in the right places, we need to expend the right energy in the right places. Energy is a fundamental part of life and is routinely measured in nearly every context, from our home heating bills to factory efficiencies to the thruster lift on NASA space shuttles.

For most of us, however, measuring the amount of energy we personally expend in the different areas of our lives is no easy thing. If you are at all like me, we rarely (if ever) do it. But like time, energy is a finite resource, and until we understand where we are spending this resource most freely, we are unlikely to be able to achieve excellence in the most important areas. Ultimately we will be unable to achieve our missions. So we need to take a step back and examine how we are using our precious energy.

There are two things that can help us get a handle on energy: 1) focus and 2) planning. We need to know when we focus—when we are actually engaged in an activity, pursuing it in a focused and deliberate manner. For example, we could be at home, spending time physically alongside our children while at the same time checking our email or making phone calls. In this instance, we are with our families but not engaged with them. Or we could be at work, spending our free hours checking the latest sports news articles, social-networking updates, or health-care tips. Again, we are at work but not engaged in work.

Conversely, we may be spending a significant amount of energy in an area without spending much "formal" time in it. For example, we might be bodily at work but mentally daydreaming, planning an upcoming vacation in our minds. Or we might be at dinner with friends but find that the only thing we can think about is the presentation at work tomorrow. We might be in a library by ourselves, writing emails and thank-you notes to friends. Or we could be at home with our children, fully engaged with them while the rest of the world disappears for the twenty minutes before they go to bed. In each of these cases, the amount of energy we spend on an area may dwarf the amount of formal time that we spend obviously engaged in it.

Yet another way of gauging energy is to ask ourselves how deliberately we approach the various areas of our lives. For example, if we approach our family with a significant amount of forethought and planning—building a values statement, outlining questions to ask our children during the week, constructing a date-night routine with our spouse, etc.—then we are probably spending a good amount of energy on our family even if we are not spending a large amount of time with them. Conversely, if we are spending significant time at home and doing nothing but watching television, then we are probably not spending much energy on our family. The same principle works in all other areas. Now it is time to ask ourselves the hard questions.

Reflection Questions

1. What do you think it means for you to expend energy?
2. What activities drain your energy—that is, leave you tired mentally and physically?
3. What activities restore your energy?
4. In which areas of life do you truly focus?
   - Family?
   - Work?
   - Friends?
   - Community?
5. How deliberately do you approach each of the above areas?
6. In which areas are you most naturally likely to plan?
7. In which areas are you most naturally likely to take life as it comes?

We can all choose to be a Joseph, someone who achieves excellence in all circumstances. No matter what we think, we have no real idea of what life has in store for us. Try as we might to connect the dots in advance, life is too unpredictable for us to base our level of excellence on the perceived commensurate level of reward. So we need to give our absolute best every day at whatever task we have in front of us, no matter what the circumstances. We need to challenge ourselves to purse an unflaggingly demanding—but unfailingly achievable—goal: to fill the unforgiving minute with sixty seconds' worth of distance run. We need to be able to state with confidence at each day's end: "Today I have given all that I have."

And as we seek to do these things, we need to take the next step and build out the virtue that helps govern our best efforts.

SUMMARY

- Great leaders consciously strive for excellence in all areas of their lives, and the lives that they lead reflect their commitment to this virtue.

- Contrary to what many believe, excellence is defined by the input, not the output. Great leaders are thankful for the day that they have been given and seek to give their best effort with every minute of the time allotted to them. They pursue their best as a worthy end in and of itself, regardless of the result it produces.

- Excellence sustains the drive that mission inspires and humility guides. Excellence gives a leader an achievable short-term goal every day, which produces perseverance in pursuit of a longer-term goal and gives a leader hope from one day to the next. Together, perseverance and hope inspire others.

- We must be balanced as we pursue this virtue. It is not enough to be excellent in one area while neglecting others. If we hope to sustain our leadership over the long run, we must be excellent at home, at work, with our friends, and in our communities.

- Excellence allows a leader to be content in all circumstances, to maintain composure, and to remain steadfast. Those, in turn, ensure that a leader makes consistent choices and trade-offs and thus keeps their integrity. Excellence also helps a leader to become increasingly competent at their tasks, preparing them for increased responsibility.

---- ★ ----

CHAPTER 4

KINDNESS

A man on a journey is robbed, beaten, and left for dead on the sidewalk of a lightly traveled street. But he isn't dead, just badly wounded, unconscious, and unable to take care of himself. Time passes, and eventually another traveler comes down that same street. It's a lawyer, and she's in a hurry. She notices the body but doesn't stop to help. She's already late for an important meeting, and besides, she knows all about regulation but nothing about medicine. She could prosecute the offender, but she can't help the offended, at least not professionally. She makes a note to call the police when she gets to her destination—if she has time before the meeting starts. Besides, the public service system works, and it's likely that someone who's better equipped to handle the situation will stop by before she can even make a call.

Twenty minutes later, a pastor, also hurrying to his destination, notices the prostrate body. He'd like to help, but he's also running late. If he doesn't make it to his megachurch in the next ten minutes, there will be no one to deliver the message, and the two thousand people in the auditorium will sit mute, waiting to be inspired. Eventually they'll become restless, maybe unruly. It's possible that people attending for the first time will be so disappointed that they'll never come back and never have the chance to hear the message of grace and redemption the pastor has to give. He, too, passes without stopping. In fact, he crosses to the other side of the street, because he knows that if he gets too close, he'll notice the beaten man's face. He would rather not do that. If he can put a face on the tragedy lying on the ground in front of him, then he'll be that much more likely to stop, or at least to feel guilty about not stopping.

About an hour after the pastor's departure, a man recently out of prison hustles down the street on his way to work. It's only his second week on the job, and he really doesn't want to be late. He's lucky even to have the gig. He doesn't want to do anything to risk it. His parole officer helped him find it, and in return the officer expects perfect attendance. However, the ex-felon notices the body and stops.

He stares for a second, and then approaches and kneels down. He tears up his T-shirt, and with what little skill he has he applies clumsy bandages to the open wounds on the man's head. He runs to the street corner and hails a cab. It's a sixty-dollar ride to the nearest hospital, but the man doesn't mind. He loads up the unconscious victim and rides with him the whole way to the hospital. When he gets there, the felon waits until the man has been admitted to the emergency room, and then he leaves his name, address, and phone number with the attending nurse. He asks her to update him with the beaten man's status as soon as she knows it. He also offers to pay whatever portion of the hospital bills he can. Then he leaves and calls his new boss and his parole officer, letting them know that he'll be late to work that day, and why.

This story is a modern version of the parable of the Good Samaritan, which has resonated through the ages because of its beautiful illustration of unexpected kindness. In some professions—nursing, religious ministry, social work, to name a few—kindness is unspokenly assumed to come with the territory. This doesn't seem to be the case with leadership. In fact, it sometimes seems that leaders need kindness's opposite, a ruthless ability to push a team and discard its flagging members the minute they fail to keep up. It sometimes seems that kindness is a soft trait in a hard world, a virtue that leaders cannot afford lest they appear weak, undisciplined, or unfair. Indeed, society often rewards—and sometimes lionizes—unkind leaders, deeming them "tough," "no-nonsense," or "hard-nosed," to name just a few of the often-used adjectives. To lead, it seems, one cannot afford to be kind. However, like many other popular leadership notions, this one is entirely untrue. The best and most effective leaders are those who practice kindness regularly and intentionally. Over time, they produce the best and most effective teams.

Shockingly enough, one of my first adult experiences with the effectiveness of kindness came at Officer Candidate School—the unlikeliest of places—and it came from one of my sergeant instructors—the unlikeliest of people. It was a hot and humid day in June, and my classmates and I were barely two weeks into the program. Every day was a whirlwind of chaos, and every one of us, me included, was operating in a state of sheer panic at best and dread terror at worst. None of us understood anything at all about our new military environment. Every minute—waking and sleeping—was controlled by our nemeses, the sergeant instructors. We were never away from their watchful eyes, and we could never do anything right. We were screamed at, taunted, harassed, and made to endure both physical and psychological punishment for any mistake, real or imagined.

It was in that pleasant setting that I stood fearfully in formation on that day in June, rigidly at parade rest on the hot asphalt tarmac in front of the dining hall. Each platoon held its ground as its fellows were released to eat. During that time, each officer candidate had to stand as motionless as possible until it was their platoon's turn to sprint off the asphalt and into the dining hall in order to shove as much food down their throats as possible in the five or so minutes allotted. As I stood in formation, waiting for our turn, I realized that I had been complying with our instructor's commands to "push water" much too enthusiastically. An overwhelming urge to use the restroom overcame me. The only problem was that there was no such thing as a bathroom break while waiting to eat. You stood, neither speaking nor moving, until it was your turn to be released. As I was still operating in a state of abject fear, I tried my best to comply and said nothing about my biological needs. Unfortunately, after about forty-five minutes, my needs won the day. I urinated in my pants.

As the stain spread slowly across my trousers, a sense of shame erupted. I wondered just how long it would take my fellow candidates to notice that I had reverted to being a two-year-old. We were all insecure enough as it was, waiting to see who wouldn't make the various cuts, who would wash out of the training and prove unfit to be a Marine. We were on high alert for weakness in our fellows, since their weakness increased our chances of success. This failure would put me on an even worse footing with my peers. I assumed that it would only be another thirty seconds or so before one of my sergeant instructors would notice and begin ridiculing me, loudly, publicly, and shamingly. I held my breath and waited for the humiliation to begin.

It never happened. One of my sergeant instructors, Staff Sergeant Shusko, noticed almost immediately what I had done. I noticed that he noticed, and I waited for the painful reaction. It never came. Instead the staff sergeant walked up to me and quietly instructed me to run back to the barracks and change trousers. No one else heard him, and he said it so matter-of-factly—almost in a peer-to-peer manner—that at first I couldn't believe that he was treating me like an actual human being. Once I realized that he was serious, I took off running. The rest of my platoon never even noticed what had happened. Shusko's reaction spared me the humiliation.

With not enough time in the program to prove myself yet, Shusko had shown me a kindness that I did not deserve. Soiling myself while standing in formation was no small thing, yet he overlooked it and allowed me to retain some dignity in front of my peers and the other instructors. It was at that moment that I realized that our staff sergeants were more than just sadistic tormentors whose sole aim in life was to make us miserable. I realized then that they were professionals who put on whatever role was necessary to teach and screen us. That brief kindness, and the flash of insight that accompanied it, helped me to make it through the next seven weeks and become a Marine officer. Every time that the demands seemed overwhelming or the instructors seemed crazily unrealistic, I thought back to Staff Sergeant Shusko and his unexpected kindness. I realized that nothing they were putting us through was pointless or mindless, that everything, however difficult, had purpose behind

it. Shusko's kindness helped me make it through the hell of Officer Candidate School and achieve my dream of becoming a Marine officer.

I experienced the effectiveness of kindness in a nonmilitary context
less than two months into my first civilian job. I'd been given a company
car (a blessing, given that I had totaled my own car while driving back
from my last duty station). At my company, PepsiCo, safety was extremely important, and one way of measuring safety was to track the
number of company car vehicular accidents that occurred over the course
of a month. Zero was the preferred number. Anything higher than that,
any damage to a company vehicle, was highly scrutinized and went on the
records as a black mark against the business unit that owned the car. Furthermore, the business unit had to pay for all repairs out of a budget that
was much better used for other things, such as giving employees raises.

It was around four o'clock on a winter morning when I backed my
brand-new company car out of my driveway and into my neighbor's car.
It was dark, and hazy, and my coffee hadn't taken full effect yet, but the
conditions didn't matter—I had just ruined the back half of a brand-new
PepsiCo vehicle, and it had taken me only a mere two months of employ-
ment to do it. What was worse, I had only had my new car for about three
weeks.

I was horrified, and nervous, and since it was four o'clock in the morning when I decided to play demolition derby with company property, I
had two and a half hours to mull over worst-case responses from my boss
when I called. I assumed that he'd marvel at how it had taken me three
whole weeks to wreck my vehicle; ask me pointedly how it was that I clev-
erly managed to hit a stationary car; and remind me of the going rates for
new bumpers and back quarter panels. I assumed that he'd point out that
my region had had a great safety record going until I saw fit to break the
streak. By the time 7 A.M. arrived, I felt thoroughly miserable. Still, I
made the call to my boss, Danny Richardson. He picked up after the second ring, and I told him what had happened.

There was a long pause after I finished my story. I braced myself for
the worst. Then Danny spoke:

"Donovan, I'm about to make you feel a whole lot better. Did I ever tell you about the time I totaled my company car with a front-end loader? Tore the top right off it. . . ."

Danny then proceeded to relate to me the fine details surrounding an incident in which he had essentially driven a bulldozer through one of his very first company cars. He pointed out that by comparison my accident was pretty pathetic, that he had already outdone me and more in the course of his storied career. Given his vast experience, he next told me exactly what I needed to do, step by step, to handle the situation properly and to get my car repaired.

I had expected some sort of reaction from him, but not this one. By all rights, Danny should have ripped me up one side and down the other, but he didn't. He chose to be kind to me in a moment when I was hurting. When the time came to explain to higher-ups what I had done, Danny defended me as a great employee who had made a simple mistake. He sacrificed his time, his energy, and his reputation to defend me, and I have never forgotten it. From that day onward, I did anything that Danny Richardson asked, solely because he was the one asking for it. I never forgot that he was there for me when I needed him; that he took a risk for me when I didn't yet deserve it. For as long as I worked for him, my goal was to be someone who deserved the kindness he had shown.

THE FOUR COMPONENTS OF KINDNESS

My response to Danny is not unusual. In fact, it is a pretty standard reaction to undeserved and unexpected kindness. Far from being a leadership vice, kindness is a leadership virtue, and it is absolutely essential if we hope to be successful over the long run. However, kindness is an easy virtue to misapply, or to fail to apply. Some will try to substitute weakness and diffidence for it. They will try to avoid responsibility and call that avoidance kindness. Others will confuse kindness with weakness and diffidence, so they will avoid it like the plague. Some will think that kindness begins and ends only with emotion. Others will think that it is simply that most squishy of designations—as embodied in the term *nice*—and thus not give it much thought at all. Kindness may be good in theory, but what exactly is it in practice?

Put simply, kindness is an emotion put into action in a particular way. The virtue of kindness has four elements: compassion, action, grace, and sacrifice. If we think back to the story of the Good Samaritan, in our version the ex-felon had them all. First off, he felt compassion, defined as a deep emotion that stirs one to action. The felon looked at the wounded man, and he immediately stopped what he was doing. He felt something deeply. It made him pause. However, the Good Samaritan did not stop at emotion, which is where many assume that kindness begins and ends. In our example, the good ex-felon actually took action in accordance with his feelings.

He crossed the street. His feelings caused him to make a decision, and his decision caused him to change his original plans. The Samaritan then undertook a series of purposeful, focused, and effective actions to achieve a deliberate end. He tore apart his own clothing to administer first aid, hailed a taxi to provide transport, and then rode to the hospital to ensure care. Our felon did not act randomly. He did not walk over to the unconscious man, whisper words of encouragement, and then leave. He did not buy him ice cream or sing him a song to cheer him up. He did not flip a coin to help decide whether to engage, or how to engage. Instead, our protagonist carefully considered what the wounded man needed and then took action to achieve that end. This is what kindness in action is all about: taking the right actions to meet the right needs in a focused and deliberate manner.

Throughout it all, the Good Samaritan showed grace by acting in the best interests of someone who had done absolutely nothing to earn it. The Samaritan had no idea who the man was before he took action, and he still had no idea after he left. He could not predict whether any of his efforts (or money) would be repaid. He did not even know if the unconscious body lying on the sidewalk belonged to a good person or an evil one. The victim might have been mean and cruel or a wanted criminal. He might also have been a wonderful father of four. The Good Samaritan took action regardless, without knowing whether the helpless person deserved it or not. After all, no matter what the circumstances and no matter who the person, when someone has earned kindness and we therefore respond in kind, our response becomes something less than the virtue we are seeking. Our response becomes something more akin to remuneration, that is, repayment of a debt incurred for services rendered. If we wish to truly be kind, then we have to be kind to people who may or may not merit it.

Finally, throughout the entire process, the Good Samaritan sacrificed. He gave his time, his energy, and his money to ensure that a complete stranger was cared for. Kindness, whether large or small, always involves a sacrifice. Perhaps it's just the time you spend listening to someone talk about their family or writing a thank-you note, which may be time you don't have. Or perhaps it's the energy expended to walk a young leader who has just wrecked their company car through the process of fixing it. Perhaps it's a portion of your salary that you give away to a cause, or a person, who has never done anything for you. Whether we give our time, our talent, or our treasure, something has to be sacrificed if true kindness is to be administered.

An amazing illustration of all the components of this virtue—compassion, action, grace, and sacrifice—came out of the brutality of the Holocaust and World War II. The story starts in the Netherlands. On May 10, 1940, Germany invaded the small country, infiltrating Wehrmacht soldiers across boundary lines by kitting them in Dutch uniforms and conducting one of the war's first large-scale paratroop invasions. The move came as a shock to the country's residents. After all, they had not engaged in hostilities with any European nation since 1830 (the Netherlands had avoided a German invasion in World War I), and they had maintained a policy of strict neutrality ever since World War II broke out. In fact, the Dutch had gone so far as to shoot down British warplanes that had passed through their airspace. What is more, Germany never bothered to declare war on the country. Germany simply invaded. Four days later, the Netherlands surrendered after the Luftwaffe gutted Rotterdam in a massive bombing campaign and then threatened to do the same to every other Dutch city. The soldiers immediately laid down their arms.

Throughout most of the first year of the occupation, the Dutch Jewish population was treated with a fairly light hand. However, all of that changed in February 1941, when the Germans cordoned off the old Jewish quarter in Amsterdam and rounded up 425 Jewish men for deportation to extermination camps. Only two escaped the raid. However, in this Jewish ghetto, called Haarlem, there lived an anomaly: a family of Christian jewelers, members of the Dutch Reformed Church. At the time of the roundup, there were three of them together: the father, Casper ten Boom, and his two daughters, Corrie and Betsie, both in their late forties. For years, the family had been active in their church, and they were known throughout the Jewish quarters for their charitable work with the disabled. In fact, the Christian family's neighbors regularly invited them to participate in their Sabbaths, and they studied the Hebrew scriptures side by side.

Despite being members of a different religion, the Ten Boom family was not immune from persecution. Shortly after the German invasion, the Nazis banned Corrie's club for young girls. Still, things remained fairly quiet for more than a year. Then, in May 1942, a well-dressed woman came to the door of the Ten Boom shop and asked for temporary shelter. She was a Jew, and her husband had been arrested and her son had gone into hiding. For several months previously, the Ten Booms had been arranging temporary shelter in the countryside for Amsterdam's persecuted Jews. Word of the Christian family's kindness had spread throughout the Jewish community. Now, with the woman at their doorstep, they were faced with a different need: the need to allow someone to live under their own roof. To do so would place the family at great risk—anyone caught hiding a Jew was subject to the harshest possible reprisals from the German and Dutch authorities. Nonetheless, Casper readily agreed to help.

From that point onward, the Ten Boom family became the center of an underground smuggling ring that stretched throughout Holland. They constructed a hidden room in Corrie's bedroom to hide the Jewish families waiting for passage out of the country. They dealt a brisk trade in smuggled ration cards, so that those who would not otherwise eat could do so. They placed their lives at risk, again and again, so that they could help thousands escape the Nazi terror. Not all Christians were as kind to the persecuted, or as brave. Corrie recalled asking a pastor to hide a new mother and her infant. He refused: "No, definitely not. We could lose our lives for that Jewish child." Casper did not hesitate. He took the child from the mother, put the baby's face against his own, and, according to Corrie's writings, replied: "You say that we could lose our lives for this child. I would consider that the greatest honor that could come to our family."

Casper was to get his honor. After nearly two years of hiding Jews, the family was caught in February 1944 and sent to the Schenevingen prison. Ten days later, Casper died in jail. Betsie and Corrie survived, and both were soon packed off to the Vught concentration camp in the Netherlands. Eventually, they were moved to the notorious Ravensbruck camp in Germany. On December 16, 1944, Betsie died of illness and privation. Corrie, however, survived. Due to a clerical error, the Germans released her just one week before all of the Ravensbruck women in her age group were killed. Eventually Corrie made her way back to Haarlem, where she started a rehabilitation center for concentration camp inmates.

Of the Netherlands' estimated prewar population of 140,000 Jews, around 105,000 were killed—a full 75 percent. Every Jew that the Ten Booms saved would otherwise have had a three-in-four chance of dying during the war. The Christian family gave their freedom and their lives during the war so that others—anonymous, unknown others, ones of a different faith, even—might live. They put their emotion into action, sacrificing everything they had in order to do so. Their kindness saved thousands, perhaps even tens of thousands. Eventually the queen of the Netherlands knighted Corrie for her family's work in the Dutch resistance.

LEADERSHIP IMPACT

Kindness like the Ten Booms' can help thousands, or it can help just one. It can involve life-altering sacrifice, or it can take just five minutes of spare time. It can be doled out to strangers, or it can be gifted to close friends. But no matter what the scope, scale, and effectiveness of this virtue externally, kindness always has a profound effect on the practitioner. For a leader, kindness is worth pursuing as much for its transformative effect on the individual giving it as for its transformative effect on the team at the receiving end. In fact, if a leader were purely selfish, and they wanted to pursue only that which would benefit them, heedless of whoever else was hurt or sustained thereby, they would still be better off pursuing kindness. Why? Because, quite simply, its effects on those who pursue it are nothing short of transformative.

Kind acts, in the first place, increase a leader's joy. When you know that you have deliberately lifted someone else up, and that you have sacrificed to do so, it produces a sense of accomplishment and altruism that is wholly independent of the recipient's response. Think of the last time you wrote someone a thank-you note for something that they did well, or the last time you told your wife that she looked pretty, or your husband that he did a nice job, or your friends that you were proud of their children's accomplishments. If you have ever served in a homeless shelter or built homes for those without them, then you know how it feels to help someone whom you do not know, someone less materially fortunate than you. Take a moment to think about how these acts of kindness to friends, peers, and strangers no doubt made you feel, and then try to imagine encountering that feeling every week, or every day.

Much like excellence, kindness is a virtue that does not hinge on external circumstances, or desired outcomes, to yield its benefits. You can be kind, and receive the internal benefits of doing so, with no regard for how the object of your kindness responds and no regard for the situation in which you find yourself. So, should we pursue kindness, we will once again find ourselves with a goal that is achievable every single day. Knowing that we have an attainable target, one that produces deep feelings of satisfaction, will increase our own happiness over time.

That joy also helps reinforce a sense of purpose, which sustains pursuit of mission and the drive for excellence. When we receive positive reinforcement on a daily basis, it helps us believe in what we are doing, even if we do not see our mission's ultimate end coming to fruition in the near term. When we see that people are responding well to kindness, and we see the results improving their lives, it helps us give our best every day, because our best produces visible, tangible results.

Kindness also reinforces reflectiveness, for it forces us to think of the needs of others and how we can meet them. If we are pursuing it, kindness helps us analyze our actions throughout the day to ensure that at least a few of them meet the criteria outlined for this virtue. And kindness reminds us of the infinite worth of people, and, by extension, of ourselves as we seek to meet the needs of others. Taking time and energy to help someone who needs it helps us to remember that people are worth helping, that they are not simply tools to meet whatever emotional, professional, or personal need we have.

FROM FEAR TO LOVE

But the important point is that kindness has transformative effects not only on us, but on the teams that we lead. As we move to try to practice this virtue regularly, our team members will at first be almost universally surprised. Most of them will probably be guarded, jaded, or on edge—most of the time, nothing comes without a price tag. It will be hard for people to believe that a leader would sacrifice time, energy, or money with no corresponding demands or expectations.

Many will also take a wait-and-see attitude, one that anticipates a quick start and an equally quick finish. To sustain kindness over time takes deliberate effort, and nearly everyone has seen a new initiative, attitude, or plan be announced with great fanfare, only to die on the vine later as the pressures of daily life choked out the effort needed to sustain the change. So, team members often adopt a guarded, show-me attitude. They will wait to see if kindness can be sustained before they believe that a leader truly intends to make it a habit.

Once we prove that kindness is no passing fad, the effects on our teams are nothing short of transformative. People make amazing behavior changes, life changes, even. Nothing better illustrates the life-altering power of kindness than the story of two different boys—in two different cultures and countries—who shared the same dream. In the early 1900s in a small village in Eastern Europe, an altar boy served faithfully in hopes of becoming a Catholic priest. One day, that altar boy was assisting the head priest with communion when the unthinkable happened. The boy accidentally knocked the chalice full of communion wine off the altar and onto the floor, ruining the carefully scripted Mass. The priest, angered, struck the boy with the back of his hand and told him never, ever to come back. The boy left and obeyed. He never did come back, and he grew up with an implacable hatred of the church.

In El Paso, Illinois, another altar boy, just three years younger, had the same dream of becoming a priest. And the same thing happened to him—he spilled the communion wine off the altar in the middle of Mass, shocking the participants. The boy burst into tears. This time the reaction from the priest was very different. He showed no anger. Rather, he knelt beside the boy, put his arms around him, and told him that everyone makes mistakes, that God loves them regardless, and that he, the priest, was confident that one day the young man would himself become a wonderful priest. Those different reactions—one harsh, one kind—drove two very different outcomes. The first altar boy became Marshal Tito, the atheist, communist dictator of Yugoslavia. The second one became Archbishop Fulton J. Sheen, one of America's most influential and beloved clergymen.

Though kindness may be off-putting at first, as people wait for the other shoe to drop, or for a leader to stop making the effort, it eventually has an extraordinary effect on the lives of people. First off, kindness makes people feel valued both as individuals and as team members. And when people feel that they and their work are appreciated, the effort they put forth to achieve common goals is intense. They see that someone is paying a price for them—the most certain indication of value in this world—so they don't mind paying a price themselves for something important.

It is when people are asked to sacrifice for a certain end but they never see any sacrifice on their behalf in return that they become jaded, demotivated, and halfhearted. After all, why should they be asked to pay a price for others when no one will first pay a price for them? Kindness prevents this outcome because kindness helps give people a reason to give their best. After my boss Danny showed me grace there wasn't anything that I wouldn't do for him. No matter how hard the task, I did my best to take it on because Danny was the one asking and because Danny had once paid a price on my behalf. I never forgot the time that he stuck his neck out for me—a brand-new employee who did not deserve it—and in return I tried to be the kind of man who would one day deserve his undeserved kindness.

The importance of this sense of being valued cannot be overstated. Many studies have revealed that the number-one reason people quit a job isn't, actually, the nature of the job itself. Rather, it's the person for whom they work. People don't quit companies; they quit leaders. But if a leader is kind, and if people feel valued, then they become extremely unlikely to leave. All of the money, time, and energy spent discussing salary increases, merit-based bonuses, noncompete and nondisclosure clauses—everything used as a Pavlovian system of rewards and punishments to stimulate loyalty—is wasted if a leader is unkind. But if a leader is kind, then their teams are far less likely to leave them no matter what the blandishments offered. All of the above become irrelevant, and the energy wasted on them can be reallocated to more purposeful endeavors. As it turns out, compassion, action, grace, and sacrifice are compelling reasons for one to dedicate one's work and life to a mission and a person.

In addition to loyalty, kindness also spurs risk-taking, because kindness makes a team feel secure. After all, they have seen grace in action. If someone knows that a well-intentioned mistake, made because they tried and failed, will be forgiven, then they are much more likely to keep trying.

Not only is a person more likely to try the tried-and-true, but they are also more likely to try new things. Thus kindness helps spur innovation and creativity throughout an organization.

Kindness from a leader also makes a team more willing to extend kindness to others. If the person at the very top takes the time to sacrifice their time, talent, or treasure for their team, then they set a standard for expected behavior. In turn, this type of behavior across a team fosters cohesion and trust, which speeds efficiency. Time-consuming bureaucracy and internal controls have their place, but they are only a substitute for trust, implemented to minimize the damage from those who cannot be trusted. In an environment characterized by kindness, though, trust can substitute for bureaucracy. A handshake can take the place of a fifty-page contract (and fifty thousand dollars' worth of legal fees). Ultimately, then, kindness engenders loyalty, spurs innovation, and speeds efficiency, all of which allow high performance to be sustained over time. Contrary to what many might think, a high-performing team is marked by kindness.

Unafraid of unwarranted repercussions, secure that they are valued for more than just the results they produce, and placed in an environment of self-replicating kindness, a team becomes increasingly likely to operate out of a love of gain. In today's day and age, most teams do not operate this way. Most teams operate on the un-kindness principle, one that motivates through fear of loss—that is, "If I don't do this task, or don't perform in my job assignment, or keep this person happy, then I will lose my job, my title, my bonus, someone else's respect, etc."

But fear of loss is exhausting. People burn out, and they exist in a constant state of anxiety. Creativity dies, because the downside for failing at something new is greater than the upside for succeeding. Everyone waits for someone else to take the initiative, to make a mistake so that they can learn what not to do. Most team members will try to avoid taking responsibility for any decision, the better to avoid any ownership of something that might fail. Decisions are postponed and hard choices are avoided.

No doubt, operating in un-kindness mode can produce strenuous effort: fear is a powerful motivator, at least as powerful a motivator as love. However, fear-based effort can only last for so long, and people will only give up so much of themselves. They will not tap into top-level effort, the kind of effort that produces excellence day after day. They will not give their absolute best and go the extra mile, because they are not inspired to do so. Eventually they will give just enough to get by, carefully husbanding their energy to sustain themselves as long as possible.

Very few institutions have applied the un-kindness principle more rigorously than did the Soviet army during World War II. At the frontline level, individual initiative was heavily discouraged and rarely, if ever, rewarded. At times, it seemed that the Soviet army's greatest fear wasn't losing a battle to the Germans; rather, it was soldiers questioning Soviet ideology or the wisdom of their superiors. Political officers were assigned to most major units, and they served both as thought police and as tactical decision makers. Russian military commanders had to worry not only about whether their decisions would meet with success on the battlefield but also about whether those decisions would anger their political superiors. In a sense, they fought two battles—one against the enemy, and one against their minders.

In this model, success was rarely rewarded, but failure was harshly punished. Seasoned combat leaders were sent to prison for offenses as trifling as writing letters questioning Stalin—something that happened to later Nobel Prize–winning author Aleksandr Solzhenitsyn—or killed for failing to obey the orders of their political officers. Punishment battalions were formed to shoot wavering soldiers in the backs if they retreated. Frontline commanders became terrified of taking decisive action that had not been vetted by both the political and military chain of command at the highest levels.

The results were glaring. The Soviets very nearly lost their first major offensive to Finland, a tiny nation that by rights should not have lasted a week against an army with three times as many soldiers, thirty times as many aircraft, and one hundred times as many tanks. The German forces, also smaller than the Soviets but emphasizing flexibility and individual initiative, pummeled the Russians until halted by the cruel winter and

Hitler's poor decisions. Thus one of largest, best-equipped armies on earth was twice humiliated in large part because it operated entirely under a fear-of-loss philosophy.

This same philosophy cripples companies as well. At one of my former employers, manufacturing mistakes began to rise suddenly. So the senior executives, myself included, decided to institute review councils. We would determine who was the most likely to blame for the mistakes, haul them in front of the council early on a Friday morning, and question them about what had happened and why. If punishment was warranted, we implemented it. Yet we rarely did the converse—praise and reward people when we completed a project ahead of schedule and ahead of budget. We gave our employees few incentives to perform better by trying something new but every incentive to avoid making a mistake by trying something new. Innovative thinking and experimentation declined precipitously. Employees kept their heads down and stuck to the tried and true. More than once I heard people respond to requests by saying, "No way. I don't want to try that because I don't want to be here on Friday morning explaining myself."

However, kindness from a leader helps migrate people from fear of loss to love of gain. Though loss is powerful, it is limiting. Love of gain, however, helps remove limits. It helps to pull the very best out of people. It helps them to ask, "How much *can* I give?" rather than "How much *must* I give?" They will do things because they want to, because they are excited, or because it is their leader asking. When people are motivated by love, they achieve a top level of performance that they would never tap into otherwise. They make decisions in the absence of information. They take ownership when no one asks them to, and they solve problems that no one else sees. They take care of the little issues before they become big ones, and they innovate and inspire others because they love what they are doing, and it shows. Fear of loss may be powerful, but love of gain is inspiring. Only kindness from a leader can unlock the true top-end potential of their team. Those who have been treated with kindness will move mountains to return the favor.

In 1917, Alex Lurye was a young American soldier stationed in the

town of Seldes, Germany. He happened to be Jewish, and one Friday
night he decided to venture into town to worship at the local synagogue.
Alone and in uniform, Alex must have been a strange sight, to say the
least. Here was a foreigner who did not speak the language, and who wore
the uniform of the enemy of the German state, appearing in the middle of
a tight-knit synagogue. Nevertheless, a German Jew, Herr Rosenau, made
the young, lonely serviceman feel welcomed in the synagogue. When the
service ended, Rosenau invited Alex to have dinner with the entire family
in their home. Among those in attendance was Rosenau's teenage daughter, Ruth.

After that evening, time and fate moved on, and Alex was unable to
visit the Rosenau family again. However, when the war ended and he
made it back home to Duluth, Minnesota, Alex had been so touched by
the Rosenau family that he wrote them a letter, thanking them for their
hospitality. For reasons unknown, the letter was never read. Herr Rosenau
put it into a desk drawer and forgot about it altogether.

By twenty-one years later, in 1938, times had become very difficult
for German Jews. The Rosenau family was no exception, and now it included the married Ruth and her three children, the oldest of whom, Sigbert, was eleven. During a family visit to the original Herr Rosenau, young
Sigbert began rummaging through his grandfather's old desk, where he
found the letter from Alex, unopened, from twenty-one years beforehand. Intrigued by the foreign postage stamp, Sigbert asked his grandfather if he could have the letter. The old man assented.

When she noticed Sigbert's new gift, Ruth was intrigued. She opened
the letter and found the thank-you note Alex Lurye had written some
two decades earlier. Immediately she remembered the young man. She
resolved to write him back. Times were becoming desperate, and though
it was a faint hope, perhaps the young man would remember the family
from Seldes that had once invited him into their home. It was a complete
long shot, but perhaps he would even sponsor their immigration to
America.

However, the envelope had no proper return address—just the name,
Alex Lurye, and the city, Duluth, Minnesota. The Rosenaus wrote any-

way. Unbeknownst to them, in the years between the wars Alex had become a wealthy businessman and was now well-known throughout his city. The letter reached him, and he wasted little time replying. What is more, he engaged wholeheartedly in the immigration process. He spent significant time and significant money sponsoring the Rosenaus' immigration, sponsoring a family he had met for just one night some twenty years in the past.

By the summer of 1938 the elder Rosenau, Ruth, and their entire extended family had immigrated to America. Unlike so many of their coreligionists, they avoided the ravages of the Nazis. The family down to the grandchildren was spared. And it was all because of one act of kindness that touched a young man's heart when he needed it. Alex's effort on behalf of a family that was barely known to him is just one example of the power of kindness-inspired love of gain. People will give everything they have and go the last mile only if they are operating from a place of love.

REFLECTION

Kindness is personally transformative. As we pursue it, we will find increasing joy in our daily lives, and we will have a greater sense of purpose from one day to the next. We will reflect more on the things that matter, and we will be more in tune to the needs of others. Kindness also has powerful effects on our teams. They will fear failure less and will innovate and spread best practices more. They will run hard, and sometimes fall down, but they will get back up again. They will trust one another and move quickly to make decisions and take actions. They will pursue a common goal because they want to—not because they are forced to—which will make them a nearly unstoppable team. We should all be so fortunate to be part of such an organization. We should all have the privilege to lead such a team.

For all of these things to happen, though, kindness must be sustained over time. It must be much more than a spontaneous emotion. Random acts, though nice, are not enough. To be practiced effectively, kindness must be treated as a discipline, no different from anything else that we want to be good at. Some people are consistently, naturally kind; others are not. To us, it should not matter whether we are one of those few naturals. We must demonstrate kindness regularly, and we cannot rely on random acts to carry the day, or to carry our lives and our leadership.

Random or not, kind acts can be large or small. Both are powerful in their own right. Those that are large usually demand significant sacrifice of one of our resources. "Significant" will be different for different people. For a busy executive, it might mean taking an hour on the way in to work to help a stranded motorist change a tire, or an afternoon to drive a friend to a distant airport and back. For a tired father, it might mean running errands for their spouse when they would rather relax in front of the television. For a student-athlete, it might mean giving bone marrow to find a match for a classmate and for a retiree it might mean giving a very small sum (but a very large percentage) of their income to a very specific charity.

Large acts indicate the *range* of our virtue—that is, the extent to which we are willing to sacrifice to be kind to someone else. Small acts, by contrast reveal the *frequency* of our kindness, which is the necessary complement to its magnitude. If large acts tell us "how much," small acts tell us "how often." To put it another way, large acts demonstrate the depth of our kindness while small acts demonstrate its breadth. And small things added up over time can make a big difference. In fact, small acts are often more important than large acts, in part because, over time, small acts of kindness afford us ample opportunity to demonstrate this virtue to those with whom we interact most closely and most often. Spectacular kindness to strangers is nice, but routine kindness to familiars is necessary.

If we want to get better at practicing kindness, then we must acknowledge up front that doing so means that we will have to give things up *and* that we will have to give them up more often and more deeply. No matter what resource we sacrifice, we have to acknowledge, in advance, that kindness by its nature comes at a cost. Failing to recognize that tough fact up front risks eventual abandonment of the virtue in the end. Staying kind is hard. But if we know that it is hard going into it, then we are much more likely to stick it out.

As we think about where we can make sacrifices, both large and small, it is worth asking ourselves a few questions.

Reflection Questions

1. How often do we make the time to say "Thank you" for a job well done or a service rendered? How many thank-yous might we say, or write, in any given day?
2. How often do we deliberately celebrate success with our teams?
3. How often do we ask someone how they are doing personally?
4. In what circumstances are we least likely to be kind to someone else? Most likely to be kind to someone else?

Contrary to what many think, this virtue in a leader is not weakness. It is strength, a necessity even, and it is not easy to achieve. But if we patiently pursue it over time, we can achieve it, and we will be strong. More important, our teams will be stronger than we are.

SUMMARY

- Kindness is an absolute imperative for a leader, but many mistake it for weakness or timidity.
- Kindness is more than an emotion or a generalized feeling of benevolence. Specifically, it is an emotion put into action in a way that demonstrates four distinct elements: 1) compassion, 2) action, 3) grace, and 4) sacrifice.
- The rewards from kindness do not hinge on the reactions of others. Put into practice, this virtue enhances our joy, reinforces our sense of purpose, and makes us more reflective.
- Kindness has extraordinary effects on the lives of our team members. It

helps them to feel valued as individuals, which makes them extremely loyal. It spurs risk taking and makes members of the team more likely to extend kindness to one another. Finally, it increases the likelihood that people will operate out of a love of gain rather than fear of loss.

• Only when a team is operating out of love of gain rather than fear of loss will they give everything of which they are capable.

CHAPTER 5

★

DISCIPLINE

I remember pickup day at Officer Candidate School (OCS) like it was yesterday. For those who have not had the distinct privilege of being screamed at by a Marine staff sergeant, pickup day is the day that not-yet-Marine-officer candidates meet their drill instructors. The wannabe officers are, for the most part, unsuspecting civilians—mostly young, mostly college-aged—who have signed away their summer in the hopes of becoming leaders of Marines. To do so, they must spend ten weeks being screened by some of the Corps' best and brightest to determine whether these raw civilians have the potential to lead young men and women in combat. By the time pickup day slams into the starry-eyed candidates, the hopeful young men and women have been sweltering in the summer heat of Quantico, Virginia, for about three days.

Though they don't know it yet, the candidates have had a deceptively easy time. Sure, they live in barracks rooms and wear a modified uniform—slacks and an olive drab T-shirt—but they are a world away from truly experiencing OCS. They haven't yet had their heads shaved bald; they haven't been made to run until they throw up; and they haven't been screamed at from two inches away. They also haven't spent hours on their hands and knees, scrubbing the barracks toilets or the stained linoleum tile with their toothbrushes. They haven't had their food knocked out of

their hands in the mess hall because they failed to eat their fill in the allotted two minutes, and they haven't been made to fight one another with
mock bayonets. No, everything up until pickup day has been leisurely and
fairly genteel. So, on some level, the officer candidates have been lulled
into a false sense of security, deliberately. All of that changes on pickup
day.

On my pickup day, three hundred or so candidates sat in the gym, a
large building made of corrugated tin with a concrete slab for a floor.
Stacked in front of our folding chairs was everything we were allowed to
bring with us, all of our worldly possessions at OCS, packed tightly into
two large green duffel bags, called seabags. Our backs were as straight as
we could make them as an officer stood at a podium at the head of our
folding-chair phalanx and droned on with advice on how to persevere
through what was coming up. As he spoke, our future sergeant instructors
filed silently into the gym.

They lined the tin walls around and behind us and stood immobile
and ramrod straight as the major wound down his speech. The sergeant
instructors looked as if they could have stepped out of a recruiting poster.
Their torsos were perfect V's, their boots were polished to a mirror shine,
and the creases in their uniforms were razor sharp. More forebodingly,
each of the instructors wore an expression that made his face look as hard
as coffin nails. I think that the major concluded with something that was
either "Semper Fi" or "you'll probably die," but by then I was too nervous
to pay much attention. Like most of my compatriots, I was eyeing the
strange beings dressed in camouflage, and wondering which ones of them
held every moment—waking and sleeping—of my next nine weeks in
their hands.

I didn't have long to wait. As soon as the major turned from the podium, all hell broke loose inside the gym. The sergeant instructors
launched themselves from their positions against the wall, screaming at
all of us to move, quickly. Two of them attached themselves to the candidates in my area. Those Marines were clearly our drill instructors. As the
cacophony inside the reflecting tin walls of the gym reached deafening
proportions, I and the rest of the officer candidates commenced the hu-

miliating procedure known as the "Seabag Drag." Scrambling frantically, with our instructors screaming at us to go faster, faster, we grabbed at our two large, green cylindrical seabags, each the size of a punching bag, wrestled them into some maneuverable configuration, and began running. With bags slung across our shoulders and backs or improbably draped along our stomachs or just flat-out dragged along the ground, we hustled as best we could out of the building to a hot, black asphalt tarmac. As we shuffled, items dropped like breadcrumbs from our bags' overstuffed mouths. We lurched down to grab them, with our new sergeant instructors shouting at us every step of the way to hurry, hurry, hurry.

As we did our best to comply, they did their best to offer withering comments on our obvious worthlessness and laziness. Our instructors had never in their entire lives seen a group so slow and yet so sloppy. How could just forty people manage to drop so many things? We looked like a group of drunken spider monkeys or drugged pack mules. We were the most hopeless group of pathetic losers our instructors had ever seen. We would never make Marine officers at this pace. We should probably quit before we were fired. As we continued our mass panic, the sergeant instructors continued to grace us with these and other similarly helpful suggestions and observations.

The humiliation and the frantic scrambling and shuffling continued until we arrived at the parade deck, several football fields' worth of hot black asphalt. We ran to the tarmac and lined up in three rows of about fifteen men each. Our instructors screamed at us to dump everything we owned out of our seabags and onto the sticky asphalt. We complied. As soon as we started, we had already failed for slowness. We were told to pack everything back up again. This time our repacking was slow, so we had to dump everything again in order to continue to get better. The instructors prowled around, inspecting the spilled contents on the ground. They had a number of opinions that they screamed at us.

"Oh my God! What do we have here, Candidate? Is this your security blanket? Did your mommy pack your bag for you? I'll bet you suck your thumb at night . . ."

"What is this trash? Do you even know where you are, Candidate

Metrosexual? Do you think you're in a beauty parlor? Are you hoping for a nice perm? Maybe a mani-pedi? Are you so dumb that you don't realize that hair gel is useless when you have no hair . . ."

And so on. We dumped, we repacked, and we dumped again. The sergeant instructors controlled our every move, and nothing we did could possibly be good enough or fast enough for them. We were useless at everything we turned our frantic, shaking hands to. It was a preview of things to come. Just a few days later, we all stood at attention in our platoon barracks, presenting ourselves for inspection to the instructors. To a man, everyone in our forty-man platoon failed that inspection. We'd spent hours prepping, staying up until two or three in the morning (wake-up was at five) to make sure we had no faults, that our boots were polished to a mirror shine, that our uniforms were immaculate, and that our weapons had no dust or dirt anywhere. It didn't matter. The instructors found something wrong with all of us.

The following weeks passed in a blur. My head was shaved bald—as were all of ours. We lost our individuality. I found myself doing push-ups for infractions real or imagined. I crawled half-drowning on my back through a trench filled with water, with barbed wire just centimeters from my face, at night, while explosions filled the air. I was made to take off my gas mask in a chamber filled with tear gas; I waded through mud and water and filth up to my chest; I ran until I threw up and then ran some more. I once screamed until I couldn't talk for three days. I did all of this because my instructors told me to. And I hated them for it.

It wasn't until I graduated that I realized what our sergeant instructors had been doing. They were taking civilians and instilling in them the discipline that the Marine Corps—a unique institution dedicated to fighting wars—demanded. They were teaching us that we had to conform to a set of standards, every day. These standards demanded more from individuals than anything else we had ever known. If we didn't discipline ourselves, and uphold the values the Corps demanded, then the organization would cease to function.

When life and death are at stake, there can be no room for debate around basic assumptions, assumptions like "no Marine left behind" or the more prosaic "weapons must be cleaned every day." All Marines must buy into the core values of "honor, courage, commitment," or else they will be expelled. These values form the backbone of the institution and explain everything it does, from the publication of doctrine to the execution of battlefield plans. They unify disparate individual members by explaining, clearly and simply, what will be expected of them at all times—whether one is in the classroom learning, on the battlefield fighting, or out of uniform relaxing, the core values must be followed. For example, members do not get to choose whether they want to quit a shift even after forty-eight hours of sleeplessness; commitment demands they continue. Leaders are not allowed romantic engagements with those in lower ranks; honor demands that they never leverage their position for personal gain. Being undisciplined is not an option, we were told, because failure to be disciplined can, and will, result in death.

On one particularly grueling road march, our sergeant instructors told us the story of "Lieutenant Smith," a real-life infantry officer in Vietnam. Before going overseas, he was advised by returning veterans to practice hiking with a pack on his back for hours. Smith ignored the advice because it was difficult. When Smith got to Vietnam, on his very first mission with his platoon he had to hike for more than ten miles through thick jungle. After about five miles of hiking, his lack of physical conditioning came through. Smith fell over, exhausted and unable to continue. The entire platoon halted, formed a security perimeter, and called in a helicopter for a medevac. As the helicopter touched down, the Viet Cong launched an ambush. Most of the men, including Lieutenant Smith, were slaughtered, and the helicopter was downed—all because one leader had failed to discipline himself to adhere to the proper standard before crisis arrived.

Three years after I graduated from Officer Candidate School, I led my own infantrymen in combat. I realized then what I should have in OCS: that our instructors were doing much more to us than instilling the basic organizational discipline common to every Marine. They were also instilling in us the disciplined mindset and the sense of responsibility that we needed in order to lead. That responsibility was significant. It meant that we had to take care of our men in body, mind, and spirit, and return them to their families better than we received them (if combat circumstances allowed). We had to accept that as leaders everything that our Marines did and failed to do was ultimately on our shoulders, regardless of whether we had a hand in it or not. And we had to take care of ourselves, to make ourselves the best people we could be, mentally and morally.

After all, our instructors weren't training basic Marines. They were training Marine officers, and these future leaders would be called to higher standards of personal discipline than would all those they led. If the officers could or would not set the example, both in their own lives and in the lives of their men, then hundreds (and perhaps thousands) of young men and women were at risk of losing their lives.

DISCIPLINE DEFINED

Most of us associate the word *discipline* with "punishment," and so it has generally negative connotations. It was not always so. The word itself originates from the Latin *disciplina,* meaning "teaching" or "learning." In thirteenth-century Middle English, the word *discipline* first entered the English lexicon. It was used as a reference to the systematic instruction given to pupils to train them in a craft or to teach them to follow a particular code of conduct or order. *Merriam-Webster's Collegiate Dictionary* lists several definitions for the word, including "orderly or prescribed conduct or pattern of behavior" and "training that corrects, molds, or perfects the mental faculties or moral character." Many people think that military discipline is just another form of extreme and unusual punishment, but that is not the case. When the Marines refer to discipline, they mean training and behavior. Over the past two centuries, the Corps has honed its training to a nearly exact science so that the behavior it produces will be as consistent as it is institutionally possible to achieve. The stakes are high. If the training fails and the resulting behavior is improper or inappropriate, then young men and women will die.

Because of this, the Marines hold their leaders to higher standards of discipline than they do the rank-and-file, and they train their leaders more extensively. Noncommissioned officers go to specific leadership schools as soon as they pin on their rank. Regular officers spend at least a year learning not only their specialty (infantry, artillery, supply, etc.) but also general leadership principles. They cannot afford to be undisciplined, and they cannot afford to fail.

In Iraq and later Afghanistan, I was supremely conscious that if I couldn't demonstrate high standards of discipline, then the basic standards that I asked of my Marines would not be followed. When it came to discipline, I had to go above and beyond what was required of others. If I stopped cleaning my rifle every day, for example, my men would start doing the same, and when we most needed it, our equipment would let us down. When I failed, and fail I did, it was not I who suffered most. It was my men. Discipline was crucial to our survival, and I quickly learned that if the team was to embrace this characteristic, then the leader had to embrace it at a higher level.

TWO HALVES TO THE WHOLE

Though the stakes outside of war are not always life-and-death, the pursuit of discipline is supremely important for all leaders. If we hope to become servant leaders, then we must be disciplined no matter what the context. But before we set off in pursuit of this virtue, we need to try to understand what, exactly, it is. Discipline is far more than creased pants, spit-shined shoes, and lots of yelling.

Fundamentally, this virtue comes in two parts, ethical and executional, with the first laying the foundation for the second. At its heart, ethical discipline means ensuring that common beliefs on right and wrong are accepted and shared across a team. In addition to the moral benefits inherent in doing what is right, a common ethical foundation has significant practical benefits. Most important, agreement on ethical issues speeds up alignment and decision-making. When a team sees eye to eye on the most fundamental of issues, progress can be made much more rapidly when deciding what to do in a difficult or ambiguous situation. Without ethical alignment in advance, however, it becomes very hard for a team to decide quickly on a course of action. They can spend endless time debating right and wrong before they ever get around to deciding what to do and how to do it.

Nearly thirty years ago, the leadership of Johnson & Johnson provided an excellent example of what a leadership team can do quickly, and under great duress, when they all agree on issues of right and wrong. On September 29, 1982, a man in the Chicago area died after taking cyanide-laced capsules of Extra-Strength Tylenol. Within the next several days, six other people in the same area died of the same poison. The first alert that the leadership of Johnson & Johnson had of the impending disaster was a phone call from a local Chicago news reporter informing them that a medical examiner had just given a press conference claiming that people were dying from poisoned Tylenol, and did the company care to comment?

The news traveled quickly to the chairman, James Burke, who immediately convened a seven-person strategy team. Their task wasn't easy. They were faced with an issue, which, if improperly handled, could result in the deaths of hundreds, possibly even thousands if the contamination was widespread. At the time of the poisonings, Tylenol had 37 percent of the analgesic market, and it accounted for 17 percent of the company's net income. But recalling every single bottle of Tylenol—the only certain way to prevent further poisoning—might be not only unnecessary but also cost the life savings of thousands who depended on the financial health of the company. Pulling every single bottle of Tylenol off the shelves nationwide might be a death blow from which the drug would never recover.

Without knowing the scope of the problem, and with the clock ticking too quickly to allow the time for a proper investigation, the strategy team had a decision to make: should they recall all, some, or none of their potentially poisoned product? In many ways, the decision came down to a fundamental choice: lives versus livelihoods. There was no time to do a lengthy, time-consuming investigation. The decision had to be made quickly.

In later interviews, all members of the strategy committee referred to Johnson & Johnson's company credo as a touchstone that helped them navigate through the crisis. Written in 1943 by Robert Wood Johnson, the credo had helped guide the company for nearly four decades. It begins with the following statement:

> We believe our first responsibility is to the doctors, nurses, and patients, to mothers and fathers and all others who use our products and services. . . .

Though it seems such a trivial thing—mere words on a piece of paper—the credo had a profound impact on the leadership team and their decision. Because it had been accepted by all of the members as true and necessary before the poisonings broke out, the credo had prealigned the decision makers on fundamental right and wrong, on that which took priority above all else in the company. In many ways, the credo was a sort of corporate code of conduct, one that helped define Johnson & Johnson's overarching company mission and responsibilities. As a result, the credo helped the key decision makers know what they needed to do when the crisis hit. After all, Robert Johnson had spelled out the company's beliefs thirty-five years in advance of the company's greatest test.

So, when people started dying in Chicago, there was no debate on what mattered most. No one second-guessed the fact that the welfare of "doctors, nurses, and patients . . . mothers and fathers" was more important than other criteria, including profits and employee retirement funds. No one made the argument that each life was worth a certain amount in a lawsuit, for example, and that the company could break even without a product recall so long as deaths remained below a specific, acceptable threshold. Where it mattered most, the team had absolute agreement on their ethical foundation.

So James Burke and his strategy team decided on a course of action that was nearly unheard-of before 1982: a full-blown product recall.

First, they alerted consumers across the nation not to use any type of Tylenol pill. Next, they stopped the production and advertising of all Tylenol and pulled the product from the entire greater Chicago area. Then Johnson & Johnson pulled every single bottle off every single shelf in America. It was the first highly publicized, nationwide product recall in modern American history. Marketing experts predicted that the drug, and the company, would never fully recover.

In its entirety, the recall, product reformulation, and relaunch cost the company $100 million. Tylenol's market share plummeted from nearly 40 percent to 7 percent. But just one year after the crisis, the drug had recovered all of the ground it had lost. And Johnson & Johnson had moved from villain to hero in the eyes of most of America.

This fortuitous outcome would never have materialized if the J&J leadership team had dithered in its decision, or if it had responded half-heartedly or begrudgingly. It would never have happened if people perceived that Johnson & Johnson cared more about profits than lives. However, the leadership team was ethically disciplined. They had established fundamental principles bracketing right and wrong well before the crisis. As a result, once the poisons hit, they had no disagreement about their priorities. They made the right decisions quickly, and the company exited the crisis stronger than it entered.

ETHICAL DISCIPLINE

If we expect a team to behave like the leadership of Johnson & Johnson, then we must also expect the team to agree on fundamental right and wrong well before a crisis hits. And if a team is to be clear on what is morally acceptable and what isn't, then their leader must first be clear. Just as important, their leader must visibly demonstrate discipline when executing right and wrong in their own lives.

Before going any further, it is worth pointing out that this chapter will not—indeed, it cannot—properly scope out a full-fledged definition of commonly accepted morality. That is the purview of a philosophy book, not a leadership one, and we do not need doctorates in ethics to lead well. What we need are ethics put into action—fewer lofty words and more noble deeds. For the purposes of moving forward, I believe that we can all agree on a common framework: a leader should not lie, cheat, or steal.

Besides, the problems that have plagued us recently, and the problems that usually plague societies at any given time, have not been ones stemming from situations where leaders have made tough moral choices when faced with difficult, shades-of-gray options. Our problems recently have been that leaders have knowingly abandoned even the most basic morality when pursuing personal gain. Most moral leadership problems do not arise from misjudging complicated ethical issues. Most arise from something much simpler: wanton disregard of common decency in pursuit of naked self-interest.

In recent times, prominent leaders have lied to customers, embezzled from clients, bribed officials (or been bribed themselves), covered up mistresses, prostitutes, and illegitimate children, cheated on their taxes, and committed whole hosts of felonies. During the recent financial bubble, for example, many Wall Street traders knowingly pawned off junk on the clients whose interest they were supposed to protect. But the traders refrained from describing the "mortgage-backed securities" they sold to customers in the same terms as they talked about them to each other—"toxic waste." Leading financial institutions lied to manipulate global interest rates in order to line their own pockets, heedless of the consequences to individuals whose homes and savings depend on these rates. Are all of these really complex moral questions?

How much better off would we be as a country if our leaders did the basic things right—if politicians paid their own taxes correctly instead of committing felony-level cheating, for example, or if church leaders could refrain from committing adultery with members of their own pastoral flock? We would be much improved if leaders, instead of pointing their fingers at the foibles of others, the maladies of society, or the complexities of choices, instead applied their accusatory and philosophical energies to their own basic ethics.

So, as leaders we should be less concerned with the finer points of complex ethics and instead focus on how we can sustain consistent adherence to clear, widely accepted moral principles. Most of us will never have to make life-and-death ethical decisions, or navigate a complex right-and-wrong dilemma where our decision affects the lives or livelihoods of thousands. However, we will all make smaller such decisions by the dozens every single day. Because they seem lower in magnitude, they can seem lesser in importance. Does it really matter if we tell someone that we've almost finished a presentation when really we haven't even started? Must we record our travel mileage as accurately as possible when we ask for reimbursement? Do people really care when we tell them that we'll handle something minor and then forget all about it as soon as we walk away? Do our children really notice it when we promise that we'll be at their games and dance recitals, and then we don't show up? Do our spouses really notice when we promise a "date night" and then we don't deliver? The answer to these questions (and all of the other ones we haven't asked) is yes. People notice the little ethical failures, and these little failures shape us over time.

To lead well, we need to apply ethical discipline to our own lives. It will help to begin by examining our adherence to the very basic standard outlined above. On its face, there is nothing novel about refraining from lying, stealing, or cheating. However, if we dig a little deeper and drill down below major, life-changing decisions and into the more mundane issues of day-to-day life, then the basic ethical challenge becomes challenging indeed. Do we make promises that we do not intend to keep (a form of lying) to avoid having to say no to someone's face? Have we ever fudged our expense reports to have our company pay for something that we should (a form of cheating)? Have we passed off someone else's idea as our own and never once given them credit for it (a form of stealing)?

A corporate leadership trainer once told us about a promising executive he was coaching. On the yearly leadership survey, this executive was ranked extremely low on the integrity metric by his team, surprising both him and his reviewers. "How can this be?" the man asked. "I don't lie on a regular basis."

The trainer thought for a bit. Then he replied, "Yes, but do you make easy promises, ones that you have no intention of fulfilling, to avoid an argument, avoid a conflict, avoid an assignment, or avoid saying no directly?" the trainer replied.

The light went on. "I do that all the time," the executive replied. "It's how I get out of doing what I don't want to. It's how I avoid conversations I don't want to have." The man had hit on a key point: unkept promises are often viewed in the same light as outright lies no matter how good the intentions. Whereas sometimes promises are made to avoid conflict, at other times they are made with the full intention of being kept. Unfortunately, the recipient of the promise cannot peer into hearts to determine intentions. All that they can see are outcomes, and in that department a well-intentioned promise unkept is no different from a conflict-avoiding promise unkept. Circumstances may sometimes prevent us from keeping our promises, but the end result is still the same: promises that don't come true.

The little things matter. It's easy to believe that when the major ethical decisions come around (for example, should I use accounting tricks to inflate this quarter's income? should I tell a customer a lie to gain a multimillion-dollar deal? should I cheat on my spouse?) that we'll make the right decisions. But if we don't practice making small choices right every day, then it's highly unlikely that we'll be ready to go when it's time to make the big ones. Furthermore, our teams notice every little minor compromise we make. They remember it when we tell them we'll follow up on something and then we never do so. They notice when we tell someone that we're working on something—or that our team is working on something—and we really aren't. They remember promises unkept. Countless times my crying children have pierced my hearing with those simple words that every parent is familiar with: "But you promised . . ." Every ethical choice that we make, large and small, is noticed and remembered by those we lead. They assemble a moral impression of us based not on what we say, but on what we do. And as we take action, we build our own ethical foundation out of the bricks of small, almost unnoticeable daily choices.

In Officer Candidate School and then again in the Marines' basic officer course, it was made very clear to us that the greatest sin that could be committed was an "integrity breach." Most commonly, an "integrity breach" took the form of a lie, but at its heart it was anything that drove a wedge between our professed beliefs—honor, courage, commitment—and our daily actions. Most often, we failed by lying, usually to cover up mistakes or gaps in knowledge. When, for example, a screaming gunnery sergeant is two inches from your face, demanding to know why you failed to carry out a specified order, particularly one from a peer, it is very easy to say you never received such an order, or that you did not understand. Shifting blame to someone else often seems the best option for getting yourself off the hook.

However, as I soon came to find out, sacrificing integrity is almost always a significant long-term loss. Candidates who were determined to have outright lied were almost always jerked out of training, hauled in front of an officer board, and harshly cross-examined to determine whether they could remain in the training. Usually, the board summarily kicked them out. Executional mistakes, on the other hand, were well tolerated, expected, even. People could fail woefully at basic skills, including marksmanship, and still be allowed repeated chances to improve, try again, and continue the training. It usually took only one integrity breach, though, to end a prospective Marine officer's career.

I did not realize what was happening at the time, but I do now. The Marines were teaching their future leaders the supreme importance of ethical discipline. If we could learn it in a relatively low-stakes training environment, with plenty of oversight readily at hand, then we would be better able to practice it in the chaotic environment of combat. There, instinctive ethical choices make the split-second difference between humanity and atrocities. Failures cost lives; successes save them. This is precisely why the Marines had instilled in us a nearly instinctive dread of ethical misconduct, of "integrity breaches." If we developed the discipline in peace, we were most likely to employ it in war. And while imperfect (even one failure is one too many), the Marines have proven in more than a decade of war to be one of the most moral, humane fighting forces in history.

I am not proposing here that leaders be saints—everyone makes moral mistakes, and leaders are no different. I am only asking that leaders try to discipline themselves to be consistent in the small decisions before they take a stab at the large ones. Consistency matters. After all, if we lead others, whether in the workplace or at home, we have an audience everywhere we go. The actions we take, and the decisions we make, set the example for what is permissible to our teams.

EXECUTIONAL DISCIPLINE

In the summer of 1914, a British explorer named Ernest Shackleton reportedly placed the following advertisement in the London classifieds:

> Men wanted for hazardous journey. Low wages, bitter cold, long hours of complete darkness. Safe return doubtful. Honour and recognition in event of success.

On August 8, 1914, Shackleton and fifty-six others left British waters to attempt the last feat remaining in the heroic age of Antarctic exploration: a journey across the continent via the South Pole. Misfortune followed hard on their heels. On January 15, 1915, Shackleton's ship, the *Endurance,* found itself frozen into an ice pack in the Weddell Sea. For several months, the ship held together and the crew stayed put. The conditions of the crew's sojourn were trying, to say the least. They endured days of near-continuous darkness and nights of hypothermia. By the time June rolled around, the temperatures were a balmy minus 17 degrees Fahrenheit. The crew and the ship persevered, but the Antarctic would not be denied. On October 24, 1915, the ship finally succumbed to the pressure of the ice around it and began sinking. The sailors were now marooned on an ice floe in the Antarctic.

The harsh conditions became even worse. The crew left their ship's berths for reindeer or wool sleeping bags laid directly on the Arctic ice. They slept in overcrowded tents. Most of their provisions sank with the ship itself. Immediately Shackleton instituted a strict routine. Supplies were rationed—every man ate the same amount of food served to them in the same aluminum mug. They had three utensils: a spoon, a knife, and their fingers, and no man took more than his due. Shackleton himself went out of his way to demonstrate his willingness to do menial chores. He dutifully took his turn to serve as "Peggy," the person who carried the pot of food from the cook to the tent, and when he found out that the cook gave him preferential treatment because of his leadership status, Shackleton became furious.

The routine could not hold forever. As the ice pack opened up, the stranded crew was forced to move their makeshift camp. Christmas Day 1915 found the men awake at midnight, pulling the three lifeboats and everything else they needed to survive across the Antarctic ice. To move the boats, they literally strapped themselves into harnesses and pulled like sled dogs. Their boots, leather ankle-highs with gabardine reaching to the knees, soon filled with water. In this state, each shoe weighed almost seven pounds. The crew cut their way through mounds of ice caused by high-pressure ridges, covering less than one thousand grueling meters per hour. At 1:30 A.M. on the next day, the first man quit.

Shackleton would have none of it. Hurrying back from his position at the head of the column, he pulled the man aside and reminded him in no uncertain terms of his responsibilities and duties. The mutineer was soon back in position pulling a heavy lifeboat. Before they turned in for the evening, Shackleton mustered his entire crew and read aloud the articles they had signed back in England, before they joined the expedition. From then on out, there were no more mutinies.

Shortly thereafter, the ice floe became especially treacherous, and Shackleton instituted a "watch and watch" system. Half of the crew would be awake at all times, with all of their winter clothes on and their gear fully stowed. The shifts were four hours on and four hours off. It was a grueling pace, but not a single man refused to stand his turn. A few days into the exhausting new routine, their provisions began to run low. Every-one was put on a starvation diet. Lack of food was layered on top of lack of sleep. Still, they persevered.

On April 23, 1916, the ice opened up enough for Shackleton and four others to attempt a daring dash for help. They set off in a modified, open-top lifeboat for the whaling station at South Georgia Island, cross-ing eight hundred miles of some of the worst, storm-swept seas on earth in the process. Once they landed, however, they had to cross the island to reach the whaling station on the other side, which would require a tra-verse of some of the globe's most difficult terrain outside of the Himala-yas. They had only a small bit of rope and a carpenter's adze to assist them. Nonetheless, the team made it safely, a feat that has confounded modern mountaineers who have attempted the same thing with much better equipment. The entire crew of the doomed ship was rescued just a few months later.

The men of the *Endurance* stand as a testament to executional disci-pline, defined in this context as *strict adherence to nonethical organiza-tional standards, rules, and expectations.* When asked to do something, they did it, and everyone did what was asked. Some men were better and some were worse, but no one ignored the rules. When it was time to pull the lifeboats, the men strapped their weary bodies into the harnesses and pulled. When it was time to cut rations, they did so, with each man taking his share and no more. There were no brawls or food stealing. When it was time to stop sleeping and stand watch, the men left the relative warmth of their shelter and stood for their allotted shift.

Most of us will never find ourselves struggling for survival in the Antarctic, with our life dependent on whether we can stay alert during our four-hour ice watch. However, no matter what context we are in, organizational standards abound, and they are important—for exam-ple: workday start time, office dress codes, home cleanliness, or meeting punctuality. For most of us, the standards embedded in our settings are unlikely to determine whether we live or die, but they can determine whether we succeed or fail as leaders.

If we hope to maintain credibility over time, then we must adhere faithfully to the same organizational expectations that our context asks of our teams. In basic training, for example, Marine officers have to learn how to march in formation, in full dress uniform and with ceremonial swords. They even have to pass a drill exam. Like many others, I often wondered how properly saluting with an antiquated weapon and meticulously decorating antiquated clothing would make me a better leader when the bullets started flying. I also wondered how scrubbing my room's linoleum floors until they were bone white, or cutting my hair nearly bald every Sunday, or any one of a hundred other small, mindless rules that I obeyed every day would in any way help me to be a better leader of Marines.

I asked one of my instructors these questions, and I never forgot his answer. First off, he told me, you do these things because you will eventually expect your Marines to do them. You need to understand what they are doing and to do it yourself. What is more, he continued, by training yourself to stay disciplined in the small things, you make it a habit to stay disciplined in the large ones. If you are accustomed to shaving every day, for example, then cleaning your rifle every day will not seem like much of an additional burden. Finally, he told me, if you can demonstrate discipline in the small yet obvious areas, those who observe you can trust that you are equally disciplined in the more important, yet largely hidden, areas of leadership. If someone notices that you cannot bother to get a haircut just one time a week, then how can they trust that you will plan your mission orders thoroughly every single day? Just like with ethical discipline, small failures can have large consequences. Being faithful in the little things prepares us to accept greater responsibility in the big ones.

Two years later, in the middle of a firefight, that lesson hit me the hard way. We had located what appeared to be a bomb several hundred yards away, and, with no engineers to examine it, I raised my rifle to shoot it. When I pulled the trigger, the only thing I heard was a faint click. I had not cleaned my weapon in several days because I had not fired it in several days. Now sand had jammed my firing pin. My instructor's words came rushing back at me. I had allowed myself to get away from the small, basic daily discipline that prevented catastrophic failures like this one. I shudder to think what would have happened if I had been defending myself, or, worse, one of my men. We would have been shot because by failing in the small things, I had suddenly failed in a large one.

Contextual norms and rules do not always make sense (the Marines have plenty whose purpose never became apparent to me) but many do, and sometimes we only realize that in retrospect, once the rules have been broken and something has gone drastically awry. For example, we realize why the forklift drivers are required to honk *every* time they start moving only after someone on the factory floor is run over. Thus we ignore nonunderstood routines at our peril. As leaders, we have to steel ourselves to follow the small expectations that our team or organization asks of us lest we weaken the foundation that supports us, or, just as bad, make irrelevant something that may be crucial to our and our team's success—the noncombat equivalent of failing to clean our rifles every day. This is not to say that every small rule makes sense or that we should try to live with ones that are clearly useless. As leaders we can change these things, but only if we have earned the credibility to do so by demonstrating that we are changing for a reason, not simply changing because our pattern is to unmake all the rules that we are simply unable to follow.

DISCIPLINE MATTERS

Ethical and executional discipline sound great in concept, but they are all too easy to ignore in practice. We have to hold ourselves to a high standard and, by our example, hold our teams to that same standard. We have to give ourselves hard looks in the mirror to identify our failures, have hard conversations with others, and make hard daily choices. But we cannot fail to do so, because if we lack discipline, both ethical and executional, and if our teams lack discipline, then the negative effects over time are irreparable.

Most immediately catastrophic is a lack of ethical discipline. Unabated, it will destroy entire organizations as surely as the sun will rise and set. The case of Barings Bank provides a worst-case example of the often-fatal harm that lax ethical discipline can inflict on an organization. In the 1980s, Barings was the oldest investment bank in Britain. It had survived both the Great Depression and two world wars, and it listed among its clients the queen herself. As deregulation made new financial instruments available, and as foreign operations opened up new fields for growth, Barings moved to capitalize on the opportunities.

In the 1990s, Barings had entered the derivatives market in force. One of its star traders was a man named Nick Leeson, who in 1992 began managing the firm's Singapore office. In short order, he demonstrated wild success at arbitrage in the East Asian financial markets. At one point in time, Leeson alone accounted for nearly 10 percent of the firm's profits. He was clearly a rising star. Unbeknownst to the home office, however, the leader of its Singapore traders was generating his impressive numbers in large part through massive accounting fraud.

The deceit started small. Initially Leeson created a special, hidden account to cover up a single loss of twenty thousand pounds sterling arising either from an accounting error or an embarrassing mistake by one of his subordinates. Later, he claimed that he intended only to conceal the loss until he recovered it through additional trading. However, the hidden account remained open, and as Leeson made increasingly aggressive bets, he concealed more and more of his losses inside it. To maintain the fiction, Leeson falsified paper and electronic records, forged letters, and stole money from client accounts to pay for his own losses. All the while he continued to report huge profits from his trading operations.

The too-impressive numbers should have raised at least some eyebrows. However, London management turned a blind eye (or an ignorant one) to the activities of the Singapore office. By early February 1995, Leeson's activities had generated losses totaling $1.3 billion—twice the bank's available trading capital. Realizing that he had doomed his office and perhaps even the entire company, Leeson jumped on a plane to Kuala Lumpur, leaving a confession note for the chairman. The Bank of England attempted a hasty weekend rescue, but it was too late. Employee bonuses around the world were canceled, and the bank was declared insolvent on February 26, 1995. ING, a Dutch group, eventually purchased Barings for the nominal sum of one British pound.

It was an ignominious end for Britain's oldest investment bank, and it serves as a cautionary tale for all of us. Ethical failures like Leeson's usually start small, with the idea that a leader will compromise "just this once." The man responsible for the largest Ponzi scheme in history, Bernie Madoff, intended to illegally hide his losses for just a short period of time, until he could "make it up." Twenty years and $65 billion later, Madoff was still scheming. In 2008, one "rogue trader," Jérôme Kerviel, lost nearly $4.9 billion for Société Générale through illegal trading. To this day, however, he claims that such behavior was tolerated by leadership as long as the profits continued. And the hits continue—recent times have witnessed one of the largest financial bankruptcies in history, from MF Global, a firm that mysteriously lost more than a billion dollars of its customers' money, money that appears to have been illegally commingled with its own in order to juice returns. Small wonder that each passing day continues to shake our faith in our economic system and our country's leadership.

Indeed, lack of ethical discipline is so powerful that it can do strategic damage to an entire nation, as the scandal of Abu Ghraib proved all too recently. In 2004, a relatively small number of soldiers, numbering under twenty altogether, began abusing and torturing Iraqi prisoners in a facility named after the surrounding area of Abu Ghraib. The American soldiers were reservists, and they later claimed that they had had little training to prepare them for work in an Iraqi prison. One of the most prominent perpetrators, Lynndie England, was working a night shift in a chicken processing plant at the time she was called up for active duty.

Still, regardless of the executional training they may or may not have received, the reservists clearly abandoned all vestiges of basic human decency—and ethical discipline—as they handled their foreign prisoners. One soldier claimed that he believed that photographing a naked prisoner with a dog collar and dog leash around his neck was not torture; rather, he believed that it was a demonstration of the legitimate use of force. Others amused themselves by building human pyramids of naked prisoners, strapping electrodes to their charges, forcing naked detainees to masturbate in front of one another, and occasionally sexually assaulting their wards with diverse objects.

Eventually pictures of the abuse made it into widespread distribution, and the picture they painted of America was a bleak one: a nation ostensibly dedicated to freedom and human rights was allowing torture and abuse by its uniformed soldiers. Thousands were inspired to take up arms against the United States military. To the extent that America could claim any moral high ground when juxtaposed against the regime of Saddam Hussein, that moral high ground went up in smoke when the sordid story of Abu Ghraib broke. A handful of undisciplined, unethical soldiers thus managed to bring dishonor upon 150,000 of their comrades, put their fellow soldiers in increased danger, and do significant strategic harm to their nation. Lieutenant Colonel Bill Cowan best summed up the disgust felt by the rest of the country:

"We went into Iraq to stop things like this from happening, and indeed, here they were, happening under our tutelage."

Lack of ethical discipline can bring down a team, a company, or even a country. We cannot afford to let ethical failures go unchecked. Otherwise our teams will disintegrate and our missions will cease to have meaning. We cannot have reasonable disagreements over whether to lie to a supplier to get them to decrease costs, for example. We cannot allow our accountants to creatively allocate budget data to make our areas of responsibility artificially inflated. We should not hide personal expenditures from our spouses. If we do not enforce discipline in the little things we should not be surprised when we find massive failures in the large ones.

A commitment to executional discipline is just as important as a commitment to its ethical cousin. To begin with, our integrity as leaders hinges on our ability to uphold the standards we mandate. Put simply, we lose our credibility when we ask our teams to adhere to one set of rules while we adhere to another (usually more lax and less sacrificial) under cover of our leadership responsibilities. For example, we may track our team's vacation days religiously but take the extra day here or there ourselves. We may demand punctuality at our meetings but be late to those of others. We may set strict spending limits for our family members but allow ourselves the odd extra hundred dollars every now and again, because, as leaders we often assume that the rules that apply to others do not necessarily apply to us.

But they do, and executional duplicity in a leader is unacceptable no matter what the extenuating circumstances and no matter what the difference in responsibilities. Too often, leaders can use the heightened responsibilities of their roles, or their extremely busy schedules, to justify the reasons why they can't be bothered to do what they ask of so many others. Too often, their teams acquiesce. However, the problem with justifying a double standard based on role is that no matter how reasoned the rationale, the overarching standard inevitably becomes degraded. After all, if a leader can't be bothered to follow their own rules, then why should a team do so?

Worse, the higher we rise in our leadership roles, the fewer people will call us to account. They may mutter to themselves as they sit in their chairs for ten uncertain minutes, waiting for us to show up late to our own meeting. They may wonder where we disappear to in the middle of the day, knowing that they themselves have to check in and out with their managers when they leave. They may wonder why their pay is being cut while that of their executives is being bolstered. But they are unlikely to ever point out a leader's duplicity to that leader's face.

Nor are they likely to point out one another's failings, and an undisciplined team is as bad as an undisciplined leader. Lack of team discipline enables habits that hurt the team and the individual offender. Furthermore, a disciplined team is a just team. Many think that this term *justice* can only be applied to criminal misconduct, but this is a very circumscribed view of the concept. In its fullness, justice means not only imposing consequences for ethical failures but also imposing consequences for executional ones. It means establishing a fair standard up front and enforcing that standard over time.

After all, good work has meaning in part because bad work has repercussions. When there are no consequences for poor adherence to standards, excellent and shoddy work become functionally equal because they produce equal outcomes. Stated standards must be backed up with consistent consequences so that those standards have meaning in reality, not simply in theory. Most of us have become dispirited at one point in time or another because we felt that we were working hard while others failed to pull their weight alongside us. Children recognize double standards instinctively. For those of us who have little ones, think of how often we have heard a child trying to get out of punishment by claiming that "you didn't punish my sister/brother for that. That's not fair." For those of us without children, think of how often we have heard, "But in the past nothing was ever done to anyone for that . . ."

Thus, when lack of executional discipline becomes pronounced, individual leadership credibility disappears and justice goes by the wayside. Additionally, there are three other things that happen, each with catastrophic consequences for a team. First, all organizational standards become confused and then irrelevant. When people see that nothing happens to someone who repeatedly ignores either written or unwritten standards, then they realize that those standards do not matter. They too begin to ignore them. Like a virus, nonadherence spreads throughout an organization until no one knows what matters or what doesn't. In recent times, Wall Street traders sold products that they knew were ticking time bombs because, no matter what their firms said about integrity, they also knew that everybody else around them was selling bombs and making money. An organization that fails to enforce its values loses its ability to create them. Instead it cedes its values to the whims of individual decision makers.

The second consequence of failure is that people lose their personal commitment to the team's welfare and mission. When we see that team members are taking advantage of the system—and taking advantage of our own hard work—with total impunity, then we often stop caring about what happens to the team. We move from a "we're-all-in-this-together" mentality to an "I'm-going-to-get-mine" one. The mission becomes subordinate to individual self-interest. Indeed, in the absence of discipline, self-interest becomes the mission. It is impossible to row a boat if all of the sailors man their oars at different times, in different ways, with different levels of intensity. At best, the vessel will stutter-stop. At worst, it will go in circles. And if enough time passes with no progress, then individuals will take to the lifeboats and head off in whatever direction seems best to them. So it is with an undisciplined team. It will never reach a goal before its members head for the exits.

Third, without executional discipline, a leader's own priorities become impossible to discern. If we cannot train ourselves to do what we say is important—to demonstrate our values by our actions and our sacrifices—then we cannot expect our teams to intuit what it is that we hold dear. If we uphold a double standard, one for us and one for everyone else, then no one will know where the real standard lies. If we do not punish ethical or executional breaches, then people will begin to believe either that we are stupid and unobservant (the generous interpretation), or that we are weak, or that our stated personal values do not mean anything to us, since we cannot be bothered to make the time to uphold them.

However, if we can get our teams and ourselves to stick with what we've outlined, we will find that the rewards are well worth the effort. First off, we will find that our teams become more committed to the standards we want them to uphold as they watch us expend time and energy to uphold these same standards. Our stated missions will also become more meaningful, because we make the time to actually pursue them. Morale will increase, because discipline imposed around reasonable standards creates a sense of fairness. If people see that adherence is met with impartial reward while infraction is met with impartial punishment, they know that the playing field is level. As a result, they are more likely to give their level best.

Consistent discipline also ensures order and keeps chaos at bay. Imagine a world where the amount of gasoline that makes up a "gallon" differs at every fuel station. Customers could pay the same amount at two different stations and receive two different amounts of gas. Commerce—and traffic—would slow to a trickle. Time and energy formerly expended transiting from one point to another would instead go toward arguing about definitions. Individuals wouldn't trust the numbers on the pump—they would double-check everything with their own measures. They might even go so far as measuring out their fuel, one gallon at a time, before putting it into their cars. Car owners would haggle with fuel station attendants. Lines would stretch for blocks, perhaps miles. Productivity would plummet. Violence would skyrocket.

A team without standards is no different than a nation without standard weights and measures. Without agreement on the fundamentals, most effort goes toward simply surviving disorder rather than making progress toward useful ends. Not only do productivity and progress come with justice, but so also do increased speed of decision making, idea generation, and overall innovation, since no time is lost debating fundamentals. Thus discipline among a team helps it execute its mission more effectively and react to events more quickly. People do not have to fight through chaos just to get their jobs done, or to even know what their jobs are in the first place. They will not spend time wondering why something happened to them that did not happen to someone else, because they trust that things are fair and consequences and awards are equally apportioned. Their trust in one another will also be higher, because they know that most of the people to whom they are yoked are pulling their own weight. A disciplined team is a trusting team, and one that can cycle more quickly than most.

Finally, a disciplined team will also go home at the end of the day feeling good about what they have accomplished with each day's time. They know that they are members of an organization that has integrity, one that means what it says and that does not send mixed messages in public and in private. For example, a company that publicly touts its commitment to social welfare while privately pushing its employees to pad their numbers cannot hope to inspire its members over time. People know when ethics are sacrificed for profits. They know when they are working for a company that says one thing and does another. But if an organization has discipline—both ethical and executional—then it and its leadership have the ability to keep their team members satisfied with the state of their own personal integrity. Everyone knows that as they push for achievement, everybody will be held to the same standard, and accomplishing the mission will not come at the cost of everything they hold right and true.

DISCIPLINE VERSUS KINDNESS?

But how do discipline and kindness coexist harmoniously in a leader? On one level, these two virtues seem to contradict each other. After all, maintaining discipline, both personal and corporate, requires some level of punishment. Kindness implies the opposite—not punishing people when they might very well merit it. Yet kindness and discipline are complementary, not contradictory. Over the long run, it is impossible to be kind to a team and be undisciplined.

Consider the following question: are we kind to our team when we allow one member to consistently violate the rules or to consistently perform below their peers, so that their peers have to pick up the slack, day in and day out? In a military or a survival context, tolerating one person who falls asleep on watch can mean that ten people die. Is that price worth the "kindness" of allowing the shirker to avoid punishment, either pre- or post-incident? In a less extreme example, is it kind to a team to allow someone to consistently work one-half of the expected hours yet be paid the same as their peers? Is one person's lack of discipline a kindness to the team members who depend on them? I would argue that it is not. By failing to hold one person accountable, an entire team is now treated unkindly.

Rather than contradicting kindness, discipline actually complements it. In fact, if done fairly, the act of punishing the individual can be a form of dispensing kindness to a team and to that individual. For the team, discipline ensures that everyone is taken care of, in the same way, and according to the same standards. Un-discipline means that only certain people are taken care of, capriciously and at the expense of everyone else. Un-discipline therefore creates an uneven playing field, with different players bound by different rules and a group of bewildered referees doing nothing. In this sort of environment, would we be surprised if the strongest team members quit because they could no longer enjoy a game whose rules change constantly?

Discipline also complements kindness at the individual level. In the short run, allowing someone to persist in poor performance, organizational ignorance, or general misconduct can seem like kindness. However, it is anything but. If we see someone unknowingly walking off the edge of a cliff, are we kind if we allow them to continue to do what they want, even if it leads to their death? Enabling and empowering are two very different things, and when we allow individual team members to continue to flout just and fair standards, we are not empowering them. Rather, we are at best enabling their underperformance and at worst hastening their self-destruction. In the long run, then, imposing individual discipline is the kindest thing we can do for our teams. We take the time and make the effort to try to make them into their best selves.

Not every infraction has to be punished, however. In plenty of cases, mercy should be extended, particularly when it comes to issues of judgment rather than issues of ethics. When people make well-meaning mistakes or fail to abide by the standards of executional discipline, we can decide to be kind and shield them from the consequences. However, if a pattern emerges, kindness cannot prevail forever, and discipline must take over at some point in time.

In the cases of ethical failures, though, the situation is different and the rope must necessarily be shorter. It is fairly easy to apply mercy to someone who simply made the wrong practical call while trying their hardest at a well-intentioned initiative. It is much more dangerous to give a second chance to someone exposed as knowingly lying, cheating, or stealing. For example, we shoulder much less risk when we forgive an accountant who accidentally put an expense into the wrong category than we do when we forgive an accountant who knowingly concealed expenses.

We can have very little room for moral misconduct, and in these situations, kindness can rarely last long. In fact, it should not be applied after more than one of these mistakes.

REFLECTION

Like the rest of our virtues, we must engage in the pursuit of discipline in, well, a disciplined fashion. First, we have to practice and apply this virtue to ourselves. Next, we have to model it, and instill it, in our teams. We also need to focus on both halves of the disciplined whole. The executional without the ethical is directionless, but the ethical without the executional is ineffective.

Reflection Questions

Ethical Discipline:

1. When was the last time I promised someone I would do something—something well within my control—that I didn't follow through on? ("I'll be at your game," "I'll be home by seven o'clock tonight," "I'll have that on your desk by noon," etc.)
2. When was the last time I told someone I would do something that I had absolutely no intention of doing? ("I'll call you next week," "We'll get together this month," "I'll probably be there," etc.)
3. When was the last time I shaded the truth, or withheld crucial information, when I was afraid of what the full truth would mean?
4. How often do I do any of the above?

Executional Discipline

Even as we reflect on ethical discipline, we cannot forget about its executional counterpart. This component to discipline is less objective and more context-dependent, and success in this area is as much about understanding and enforcing what is already in place, or what we already know is necessary, as it is about applying new standards of behavior.

1. What are the most common standards (and they are rarely found in a handbook or manual) in our organization? (For example, are people usually early, on time, or late to events? What are the common dress codes?)

2. What are the most common disappointments expressed? (Do people regularly complain about meetings not starting or ending on time? Do they mention how often other members show up late?)

3. In light of the answers to the above two questions, what should our personal top-five rules for ourselves be? (For example, "My meetings will always start and end on time.")

The virtue of discipline, both executional and ethical, is a crucial one if we hope to be successful as leaders. We must start with ourselves first and only then move on to our teams, for if we cannot practice what we preach, then what hope have those who follow us? But if we can do so, painful though it may be to begin and difficult though it may be to maintain, we will find that we perform a tremendous service to our teams. We make all of their hard work mean something. We keep chaos at bay, their missions meaningful, and everyone moving in the same direction. We set up an even playing field for all who wish to succeed to be able to do so. Most important, we allow our teams to go home each night with their heads held high, secure in the knowledge that their efforts have been in the service of an organization whose ethics they can trust.

SUMMARY

• Discipline is a paramount virtue for a leader. At its heart, discipline revolves around teaching and instruction rather than punishment and correction, and its whole purpose is to make an individual and a team as effective as possible in a given set of circumstances. Discipline produces predictable, repeatable behavior that conforms to high ethical standards and effective organizational norms.

- There are two components to discipline: ethical discipline and executional discipline. The first component calls leaders to be truthful, honest, and fair in both large and small decisions. The second calls them to understand, outline, and abide by the nonmoral standards that their organizations, and their teams, deem essential for success.
- Failure to apply ethical discipline to our own lives and to the lives of our team will ultimately cause catastrophic failure in both areas. Lack of ethical discipline has humiliated prominent leaders, destroyed gold-plated companies, and even damaged the strategies of sovereign countries.
- Failure to apply executional discipline to our own lives and the lives of our teams will destroy our individual credibility, obscure our broader mission, make our priorities as leaders confusing and irrelevant, and cause people to lose commitment. Rather than working on common goals and heading in a common direction, our team members will do whatever it is that they believe is in their immediate best interest.
- Discipline complements kindness. For the team, discipline ensures that everyone is taken care of, in the same way, and according to the same standards.
- For the individual, imposing individual discipline helps them avoid failures and helps make them into their best selves.
- The rewards of discipline are great. It helps a team become committed to the same standards; it keeps chaos at bay; and it increases the speed of decision-making and innovation at all levels. Discipline among a team helps it execute its mission more effectively and react to events more quickly. Most important, however, it helps all of us go home each day feeling good about ourselves and what we have accomplished with that day's time.

★

CHAPTER 6

COURAGE

In the fall of 2003, Corporal Jason Dunham returned home from Iraq. He had been a squad leader in that year's spring invasion, a man in charge of twelve other men. They had been lucky—and good—throughout the war. By the time the Corps exited Iraq entirely in late 2003, the squad had not lost a single man, and Dunham had done everything he set out to do in the Marines. He had risen to the rank of noncommissioned officer in four short years. He had led his men bravely through some of the most difficult fighting of the invasion. He had accomplished his mission and brought home all of his Marines. So, his goals achieved, Dunham prepared to exit the Corps. His contracted four years were up.

Then Jason learned that the Marines would be returning to Iraq in early 2004 and that his squad would be among the first wave to head back. For most of his men, the war was not yet over. Unlike Jason, they still had several years to serve out. After thinking over the situation, Dunham told his mother that he didn't feel good about his men going back into combat without him there to take care of them. So he reenlisted, volunteering for an additional two years and one more combat deployment. In return, he got to lead his men again.

Dunham and his squad left for Iraq in February 2004. They were stationed in Husaybah, in Anbar Province, in the country's volatile west-

ern region. At the heart of the insurgency that gripped the nation that
year, Anbar was one of the country's most dangerous areas. On April 14,
2004, Dunham and his squad were patrolling on foot when they came
under fire. Heading south to cut off their ambushers, they came upon a
seven-vehicle convoy exiting the scene. What follows is directly out of
Dunham's posthumous citation for the Medal of Honor, America's highest award for valor:

> Corporal Dunham and his team stopped the vehicles to search
> them for weapons. As they approached the vehicles, an insurgent
> leaped out and attacked Corporal Dunham. Corporal Dunham
> wrestled the insurgent to the ground and in the ensuing struggle
> saw the insurgent release a grenade. Corporal Dunham immedi-
> ately alerted his fellow Marines to the threat. Aware of the im-
> minent danger and without hesitation, Corporal Dunham
> covered the grenade with his helmet and body, bearing the brunt
> of the explosion and shielding his Marines from the blast. In an
> ultimate and selfless act of bravery in which he was mortally
> wounded, he saved the lives of at least two fellow Marines.

Dunham gave to his men and his mission the last full measure of devotion, but this final act of courage was much more than a simple split-
second decision. It was the result of time and training and character built
one difficult experience at a time. Its genesis was a year earlier, when Jason
volunteered to lead again and return to war. This decision was particularly difficult because Jason, unlike many others who went to war that
year, had already faced down combat. He knew with absolute certainty
that he was placing himself at risk of grievous harm, because every combat veteran knows that wounds in war are mainly a function of the law of
averages. Enough firefights multiplied by enough exposure equals certain
wounds or death. Yet Jason returned anyway, fully aware of the trade-off
he was making. This deliberate decision to embrace risk to lead well high-
lights Dunham's courage as much, if not more than, his split-second decision to jump on a grenade. Dunham's courage, expressed through his

actions, gave everyone who cared to notice the visible, indisputable proof of his values.

TWO TYPES OF COURAGE

The Marines define Dunham's actions as *physical courage:* risking life and limb in pursuit of a worthy mission. Physical courage is universally respected; after all, there are few better ways to demonstrate that you mean what you say than to put yourself bodily on the line for your values. While Dunham's example is one of the most dramatic, there are many other ways to demonstrate bravery that are more relevant for day-to-day life. Unfortunately, most of us gloss over courage when we think of leadership in the modern world. If, by some chance, we do dwell on it, we usually dismiss it as an honorable but largely irrelevant virtue, appropriate for the battlefield but not the business world. Firefighters and policemen may have the chance to be brave, but lawyers and accountants do not, nor do they particularly need to be. Courage might be useful for people who live anachronistic lives, but it is largely irrelevant for those of us in a comfortable modern world. So most of us believe that while courage is nice, it is cleverness that counts. But nothing could be further from the truth.

What's more, physical courage is not the only way to demonstrate this virtue. There is another equally important form of courage, and it is this form that we will all have the chance to embrace or avoid in our day-to-day lives. It is called moral courage. This courage does not risk lives; rather, it risks livelihoods. It does not push through physical pain, but it does accept emotional trauma. It may not incur bodily harm, but it may require difficult, even life-altering decisions to be made in a matter of seconds. Put simply, moral courage is that form of courage that overcomes fear to speak the truth to power, even—and especially—when power doesn't want to hear the truth. In so doing, the morally courageous put their positions, their reputations, and their ability to provide for their families on the line. While all of these may be recoverable (unlike life and limb), they are substantial sacrifices nonetheless.

Cynthia Cooper was someone who made the sacrifice. It was early 2002, and she was working as an internal auditor for telecom giant WorldCom. Enron had filed for bankruptcy just a few months earlier, and legislative pressure had built up in Congress to do something to tighten corporate regulation. Commensurate pressure to cover up accounting fraud had arisen within parts of the business community, including, as it later turned out, WorldCom. As part of her normal responsibilities, Cooper was investigating unusual accounting entries at WorldCom's wireless division when she noticed some that seemed particularly strange. She brought her concerns to Arthur Andersen, the firm's external auditor, but a partner told her not to worry, that any aggressive entries she noticed were no doubt balanced out across the entire corporation.

The very next day, while at the hairdresser, Cooper received a call from none other than WorldCom's chief financial officer, Scott Sullivan. He chastised her for investigating the wireless entries, but he did not demand that she stop. If she wanted to continue, he told her, she would need to do something rather strange: channel all of her questions not through Arthur Andersen but through Sullivan's personal deputy. So, while getting her hair done, Cynthia Cooper encountered a life-changing moment of truth: would she continue her investigation, and, if so, would she do it the way that she knew to be right or would she bow to pressure from the CFO?

Take a moment to put yourself in Cynthia Cooper's shoes: your boss's boss, also the company's second in command, has just reprimanded you for how you have handled yourself. Still, he has not outright demanded that you stop what you are doing. He has, however, asked you to divert your questions away from established channels. While strange, it is not necessarily wrong. Besides, you do not yet know that you've just stumbled on to the largest accounting fraud in U.S. history. For all you know, you've actually made a serious career error because you started asking questions without having all of the facts, unnecessarily angered your boss, and possibly jeopardized your job. So, would you keep up your investigation behind your boss's back? If you did, would you continue to probe if you realized that the results of your work would likely cost you your job and send your paycheck, your health insurance, and your retirement savings up in smoke? Would you continue if your peers pressured you not to, if your friends at work ostracized you, if your family didn't support you, and if the only certain consequence of your investigation was harassment from reporters, employers, co-workers, and federal investigators?

Cooper persevered. Shortly after the warning from her CFO, the Securities and Exchange Commission sent WorldCom a request for information, and, even though no one formally assigned the request to her, Cooper decided to handle it. Working with several others, late at night to avoid detection, she and her team turned up nearly $2 billion in questionable accounting entries. They were warned off again by Sullivan and pushed gently aside by the head of the WorldCom audit committee, who offhandedly told Cooper's group to contact the new outside auditing firm, KPMG. No one was talking.

Threatened, warned, reassured, ignored, and stonewalled, Cooper and team persevered regardless. Eventually they made it in front of WorldCom's board and revealed the extent of their findings. Four days later, the company reported that it had inflated profits by $3.8 billion over five fiscal quarters. WorldCom had created the single largest accounting fraud in modern history. The SEC immediately filed a civil suit against the company, and just two days later trading in WorldCom's stock was halted. Eventually the company would file for bankruptcy. Cynthia Cooper, her small team, and thousands of others were now officially unemployed.

Most of us like to believe that we would readily leap to question an ethically suspect, outright illegal, or just plain stupid plan. The reality is often more complex. In Cooper's case, speaking truth to power meant wading through difficult accounting technicalities, parsing arcane minutiae of journal entries, and battling the constant reassurance from others higher in the food chain that everything was fine. Nothing illegal or immoral was clear from the get-go, but what was also clear was that something was not right. Cooper's courage started with her willingness to persevere in pursuit of the truth even before the consequences of telling the truth became known.

Many times, however, the truth of an illegal, immoral, or ill-conceived plan is well-known up front. Even then we can rationalize a nonresponse. It is simple: the positive results of questioning a plan or a leader are always hazy and usually a long way away, but the immediate punishments for such questions are typically crystal clear and right around the corner. Furthermore, we know that if we are going to do something to act on our convictions, then it probably needs to happen immediately, which means we can expect punishment nearly immediately. Thus it becomes easy to argue to ourselves that our fears will not really materialize, or that they are overblown, so we probably do not need to take any action or speak up right away. The harsh results from doing something are usually a great deal more certain than the pained conscience that results from doing nothing. The courage to tell the truth in the face of clearly immoral or illegal requests can be hard to muster. Difficulty in the short-term aftermath, whether it is persecution, or unemployment, or even jail time, is often a guarantee.

Consider Joe Darby, the military policeman at Abu Ghraib who reported the abuses there to a U.S. investigator in 2004. He was an ABC News Person of the Week; he received a Profile in Courage award in 2005; and he and his wife now live in protective military custody because of the threats against them. Stanley Adams, a Hoffmann–La Roche executive, spent six months in jail for reporting evidence of price-fixing. Shawn Carpenter was fired from Sandia National Laboratories for voluntarily working with the FBI and the U.S. Army to help them stop hackers from penetrating U.S. security systems. Anna Politkovskaya, a noted journalist, became a vocal critic of the Russian war atrocities in Chechnya, and later, of the Putin administration. She was shot dead in her apartment in 2006, a murder that has never been solved.

Most of us will not face company-, job-, or life-threatening whistleblowing decisions like those above. Despite that, moral courage is a virtue that is easy to cheerlead in a clinical setting but hard to execute in a practical one. I have seen it exercised on the battlefield and in the business world, and I have seen it failed to be exercised. I have sat in meetings where everyone knew that the leader was presenting an unrealistic plan that could not—and would not—be supported by those listening, but no one (me included) said anything. I have worked for people who have scared me to the point that I never offered up any constructive criticism. I have crafted battle plans that were idiotic, and I've been very thankful for the squad leaders who had the guts to tell me I was an idiot. I have learned the hard way that moral courage is extremely valuable, extremely hard to execute consistently, and more rare than we would like to admit.

PHYSICAL COURAGE—EVERY DAY FOR EVERYONE

To become effective servant-leaders, we must pursue both moral and physical courage. At first glance, it seems doubtful that most of us will have the opportunity to demonstrate physical courage, let alone pursue it. To be sure, certain rarefied professions—military, law enforcement, and emergency services—afford semiregular opportunities to demonstrate this part of the virtue. It is easy to think that if we are not placed in high-risk contexts as part of our day jobs, then most of us have no chance of cultivating this part of the virtue. This thought is wrong. All of us have the opportunity to pursue physical courage, even if the opportunity to do so is not immediately obvious. We do not have to wait passively for life to present us with extraordinary circumstances to pursue this virtue.

Why is this? It is because at its heart, physical courage can be as simple as physically pushing ourselves outside of our comfort zone to walk in the shoes of our team members. At its purest, physical courage means risking life and limb as we overcome fear to perform a necessary task in support of a worthy mission. However, in a broader sense physical courage means sacrificing time and energy doing something that we are afraid of—something that is demanding and unpleasant, for example—so that we can better serve our team. Once we reach leadership roles, it is easy to forget what life is like for those we lead. Those of us with the guts to remind ourselves by taking on the demanding tasks asked of our teams have an easy opportunity to go after courage.

My old boss, Danny Richardson, was in charge of a $300 million business. He oversaw a workforce of nearly a thousand people, most of whom delivered potato chips to grocery stores and stocked the grocery shelves themselves. On major holidays, when his people were starting at midnight and working sixteen-hour days just to keep the shelves full of chips, Danny would put on some worn slacks, literally roll up his sleeves, and work side by side with his drivers at the busiest stores.

Unknown to most of them, though, Danny was a cancer survivor whose surgeries had left his body at something less than 100 percent. He had also lived through a horrific motorcycle accident that nearly gutted him. Danny's stomach muscles were barely functional. The long days spent in grocery stores exhausted him and took a toll on his already worn body. But he got his hands dirty every single holiday, and everyone who worked for him respected him for having the courage to leave his comfort zone, put himself in pain, and walk in the shoes of his people. Many of us have the same opportunity to serve our people as Danny had, but how many of us make the time to take advantage of it?

Many of us do not work in a labor-intensive industry like Danny's, but we can still demonstrate some physical courage. In my very first job in a corporate headquarters, I had to give a presentation to a group of our senior field leaders, who had flown in from various parts of the country. There would be several hundred of them in a packed conference room, and I would be up onstage all by myself, trying to earn their support. I was all of one month into my job and barely getting the hang of it, so I had no real idea of what it was I needed to say. The night before the event, I was in my office, working late to get my presentation just right. But I was not alone. My boss was there with me, reviewing every change I made and making the appropriate corrections himself—getting his hands dirty with the keyboard work, so to speak. He did not have to work side by side with me, but he did, giving of his time and energy to make me successful. He was not afraid to work a long evening or to do the menial drudge work of changing fonts and picture sizes, even though he knew he was not the best at it. It wasn't the same thing as running into a burning building to save a family, but it was physical courage nonetheless, and it meant a lot to me to have him there.

There are many other ways to show physical courage in our everyday lives without necessarily putting our lives on the line. For example, a leader can be terrified of public speaking but nonetheless make an impassioned presentation to a crowded convention center audience because his team needs someone to argue on their behalf. A parent may need to wake up early for work, but they sacrifice sleep to stay up late with their children when they are sick, or to stay up late to make sure their teenagers come home on time and in one piece. A doctor on call may dread driving in to the hospital in the middle of the night, but she does anyway because her on-site presence will reassure her team and their patients. As I write these words, my IT director is going to work every Wednesday after a two-hour chemotherapy session, because he knows that his presence inspires his team and helps them put their own daily challenges in perspective. Though many of us might think that the virtue of physical courage applies only to people with lives far different from ours, we are wrong. Nearly all of us have the chance to demonstrate this virtue, if we want to.

Some of us, however, may very well work in high-risk professions where physical courage is demanded almost daily. If so, then we have almost automatically earned the respect of those not in our field—think of the near-universal admiration for America's soldiers, firefighters, and police officers. However, we have *not* automatically earned the respect of our peers or our teams, because they know that anyone can be brave for five minutes. It is usually the smaller, deliberate acts of courage rather than the larger, spontaneous decisions that win our teams over in the long run. In Jason Dunham's case, the bravest act he took may not have been jumping on the grenade; rather, it was deciding to rejoin the Marines to relead his squad in combat after he had experienced the horrors of combat firsthand. The grenade was a nearly automatic, even instinctive decision with little time to consider the consequences. Rejoining was deliberate, with plenty of time to reflect on all the bad things that might happen as a result.

In high-risk professions where the environment allows for spontaneous displays, it is the smaller daily acts of physical courage that earn respect over time. A leader may be spectacularly brave for ten minutes, but can they be quietly brave for ten months? Can they sacrifice their own sleep to check on the welfare of their people? Do they turn down more comfortable quarters, or more posh offices, in order to live and work in the same conditions as their teams? Do they take on menial tasks to prove that there is no job they will not do? These constant, even small, acts of courage earn the respect of a team over time. They know how much harder it is to make the deliberate, daily choices to sacrifice than it is to make the one-time, instinctive decision to act.

Conversely, in non-high-risk professions, unexpected singular actions often have as much power as do the smaller daily decisions. Danny Richardson only had to spend one early morning on his hands and knees in a hundred-degree warehouse to earn my respect. One of my best district managers gained his team's attention when he showed up at midnight in a Walmart to move shelves around so that his driver did not have to. I've seen corporate vice presidents battling floods in their manufacturing facilities and driving trucks full of provisions into the heart of hurricane-ravaged cities. These leaders gained instant respect from their teams.

Still, the small things matter. Do we wake up early to help out our teams when they have a big project on the line? Do we stay late when someone needs more help than we can give them during working hours? Do we demand more comfortable conditions—or bigger offices—than those whom we lead, or do we eschew the privileges of position? In non-high-risk contexts, we all have the opportunity to demonstrate physical courage by doing things that we are nervous about, or even afraid of, even if the best that the environment allows us is small levels of physical sacrifice.

THE BUILDING BLOCKS OF MORAL COURAGE

Some of us may have to stretch ourselves to find ways to demonstrate physical courage in our day-to-day leadership roles. But none of us will have difficulty coming up with opportunities for moral courage. We've all had, I assert, the chance to take responsibility for a mistake we made, or for a mistake made by one of our team members, within the past month. By the same token, we have all had a chance to deflect responsibility and blame away from ourselves and onto someone else. We have had chances to tell the full truth or to tell something less (and maybe even lie outright). And we have all had the opportunity to tell our leaders that we disagree with their decisions, or, in the worst cases, that their decisions are morally wrong.

It is extremely hard for leaders to build credibility in this area, if only because of the simple law of averages. It takes a long, unbroken chain of right choices to build our reputations, but only one failure to tear them down completely. Just one instance of blaming our team for our mistake may cause them to conclude that we are uncaring, or cowardly, or both. Our peers need to watch us sit silently through a blatantly unprincipled rant just once before they conclude that we will readily sacrifice principles for politics. If we want to be known for our moral courage, then we have to be consistent, and we have to sustain our consistency over time.

We can help ourselves by understanding the four key components of this brand of courage. The first of these components is a clear picture of our own moral values, a picture that is painted on the backdrop of a clearly understood mission. In other words, our mission must inform our morals. And if we cannot identify our unbreakable principles before we are in the hot seat, it is a near certainty that we will fail to figure it out once the heat is on. If we do not know what keeps us going above and beyond our own comfort or ambition, then we are nearly certain to sacrifice courage on the altar of convenience.

One of the best modern-day examples of an alignment of values with mission is the American military's antitorture training, something that occurs in SERE (Survival, Evasion, Resistance, Escape) school. Though much of the training revolves around imparting technical skills—for example, the ability to make an animal trap, start a fire with flint and tender, or answer interrogation indirectly—at the heart of the school is the military Code of Conduct, a prescriptive pattern of behavior that builds on a shared mission. All technical expertise taught at SERE builds on a moral foundation, a creed common to all. Before going into the field to practice what they have learned, every student is required to memorize and recite the following:

1. I am an American, fighting in the forces which guard my country and our way of life. I am prepared to give my life in their defense.
2. I will never surrender of my own free will. If in command, I will never surrender the members of my command while they still have the means to resist.
3. If I am captured, I will continue to resist by all means available. I will make every effort to escape and to aid others to escape. I will accept neither parole nor special favors from the enemy.
4. If I become a prisoner of war, I will keep faith with my fellow prisoners. I will give no information nor take part in any action which might be harmful to my comrades. If I am senior I will take command. If not, I will obey the lawful orders of those appointed over me and will back them up in every way.
5. When questioned, should I become a prisoner of war, I am required to give name, rank, serial number, and date of birth. I will evade answering further questions to the utmost of my ability; I will make no oral or written statements disloyal to my country and its allies or harmful to their cause.

I will never forget that I am an American, fighting for freedom, responsible for my actions, and dedicated to the principles which made my country free. I will trust in my God and in the United States of America.

To some, the above words may seem trite, glib, or irrelevant. Having been through the training, I can assure you that they are anything but. The Code of Conduct was originally developed in 1955, in part as a result of the American experience in the Korean War, where our POWs fared poorly in Communist Chinese and North Korean prison camps. Put bluntly, American prisoners' survival rates were unconscionably low.

Many of the prisoners seemed purposeless, confused, and disoriented throughout the duration of their internment. Overall leadership was lacking, and the soldiers did a poor job banding together to support one another. Stories of collaboration and betrayal abound. Those who ratted out their comrades were rewarded handsomely, sometimes with prostitutes and, in extreme cases, with trips into North Korea. By contrast, those who remained loyal endured starvation, freezing temperatures, and torture.

There was one group, however, that fared far better under the strain of the camps: a brigade of Turkish infantrymen. The Turks had fought alongside their American counterparts, and many of their soldiers were captured and interned in the same camps. By all accounts, the Turks significantly outperformed the Yanks. The U.S. Army and subsequent historians have attributed a large part of the Turkish success to an informal code, summed up by a simple, unwavering belief in the importance of Turkish honor, the superiority of the Turkish soldier, and the primacy of Turkish solidarity.

Essentially, every captured Turkish soldier believed at the core of their being that they were better than their captors and everyone else in the camp to boot. They also believed that they had a duty to demonstrate this superiority. Thus, no Turk would allow another to fail, for failure was a sign of inferiority and dishonor. To the extent that the camps allowed, the Turks did everything that they could as a single ethnic bloc—taking meals, huddling for warmth, singing patriotic songs. According to most stories, not a single Turkish soldier broke rank and betrayed his fellows, no matter how brutal the conditions, how awful the torture, or how promising the rewards. Official Turkish records indicate that every single one of their soldiers made it home alive.

Without a corresponding unifying system of values, the fragmented Americans did far worse. Thus the Code of Conduct was developed. Read it in the comfort of your living room, and it seems a pretty but irrelevant document. Recite it near naked while hunching inside of a small, cold concrete box with your head still swimming from being repeatedly slapped in the face, and the code truly comes to life. I will never forget being yanked out of my box in the middle of the night, frog-marched across the prison compound to a sinister-looking office, and slammed against a wall by a burly interrogator as harsh klieg lights blinded me. The man silhouetted behind my tormentor was smoking a cigarette and wearing a beret. He asked me a question about my fellow prisoners. I was still so stunned that I didn't respond immediately, and I was punched in the stomach. For a moment, my mind blanked out entirely—a form of shock, most likely. I had no idea how to respond. I couldn't even think. The only thing I could do was gasp like a fish and make strange noises.

Then, odd though it may seem, the first sentence of the code started running through my head even as my head rebounded off the wall behind me: "I am an American . . ." The recitation helped calm and center me in the middle of a literal beating. I knew what I could do: state my name, rank, serial number, date of birth. I knew what I could not do: break the faith with my fellow prisoners, make disloyal statements, accept special favors. The code told me in advance what I could and could not do, and, as a result, it helped me know how to respond and how to handle a situation far beyond the limits of my own control. Knowing my own unbreakable principles—the first component of moral courage—was made brutally clear to me in our mock prison camp.

Once we have identified our key moral principles, we must next resolve to embrace the negative outcomes that might result from upholding them. This resolution is the second building block of moral courage. Speaking truth to power, for example, does not fall into the realm of courage when we believe that doing so will incur zero consequences. Truth only becomes courage when we believe that our words carry significant personal risk. For example, we might think that by voicing our opposition to a nonsensical plan, our careers could be derailed or our jobs lost entirely. We might believe that by identifying cheaters in our own organizations, we will fall out of favor with peers and endure social isolation.

So, if we are to pursue moral courage, then we must embrace in advance the idea of negative outcomes. Without a doubt, there will arise specific situations in which we will be presented with the choice to incur punishment to do what is right. If we want to be brave, we must make our peace with that concept before we are presented with such a choice. It is always easier to make the right decision in the moment if we have already accepted the consequences in advance. It is much harder to do the right thing at the right time when we have neither contemplated nor accepted what might happen in the aftermath. We will find ourselves simultaneously working out the right thing to do, analyzing the consequences for doing so, and psychologically preparing ourselves to accept the negative results. We will also find that we are doing this analysis under time constraints and under significant pressure from peers, leaders, and even our own team members. Given this sort of environment for decision-making, is it any wonder that we are much more likely to analyze poorly if we have not analyzed already?

Building on this second component, the next key piece of moral courage is a willingness to bear responsibility for failure. The timeworn adage "Success has many fathers, but failure is an orphan" is all too true. The leader who is prepared to raise their hand and say "Blame me for the results" is a rarity in our current age. Most of the time, leaders who stood at the helm while the ship ran aground do everything in their power to blame something other than their own navigational prowess. They admit nothing, deny everything, and make counter-accusations. Recent headlines have featured CEOs disavowing any responsibility for the failure of their companies, politicians claiming that government inaction is the fault of anyone but themselves, celebrities blaming the pressure of fame for their behavior problems (or substance abuse), and leaders making any number of other excuses. Sadly, responsibility avoidance is no longer the exception in our culture. It is the rule.

Inherent shamefulness aside, the problem with this approach is twofold. First off, most people will never believe leaders who avoid responsibility and will never accept their excuses. If a leader bears that title when failure occurs, then, no matter what the exacerbating circumstances, people looking on will assign that leader blame because it is simple and easy to do (even if it is not always fair). After all, a leader personifies their organization. Second, in most cases leaders openly enjoy the perks of their position in the run-up to failure. Sadly, today's leadership class is not widely known for its frugality and sacrifice. Taking the perks (and the money) in the good times but not taking the blame in the bad strikes nearly everyone as blatantly unfair. A team will not long tolerate an unfair leader, and neither will an observing public.

Finally, the fourth component of moral courage is the willingness to openly admit mistakes. Most people know that everyone—leaders and nonleaders alike—makes wrong decisions that lead to failure. Given this basic fact of life, teams are usually much more receptive to honest admissions of mistakes and sincere acceptance of fault than many people believe. In fact, admission of fault often strengthens rather than weakens a leader. Not only does it help keep them humble, but it also confirms their ability to accept reality and their willingness to take advice and correction. (There is one caveat: people are forgiving provided that the mistake is one of judgment and not morality—moral mistakes are often much harder to recover from.) Admission of fault also proves that a leader is secure. Acknowledgment of mistakes does not rock their world or crack their carefully constructed façade, because they are comfortable with who they really are.

Thus, moral courage has four fundamental pillars: 1) clear identification of our own unbreakable values; 2) an a priori acceptance of negative outcomes if necessary in order to uphold those values; 3) the willingness to shoulder responsibility for failure; and 4) the open admission of mistakes. Taken together, these pillars help us steel ourselves to make the right choice regardless of our fear. Pull any one of them out and we become significantly less likely to demonstrate bravery when we most need it.

MORAL + PHYSICAL COURAGE = A LEADERSHIP IMPERATIVE

Courage, moral or physical, is not an anachronistic virtue with limited application in our modern world; it is an absolute must-have for leaders. If we can consistently demonstrate it in both of its forms, courage, like the other virtues we've explored, will have transformational effects. First off, physical courage is the most visible demonstration of values that we can possibly make. Nothing says "I care" more than putting life and limb on the line on behalf of our teams. Nothing says "my team and our mission are important" better than making sacrifices of time and physical comfort to serve something other than ourselves. Physical courage is the surest and quickest way to demonstrate that our values and our people matter to us. Thus it is also the surest and quickest way for us as leaders to earn credibility.

Physical courage is also one of the only things that penetrate a jaded populace accustomed to brave words and craven deeds. Today, the world is full of pseudo-leaders who talk well and look good—right up until the point when they are asked to actually put themselves on the line to back up their rhetoric. Most will not do it. The rare ones who actually do become a stark and startling contrast. When Pat Tillman, a star NFL cornerback, told the world that he respected our soldiers and loved our country, everyone who heard him believed him. Why? Because he forsook his multimillion-dollar football contract and put his life on the line by volunteering for the U.S. Army Rangers. When Martin Luther King Jr. stated his commitment to the idea that all men are created equal, a watching world believed him. Why? Because the civil rights leader was willing to endure jail time to prove his belief. Leaders who demonstrate physical courage have an opportunity to immediately galvanize people who have become jaded by the day-in, day-out mismatch between words and deeds in a world devoid of sacrificial (which is to say, real) leaders.

Additionally, walking in the shoes of our team by doing something physically difficult, dangerous, or demanding proves that we understand what they do and what we ask of them. For example, I have been amazed at how much insight I have gained by simply working one week on a night shift. I take for granted those who do it and how they manage their family life to support a schedule that is the reverse of most of the world. It is so easy for us as leaders to take for granted the sacrifices our team members make simply because they show up to work on time and their complaints don't reach us. Do we really understand what life looks like when you have to duct-tape your curtains together because your shift starts at

11 P.M. and you go to sleep at 10 A.M. every day? Can we really know what it is like to try to raise a family when you spend two consecutive weeks on airplanes? Can we really empathize with what we are asking of our teams, or do we just pretend that we can because pretending is better than actually trying to live it ourselves? Or did we once live like they did, and now we try our best to forget it because our rank allows us to avoid the sacrifices? If we want to lead well, we cannot pretend and we cannot forget.

Moral courage has an equally profound effect on our leadership. First off, it enables decision-making. Leaders who are afraid to fail often fail to decide when there is any element of risk involved. We have all seen them, the ones who cannot give clear direction, or even choose a direction, when they are paralyzed by the thought that whatever they choose might be wrong. They put off hard choices, or waffle and pontificate, or, worst of all, leave the decisions to be made by someone else. These leaders force their teams to make the hard choices they themselves avoid.

By contrast, leaders with moral courage have no trouble, and often little delay, in making hard or risky decisions. As a result, they react more quickly than their competition and iterate their plans more rapidly. They are also more likely to have a team that actually behaves like one—that is, all team members work along the same lines of effort because decisions have been made and made clearly. Without clear choices and clear guidance, a team may actually work at cross-purposes as different members pursue different goals by different means.

The second thing that moral courage does for a leader is build a credibility bank. Every time that a team sees their leader stand up and take a hit for them, or take a risk to do what they all know is right, or refuse to toe the company line to do what they all know is wrong, the leader gains trust. People start to believe that we mean what we say and that we follow through on our commitments. People start to trust that no matter how tough the environment, they can go home and look themselves in the mirror at night because they know that they work for someone who will never bow to pressure and ask them to do something they know is wrong. In a world where the gap between words and deeds yaws wide in leaders, those whose bravery bridges this gap have the opportunity to quickly gain and maintain credibility and the respect of their teams.

Third, moral courage helps a leader persevere in pursuit of their stated mission. If we know what we want and what we do not want, and if we have accepted the trade-offs in advance, then we will eventually find it easier to make the same decisions the same way every time. And, as we practice making hard choices, those choices will suddenly no longer seem as hard. We will find that we have made courage a habit. What once was a long and agonizing process becomes a short and painless one, because we have trained ourselves to make it almost second nature. Once training kicks in, perseverance follows.

Hard on the heels of perseverance is hope. It is when we stop trying that we stop hoping. If we fall one too many times, and never get back up, then we consign ourselves to the dirt. If we fail one too many times, and never try again, then we resign ourselves to failure. But if we do what is hard again and again, then what was once hard eventually becomes easy, and we start to envision a better place. We begin to think that our efforts may actually make a difference, if only a slight one. Belief will become action, and action will become results, and results will help reinforce belief. In the best-case scenarios, we create a virtuous cycle as beliefs and results complement one another. And even in the worst-case scenarios, the ones where the results do not come quickly or at all, the simple act of trying helps keep hope alive. If we cease trying, though, we will soon cease hoping.

Moral courage also helps us live unified lives, ones where our words and deeds match consistently over time. When we demonstrate the willingness to put our livelihoods on the line and sacrifice them if need be to stay consistent with our values, then we allow ourselves to stay true to ourselves. Too often, we want to live our beliefs right up until the point where we have to pay a price, often literally. But if we sacrifice our values, we drive a wedge within ourselves between that which we want to do and that which we actually do. The deeper we drive that wedge and the further apart actions and values become, the more our lives become disunified and the harder it becomes to live with ourselves. The more that we act in accordance with our beliefs, though, the greater the probability that we will see peace increase in our lives. As we increase our integrity over time, it becomes increasingly easier to live with ourselves.

Finally, courage reinforces discipline. If ethical discipline calls us to examine ourselves in the small areas and to hold a consistent, values-based line, moral courage helps us bear the consequences of doing so. If executional discipline demands that we hew to difficult and demanding standards, physical courage helps us steel ourselves to the sacrifice necessary to uphold these same standards. Discipline helps us maintain our credibility by acknowledging, enforcing, and obeying standards; courage helps us maintain our credibility by refusing to alter those standards no matter what the consequences. Indeed, courage married to discipline is the only way to stay consistent in our values over time.

Additionally, courage and discipline work in combination to speed up the pace of decision-making, plan iteration, and innovation. A team will fail to act if its leader does not have the backbone to make decisions, but even if the leader does, a team will fail to act effectively if it does not know the rules by which those decisions must be executed. Conversely, a team can know all the rules of the game yet still fail to move decisively because its leader does not have the guts to tell them when the game begins and ends. Discipline speeds things up by allowing everyone to play by the same rules. Courage speeds things up by getting the team off the starting line quickly. If we can layer courage on top of discipline, then we will find that we reinforce our integrity, magnify our credibility, and increase the pace at which we and our teams act, react, and innovate.

THE OPPOSITE OF COURAGE

To truly appreciate the effects of courage, it is worth thinking about what happens when a leader does not show it, which is to say, what happens when a leader is a coward. *Coward* is not a word that we hear often today, even though many of us have identified leaders we know are afraid. We use words like *accommodating*, or *quiet*, or even *indecisive* when what we really mean is "not brave." Cowardice seems somehow "extreme"—it is easy to think that the term only applies to circumstances like war, or natural disasters. It is just as easy to think that those of us who live outside the context of soldiering, policing, or other emergency professions have very little opportunity to actually *be* cowards. But the hard truth is that every one of us has the opportunity to prove ourselves a coward nearly every day of our lives.

One of the most horrifying events of the twentieth century was the massacre of Jews, Gypsies, communists, the mentally disabled, and many other "undesirable" groups throughout the territories controlled by Nazi Germany before and during World War II. The sheer scope and scale of the evil is the first thing that hits anyone who takes the time to learn about it. The second thing is that this horror was aided and abetted by absolutely normal men and women. Most of them were neither soldiers, Nazis, nor Germans. When asked by the Germans to reveal their Jewish neighbors, for example, many Polish citizens freely pointed them out. Furthermore, most historians agree that for most of those who collaborated with the Nazis, there were no systematic punishments administered for noncompliance. One might go to prison camp for actively aiding the undesirables, such as hiding Jewish refugees, but very few were ever punished simply for doing nothing. Still, most people chose to collaborate.

Historian Hannah Arendt termed this phenomenon "the banality of evil," which is a neat way of summing up the prevalence of cowardice in ordinary society. The famous Milgram experiment, conducted in 1961, lends credence to this idea. In the experiments, carried out by psychologist Stanley Milgram of Yale University, two people were asked to draw slips of paper to determine whether they would be a "teacher" or a "student." Both slips, however, said "teacher," and one of the two paired people was an actor who always took the role of student. The unwitting volunteers thus became the teachers. They believed that they were testing the effects of negative reinforcement on memory, but what was really being studied was the willingness of individuals to squelch their own morality.

After drawing their roles, the two research subjects were separated so that they could hear but not see each other. The teachers were then instructed to read word pairs to their students and to give the students options to repeat back to them. Every time a student failed to respond correctly, the teacher would administer an electric shock by pressing a button. So that they would know exactly what they were administering, each teacher was given a small electric shock themselves before the experiment began. The intensity of the shock increased with each wrong answer. The shocks would go up to 450 volts, a level at which the subjects would experience extreme pain. Teachers were allowed to administer a maximum of three of these painful shocks before the experiment was halted.

In reality, the students were never shocked, but the teachers did not know that. Each shock produced a prerecorded sound of pain from the student (whom the teacher could not see). As the voltage escalated, so did the intensity of the screams. After several shocks, the student actor would begin banging on the wall that separated them from the teacher. In some cases, the students would begin to moan about their heart hurting. If the teachers ever expressed nervousness, the researchers told them one of four things, each of which built upon the next:

1. Please *continue*.
2. The experiment requires that you *continue*.
3. It is absolutely essential that you *continue*.
4. You have no other choice, you *must* go on.

Aside from the verbal admonishment, though, it was clear to teachers that there was no other penalty for administering the punishment. So, before the experiment began, Milgram asked his Yale psychology students to guess at how many teachers would actually administer a shock that they believed would cause severe pain. Most thought that only 1 to 3 percent of teachers would progress beyond a strong shock. Surely their morality would compel them to stand up to authority before the experiment went too far. The same was true of Milgram's psychologist peers when he polled them. They believed that only a small number of normal citizens would knowingly harm someone else. But the students and the professionals were wrong. A shocking 65 percent of test subjects administered the third 450-volt shock. Similar experiments have yielded similar results. Difficult as it may be to believe, cowardice in very ordinary, very normal situations is very easy and very prevalent.

But cowardice will rip teams, organizations, and entire cultures apart. Martin Niemöller was a German pastor who began his career as a fervent anticommunist and Nazi supporter. However, when Hitler began to insist upon the supremacy of the state over religion, Niemöller began to oppose him. The pastor was imprisoned in 1937 and not released until liberated from the Dachau extermination camp in 1945. Sadly, very few of his coreligionists spoke out against Hitler, who would eventually be viewed as one of history's great monsters. Their failure, and that of others, destroyed not only their credibility but also the social fabric of their country. Niemöller described the moral cowardice in the following famous words:

> In Germany, they came first for the Communists. And I didn't speak up because I wasn't a Communist. And then they came for the trade unionists. And I didn't speak up because I wasn't a trade unionist. And then they came for the Jews. And I didn't speak up because I wasn't a Jew. And then they came for me. . . . And by that time there was no one left to speak up.

When poor decisions, or even outright evil, is left unchallenged by good men and women, the consequences for society writ large are dire. Indeed, one could argue that cowardice underpinned the spectacular crash in America's financial and housing sectors in 2008–2009. Because very few in positions of political or financial power spoke out openly against fraudulent lending, investor deception, bogus financial products, and a whole host of other problems, a country's entire economic system nearly collapsed. This failure happened in normal, ordinary day-to-day conditions. Indeed, it happened on the heels of a nearly unprecedented two-decade run of national prosperity. And just like the Holocaust, it was allowed to happen by normal, ordinary, day-to-day men and women.

In addition to corroding societies, moral cowardice also eats at us as individuals. I have failed a whole host of times in the area of courage, but one of the ones that stands out most vividly is an experience at SERE school. The school teaches students two things: 1) basic survival skills for living off the land and 2) techniques to resist torture and imprisonment. In the latter portion of the school, students are actually force-marched into a mock prison camp and treated as prisoners of war for a period of time. In my particular facility, we were crammed into small, three-foot-high square concrete boxes that served as our cells. We wore nothing but our underwear.

As time progressed, various of us were taken out of our cells and subjected to questioning, among other things. We had several women in our group of prisoners. They, too, were taken out of their cells. In our training, we had been told that women were often more likely to be subject to rape and sexual humiliation than men, and that often (but not always) this treatment was the result of a rogue guard who would be stopped by his superiors if they knew of his behavior. One of the best things prisoners could do to prevent sexual abuse was to draw attention to the offender. One of the best ways to do that was for the assaultee to simply make noise while her fellow POWs attempted to distract the guard in other ways, such as exiting their cells.

After just a few hours in the camp, our group was tested on how we would respond to such a situation. Sometime in the early evening, a guard strolled by our concrete blocks and announced in a loud, Russian-accented voice that he was going to have some fun with "good-looking War Criminal Number 11" (I have no recollection of what her real name was). It was a perfect setup: he was clearly alone and his intentions were obvious. To her credit, the woman immediately began shouting and making a ruckus. To my shame, I did nothing. Neither did the rest of my classmates.

We sat in silence in our cells for several long minutes while the fake Russian guard bragged about what he was going to do sexually to our fellow POW. When he yanked her out of her cell, we remained silent. Running through my head were all the things I could do to help out. I considered shouting or throwing myself out of the cell (there were no doors, just canvas flaps covering the openings), thereby creating a diversion that would draw attention to the rogue guard. I knew that major painful consequences were unlikely. If this scenario was anything like our training, the guard was doing something he should not be. He was more likely to be punished than I.

I tensed up, preparing to lift my flap and jump out, and then I stopped. I could hear the guard walking our comrade away, and I did absolutely nothing. It was a deliberate choice, not one that I made simply by failing to decide. I actually made a conscious decision to ignore my comrade. When I should have spoken out, I just sat in my cell and listened as the shouting receded. I withdrew into myself and tried to block out what I was hearing. To this day, eight years later, I remember that failure, and it shames me. The more that failures like this one build up over time in our lives, the more we become internally torn and the more we have trouble reconciling what we want to do with what we actually do.

When individuals do not demonstrate courage, they tear at their own souls. When leaders do not demonstrate courage, they tear at the very fabric of our world.

REFLECTION

Even though we all have the natural ability to give in to our fears, to avoid risk, and to shy away from responsibility and hard decisions, we all can overcome our natural bent. I failed the courage test in SERE school, and I have failed the same test many times since then in much less demanding circumstances because I lost sight of this virtue. We are all at risk of similar failure if we do not take the time to practice being brave.

Despite its critical importance to a leader and a team, courage is a virtue that is rarely discussed in anything more than superficial detail. Worse, many assume that this virtue applies only in very narrow, very specific life circumstances—the military or law enforcement, for example. In those contexts, though, people train to be brave. They prepare themselves to make the right decisions when life and death are on the line by practicing their decisions when the stakes are lower. Soldiers and police officers know that courage does not come naturally and that it must be taught, honed, and endlessly rehearsed.

However, apart from a few specialized professions, our broader society has lost its focus on this virtue. Yet many of our leaders apparently still feel confident in their ability to choose courage at will. The widely assumed view seems to be that courage is mostly irrelevant in normal, day-to-day life and that in those rare and extreme situations in which it is needed, we will naturally choose to do the right thing. Unfortunately, this is not true. Moral courage is needed in every facet of daily life. And if we want to be brave when the stakes are high, then we must practice courage when they aren't.

Reflection Questions

1. Think of a time when you were a coward, either physically or morally. How did you feel the next day?
2. Where do you think you have a recurring opportunity to choose courage in your day-to-day life?
3. If you were to build your own personal Code of Conduct, what would be the three or four things you would want it to say?
   - What would you want to do, at all times? ("I am an American, fighting for my freedom . . .")
   - What would you never want to do? ("I will never surrender . . . I will never accept special favors . . .")
4. How can you practice being brave?

In today's world, courage is as broadly relevant as it is little discussed, and if recent events are any indication, most leaders will fail at this virtue when placed in the crucible of tough decision-making. However, those who persevere in the pursuit of courage are much more likely to be brave under pressure. For those of us who can aspire to it, courage will earn us instant credibility with our teams and peers. It will help us make quick, sound decisions that leave our competition struggling to catch up. It will help us persevere through difficult times, and it will help us keep hope alive. Most important, it will allow us to live lives of integrity, ones in which our words and deeds form a unified whole. And as we increase in courage, we will find that our teams reap the rewards.

So, it is not enough that we be simply humble, kind, and disciplined. We must also be brave.

SUMMARY

- Courage is an often overlooked but extremely important leadership virtue. At its purest, courage comes in two forms: *physical courage* and *moral courage.* Physical courage involves overcoming fear and risking life and limb in pursuit of a worthy mission. Moral courage overcomes fear and risks livelihoods—positions, reputations, etc.—by speaking the truth to power.
- Physical courage can be applied in nearly every situation, even those outside of war, police work, natural disasters, and emergencies. In its broadest sense, physical courage can be taken to mean sacrificing time and energy doing something that we are afraid of—something that is demanding and unpleasant, for example—so that we can better serve our team.
- Everyone will have a chance to demonstrate moral courage in their lives, and this virtue is built of three components. The first of these components is a clear picture of our own moral values. The second is a resolution to embrace the negative outcomes that might result from upholding our values in all situations. The third component is a willingness to bear responsibility for failure. The fourth is a willingness to openly admit mistakes.
- *Cowardice,* while a little-used word, helps highlight the importance of courage. A brave leader must realize that every single one of us has the

opportunity to demonstrate cowardice on a daily, weekly, and monthly basis. Left unchecked, cowardice will corrode individuals, teams, and our broader society to the point at which they collapse entirely.

• Combined, moral and physical courage have a profound effect on leadership. Physical courage is the most visible demonstration of values that we can possibly make and is thus the surest and quickest way for leaders to earn credibility. This virtue is also one of the only things that penetrate a jaded populace accustomed to words without action. Finally, physical courage helps prove to our team that we understand what they do and what we ask of them.

• Moral courage enables decision-making, particularly in risky circumstances, and helps a leader build a credibility bank with their peers and teammates. Moral courage also helps a leader persevere in pursuit of their stated mission, and perseverance leads to hope, for it is when we stop trying that we stop hoping. Moral courage also helps us live unified lives, in which our words and deeds match consistently over time. Finally, moral courage reinforces discipline, and courage and discipline work in combination to speed up the pace of decision-making, plan iteration, and innovation.

———— ★ ————

CHAPTER 7

WISDOM

Imagine you are standing on a busy subway platform in a major city—New York, Boston, London, Paris, Tokyo, take your pick. You are able to observe the comings and goings of the trains. If you are a railway enthusiast then everything is quite exciting, even if somewhat confusing. If you are not an enthusiast, then everything is simply very confusing. If you pay very close attention, you may be able to discern from the arrival and departure of the subway cars something about the method of their movements—for example, they arrive at fifteen minute intervals, they can accommodate several dozen passengers each, the conductor sits in the front car. But while you may work out some patterns from inference, you will never work out all of them. Try as you might, you will never know the overarching design or the minute-by-minute decisions that inform the entire station's operation.

Now suppose you are transported to a control room a few stories above the station. There, taking up an entire wall, is a diagram of the whole subway system and the track layout for a five-mile radius around the station. Little glowing lights move along each rail, representing the movement of each of the trains. The entire map is laid out in front of you, with the real-time actions represented as you watch. You see the station through the eyes of those who control it, and instantly, the reasoning be-

hind the minute-by-minute decisions becomes clear. You know exactly
why one train was made to delay while another was made to speed up. You
can discern why one was diverted from its normal track while another was
made to lie by. You know now not just the what, but also the why.

What's more, if you look long enough you can infer the logic, and the
patterns, underlying the entire operation. If you take close notes and have
a scientific bent, you can even begin to predict the future, and to explain
it. Not only do you know why certain things happen in the moment, but
you can be reasonably certain as to what things will happen in the moments to come, what decisions will be made in the future. When it comes
to the operation of that subway station, you have become omniscient.

THE SUBWAY VERSUS THE AUTOMOBILE

Many of us believe that this sort of knowledge—a deepened insight into
the meaning and purpose of the circumstances surrounding us combined
with an ability to predict events and their outcome—is what we call wisdom. Those who possess wisdom are often thought to be masters of life's
events, just as those in the control room are masters of the train system's
operations. If we carry this idea to its logical conclusion, then a perfect
understanding of current events and an infallible ability to forecast the
future constitute wisdom's pinnacle. If we could but stand at that height,
we would understand the why behind everything that happens and the
what that unfolds from our current decisions. The more perfect our wisdom, the fewer questions we will have in life.

Unfortunately, wisdom is neither omniscience nor prescience, both
of which are entirely unattainable in this life no matter how masterful we
become. Increased wisdom rarely gives us an increased real-time ability
to understand why things happen. We cannot gain insight into the operating system of life in the same way that we can, theoretically, master the
operating system of a train network. We will not always know which trains
are running on time and which ones are running late. Nor will wisdom

make it possible for us to discern the results of today's decisions or their implications tomorrow. Sometimes we might have a glimpse of which trains are set to arrive, but many times they will arrive unbidden, or not at all.

Most vexing of all is that even at its absolute height, wisdom will not help us understand why life's *bad* events happen, particularly to good people. We may never understand why the train wreck occurs, never see the good that comes from pain. That paradox will remain a mystery no matter how many philosophers take a crack at it.

If the virtue of wisdom cannot act as a cure-all for our most perplexing gaps in knowledge, then what, exactly, does it do? Put simply, wisdom helps us to choose well in moments of decision and act correctly in moments when we need to execute decisions. While we cannot always know why things happen, or what's going to happen in the future, we can in fact make the best possible decisions in the present. We can choose the right actions with the right intentions. We can do our best with what we have and rest secure in the knowledge that our best is absolutely good enough.

Wisdom, our last virtue, is more akin to operating a car than controlling a train system. When driving, you generally do not ask yourself why a road curves this way or that, or why a bridge is placed in a certain place. You do not try to infer the reasoning behind why a particular car has swerved at a particular part of the road, or why the driver in front of you brakes erratically, or why the one to your right side is broken down. In driving, understanding the design of the road system and the intention of its architects doesn't matter. We can understand those perfectly and still have a spectacular crash. What matters, rather, is the soundness of our judgment relative to the situation in front of us and the speed and appropriateness of our consequent reactions. We do not need to understand the meaning and purpose of city planners to be successful. To be good drivers, we simply need to see clearly out of our windshields, and do the right thing at each bend in the road.

SEEING THE ROAD POORLY . . .

Attaining wisdom begins with cultivating the ability to recognize the road immediately in front of us for exactly what it is. Wisdom is founded on humility, the second of our virtues, because humility helps us to see ourselves as we truly are rather than ourselves as we wish to be. Unfortunately, it is hard for most human beings to do this naturally. And when we cannot see ourselves accurately, it is almost impossible to see the road in front of us clearly. Empirical and anecdotal evidence both bear out the sad but true fact that most of us are more likely to change facts to fit our own predetermined theories than we are to change our own predetermined theories to fit facts. Like it or not, we have a hard time seeing reality as it is, as opposed to what we want it to be.

The tragic story of the HMS *Thetis* well illustrates this fundamental problem of humanity. At 10 A.M. on June 1, 1938, the *Thetis,* a brand-new, Triton-class submarine, left its berth for a series of diving tests. As its complete safety and effectiveness had not yet been assured, Cammell Laird Ltd., the shipbuilders, retained ownership until complete testing would allow the sub to be turned over to the British admiralty. Still, most of the ship's occupants were British naval officers, with Captain H. P. K. Oram commanding. The captain had been serving on submarines for twenty-one years. The rest of the officers were also highly trained and experienced, and Cammell Laird had twenty-six of its own employees on board, all of them engineers and submarine experts. Thus the total number of people packed into the *Thetis* for the trial was 103, twice the vessel's intended capacity.

At 2 P.M., the *Thetis* dove for her first exercise. Lieutenant H. G. Woods ordered torpedo tubes numbers five and six flooded with water to simulate the weight of actual torpedoes. The submarine dove somewhat unevenly, so Woods opened the test cock of tube number five to ensure that the flooding had been successful. If water was inside, the cock should have discharged a small stream of water. It did not, so Woods logically assumed that torpedo tube five contained no water. But before investigating further, the cautious officer ordered shut the cap that would cover tube five from the ocean outside. Then Woods opened up the torpedo tube's door—the one that connected the tube itself to the inside of the submarine—to see what had happened.

Unbeknownst to the lieutenant, the test cock had been painted shut. No water could possibly emerge, even if the tube was completely full of water. As it turned out, the tube was, in fact, flooded, but the painted-shut cock had made this situation impossible to detect. Worse, when Woods had ordered the number-five cap shut, the cap itself had failed. It had only partially shut, leaving the torpedo tube open to the surrounding ocean. When Woods opened the fateful door number five, seawater flooded into the *Thetis* at the rate of two tons per second.

The sailors frantically secured other interior watertight doors, but they acted too late to prevent the front two compartments of the submarine from filling up entirely. The submarine sank nose-first to the bottom of the sea, 130 feet below the surface. In the process, the sub's signaling apparatus was irreparably damaged, cutting off its best means of communication with the outside world. By forcing compressed air into some of the ballast tanks, the sailors managed to surface eighteen feet of the *Thetis*'s stern sometime during the evening. Unfortunately, this was not enough to allow anyone to escape. And time was running out for the trapped crew. Normally, the *Thetis*'s air supply would last forty-eight hours, but today was not normal—the *Thetis* was packed to twice its standard capacity. The clean air now had a much shorter lifetime.

Shortly after the submarine came to rest on the ocean's floor, the sailors floated marker buoys. Still, they realized that in the middle of the vast ocean, two small buoys would be difficult to detect. The crew thus determined to escape via the newly pioneered Davis apparatus, an early predecessor of modern-day scuba gear. The Davis device was essentially two bags filled with oxygen and a carbon-dioxide-absorbing chemical. It accommodated two men at a time. The users would step into a watertight compartment, shut one door behind them, open another one to the sea, and eventually use the apparatus to float to the ocean's surface. The Davis gear allowed breathing underwater for thirty to forty-five minutes.

Performed correctly, this procedure should have allowed two people to escape every five minutes.

The crew selected Oram and Woods as their pioneers—Oram because he had developed a plan to pump air into the submarine from the outside and Woods because he could give a firsthand account of how the disaster had occurred. The two knew that the probability of them being found immediately was highly unlikely, so Oram bound instructions with the ship's location to his wrist in the event that he was discovered unconscious or dead. Then, at eight o'clock the next morning (Friday) the two officers disembarked.

The remaining crew quickly learned that exit via the Davis procedure would take thirty minutes, not five, because of the time required to flood and clear the exit chamber. So four men tried the next escape together. Enfeebled by lack of oxygen, they all died in the escape chamber. It took until 10 A.M. before the next two were able to escape, two full hours, or twenty times the expected cycle time, after Woods and Oram left. One of the survivors later reported that he was unlikely to have lasted another hour inside the *Thetis*. Less than twenty-four hours after the dive started, the air supply was already running out.

Incredibly, the response of those back onshore was just now getting started. The delay started with the boat scheduled to observe the dive. Despite a complete lack of scheduled indicators, the *Grebe Cock,* as the vessel was called, telegraphed the submarine's commanding fort only fifteen minutes before the *Thetis* should have surfaced, at 4:45 P.M. on Thursday. The only thing the *Grebe* asked was for a confirmation of the submarine's scheduled surface time—the telegraph was specifically worded to avoid causing alarm. No alarm was raised until 6:15 P.M., an hour after the *Thetis* should have arisen.

Even as the trapped crew's oxygen supply diminished rapidly, the shore party took its time to scale up the rescue efforts. It took until nearly ten o'clock Thursday evening—eight hours after the submarine sunk— for a full-scale search to be launched. By that point, more than a third of the *Thetis*'s air had been consumed. Still, the stricken vessel was not located until nearly eight the next morning, when a rescue ship's crew spotted the sub's stern protruding from the sea. By this time the oxygen levels inside the submarine were becoming dangerously low. But at around 8:30 A.M., Oram and Woods bobbed to the surface sporting the Davis apparatus. A pleased and secretly relieved British admiralty proudly informed the anxious public of history's first mass escape from a submarine disaster. Little did they know that the Davis escape method was taking twenty times longer than planned.

What followed next would have been comical had the results not been so tragic. Awaiting a miraculous Davis escape, rescuers had stopped all real efforts at salvaging the submarine. Even though they should have been alerted that something was amiss when no one else followed Oram and Woods to the surface within ten minutes, the Admiralty waited to take any further action for an incredible two hours, until the second set of escapees made it to the surface and delivered their grim tale. Several more hours passed as nonexistent salvage plans were hastily and shoddily developed, and still no Davis apparatus escapees emerged. Finally, at around noon on Friday, steel cables were strapped around the ship. They slipped off. A second set broke completely, and the rescuers lost the *Thetis*. The sub was not relocated until eleven that evening. By this time, nearly all of the ship's oxygen had run out. Those inside were too weak by now to drag themselves out of the hull.

Still, it took until 1 A.M. on Saturday for specially trained deep-sea divers to arrive from out of the country. They tried to cut two holes in the stern and failed miserably. An hour later, several faint taps were heard within the *Thetis*. Then, silence. At 4:10 P.M., the British admiralty—the same agency that had, just one day earlier, confidently announced the first mass self-rescue in submarine history—now somberly announced that all remaining ninety-nine members of the *Thetis* had perished. A highly trained, highly experienced crew in service to the world's most powerful navy had suffocated to death just one hundred feet below the surface of the water, in full view of their would-be rescuers.

The cause of this unnecessary tragedy: willful blindness to basic facts combined with a powerful willingness to bend basic facts to fit convenient theories. From the moment that the sub failed to signal her surfacing to the moment that faint taps inside its hull were heard, the Admiralty made all of the wrong decisions for one primary reason: they could not force themselves to admit that a major disaster had happened during a routine training exercise. At every stage, the rescue response was criminally slow, and at every step, the rescuers themselves leaped to believe whatever conclusion seemed most favorable. Thus the *Thetis*'s watchship initially failed to send out any real alarm. Thus the British admiralty latched on to an improbable, never-done-before mass Davis apparatus escape and then stopped making decisions. Thus decisions were resumed only after it became woefully apparent that the convenient orthodoxy was untrue. Thus deep-sea divers were not called until the entire crew was dead or nearly so. The British navy, ruler of the waves for the past one hundred years, was too enamored with itself to exhibit wisdom. It was too proud to see reality as it was—the navy saw only what it wished to.

Thus died one hundred men.

. . . AND SEEING THE ROAD WELL

Some thirty-two years later, NASA responded very differently to a very similar situation. On April 11, 1970, Apollo 13 launched for an attempted landing on the moon. Commanding the mission was Captain Jim Lovell, a man who was already an accomplished astronaut. The two other crew members were Fred Haise and Jack Swigert, both experienced test pilots. Initially everything proceeded according to plan. Floating high above the planet, the carefully selected, highly trained astronauts were relaxed and even somewhat bored. In fact, Haise amused himself by occasionally depressing the rocket's depressurization valve, causing a resounding boom that terrified his comrades.

Unbeknownst to the astronauts and Mission Control back in Houston, oxygen tank number two, a mere ten feet below the bored crew's couches, suffered from a crack in its wiring. For forty hours the crew drew air from this tank, but the exposed wires remained safely submerged in liquid. Some two hundred thousand miles from earth, though, the crew had finally consumed enough air to expose the cracked wiring. Shortly before preparing to sleep that night, Lovell and crew obeyed a routine request from Mission Control: turn on the fans in oxygen tank number two. A spark jumped between the cracked wires, causing a fire to break out inside of a metal tank containing liquid oxygen. The result: a catastrophic explosion.

A tremendous bang rocked the spacecraft and rousted the crew. Glancing at the instrument panel, the astronauts immediately noticed that parts of the electrical system had failed. They also noticed that a gaseous substance—their stored oxygen—was streaming from the rocket's service module. Immediately Lovell and crew assessed the situation and correctly diagnosed it as catastrophic. Heartbreaking as it was to abandon a mission for which they had so exhaustively trained with the eyes of the nation upon them, the astronauts realized that they would not be able to land on the moon. In fact, they would be lucky just to get back home alive.

Back in Houston, that realization came more slowly. Immediately after the explosion, Mission Control's instruments indicated a loss of both of the craft's oxygen tanks, the entire electrical system, and significant amounts of fuel. It was a disaster of such epic proportions that the Houston observers simply could not believe that such a thing had occurred, particularly in an overengineered space rocket that they had created themselves. So Houston latched on to a different and more convenient explanation: instrument failure aboard the spacecraft. Since they could not believe what the instruments were telling them, they chose to ignore the instruments. Put another way, Mission Control shot the messenger.

Fortunately, the remedy to an imagined instrument failure was simple: locate and fix the defective instruments. In the minds of the Houston-based engineers, as soon as the instruments were repaired, the bad news would simply disappear. The real mission would resume as planned under much more pleasant circumstances. However, twenty minutes later, no faulty instrument had been located. Unlike the British admiralty in the previous example, Houston Mission Control immediately switched its thesis to the correct one. As painful as it was for the team that built the rocket to accept that their creation had failed, they had to acknowledge the chilling new reality. The indicators were telling the truth. Less than two hours of oxygen remained on Apollo 13.

Mission Control immediately ordered the astronauts to move to the lunar excursion module. It was attached to the greater rocket body and carried its own separate oxygen supply, enough for two men for two days. Six hours after the accident, however, both the crew and mission control realized that if Apollo 13 did not speed up, she would run out of power and water before returning to earth. Once they completed the burn that increased the craft's speed, Lovell and crew turned off all power in the lunar module to conserve its energy. The temperature rapidly dropped below freezing.

Another problem soon became apparent: carbon dioxide was rapidly building up within the excursion model. The air would have to be filtered, but the lunar module had no filters left. Fortunately, the command module did. There was one problem, though: the command module's filters were round, while the lunar module's were square. Back in Houston, Mission Control frantically constructed a round-to-square adaptor out of makeshift materials readily available to the crew: duct tape, plastic bags, and cardboard. It took several hours to prototype and several more for the astronauts to actually build the thing. Once they did, the makeshift filter went to work and the crew breathed easier, literally.

Their relief did not last long. With less than a day before reentry to the earth's atmosphere, Mission Control noticed that the craft's angle was off and alerted the crew, who corrected the problem by estimating the position of the earth relative to the center of the window of the lunar module. Meanwhile, Mission Control frantically strove to come up with a plan to restart the command module's frozen power systems. Nine hours before they were expected to land, the crew finally got their instructions from Houston. Transcription took two hours and every scrap of paper the crew could find. Fortunately, Swigert, the command module pilot, had the time to dry-run the instructions once before it was time for the real thing.

Racing toward the earth at 2,000 miles per hour, the Apollo 13 crew climbed back into the frozen command module and began the laborious process of restoring power. One by one, the systems came back on line. The complicated strategy developed by Mission Control had proven successful. Fifteen minutes before splashdown, the crew jettisoned the lunar module. Then they tensed up and awaited the three-minute reentry burn, during which they would lose all contact with Houston.

The recovery team had been preparing for the past three days for the return of the Apollo 13. Ships, helicopters, and air squadrons were massed in the Pacific Ocean, but even with that level of preparation, there was still room for error. The spacecraft could potentially land anywhere within a 500-by-250-mile rectangle, and if it turned upside down, it would be nearly invisible to aircraft spotters. Apollo 13 entered the earth's atmosphere and radio blackout ensued. At the end of three minutes, there was still no word from the crew. Then, suddenly, the massed rescuers observed the reentry module descending through the cloud cover with her parachutes deployed. The miraculous had occurred: after a complete systems failure some two hundred thousand miles from earth, Mission Control and three astronauts had overcome one challenge after another—suffocation, hypothermia, dehydration, and technical uncertainty at every turn—to return Apollo 13 and its entire crew safely home.

Contrast this result with that of the HMS *Thetis,* where every passenger perished just one hundred feet below the surface of the ocean, in full view of their would-be rescuers. There are many differences in the two cases, but the primary one is the following: at every turn, Houston Mission Control adjusted its hypothesis to fit the facts and made decisions accordingly, whereas the British admiralty did just the opposite—at every turn, it adjusted the facts to fit its predetermined hypothesis, allowing it to avoid making any decisions at all.

Throughout the entirety of their ordeal, all of the Apollo 13 actors displayed remarkable wisdom. Stranded without air, heat, and light some hundreds of thousands of miles away from their home planet, the players in this drama could not know the ultimate outcome of their situation. Clearly, Mission Control had failed to predict every challenge that lay before them, and each time one difficulty was overcome another one presented itself. No one could be sure of the results of their decisions. Indeed, no one could be sure of even the next ten minutes.

Still, at every juncture, the astronauts and their Houston-based support crew consistently recognized the reality of the road they were on and made the best decisions that they could. The Admiralty did just the opposite with the *Thetis*. The ruler of the waves, a nation whose naval supremacy ensured that the sun never set on its empire, could not rescue one hundred people one hundred feet below the water. The Houston engineers managed to rescue their entire crew some two hundred thousand miles away from earth.

WISDOM AND INTELLIGENCE: TWO VERY DIFFERENT THINGS

Wisdom is grounded in humility, and springs from it. It is humility that helps us see ourselves as we really are so that we can see the road in front of us through the clearest windshield possible. It is humility that allows us to make decisions that are founded in reality rather than fantasy. But, as we have seen, cultivating the virtue of humility takes hard work. Assuming that we do the work, how do we take humility to the next step and transform it into wisdom?

It helps if we first take a look at what wisdom is not. Some may instinctively realize what we pointed out earlier—that wisdom is neither omniscience or prescience. However, even if we realize that "wisdom" cannot guarantee an understanding of current events or an ability to predict the future, we may still mistake this virtue for something else. Many people believe that wisdom is simply an enhanced form of intelligence, something grasped by those who are smarter than run-of-the-mill humanity. Not at all.

Wisdom is not superior intellect, or cleverness in action, or top-shelf education. Some of the smartest leaders of our time, people who graced magazine covers nationwide, are now wearing orange jumpsuits and picking up trash in the federal penitentiary because they made tragically stupid life decisions. Intelligence is no guarantor that the best people will choose the best means to the best ends. If intelligence leads to hubris (which it often does), and if the smartest guys in the room think that they can do no wrong (which they often do think), then the virtue of wisdom may even be less likely to be found in those with the highest IQs.

Until I joined the United States Marines and forcibly learned how little I truly know, I believed in the false notion that wisdom and intellect were one and the same. I had been educated in a technocratic undergraduate institution, and there I developed a bias toward the theory that those blessed with high intelligence and higher education would necessarily make better decisions than those without one, or both. The smart and the educated should therefore be given a greater responsibility for decision-making by society, I began to believe. Then I joined the Corps and saw true wisdom at work, with life and death on the line. In combat I realized that in many cases those who were the wisest—those who made the best decisions under extreme pressure—were often those with the least education but the greatest willingness to learn. Those who thought that they knew everything and listened to no one, on the other hand, got people killed.

I learned what wisdom really is from a semiliterate Filipino in a war-torn country far from home. Gunny Jaugan was a Filipino immigrant with barely a high school education. His Tagalog dialect was probably excellent, but his English was broken at best and unintelligible at worst. He applied personal pronouns to inanimate objects—"You see this backpack? He is all jacked up"—and scored quite low on his military intelligence test. Yet, no matter what the situation, Gunny Jaugan always seemed to know exactly what to do and why to do it.

One day in Iraq we had come back in from a hot, exhausting patrol, only to find that we had the grueling task of filling twenty sandbags apiece to help fortify our base against the constant mortar strikes. We had been wearing sixty pounds of gear and had been walking for hours in the 130-degree heat. Our uniforms had been soaked through with sweat two and three times over during the day, but it didn't matter. The sandbags needed to be filled because the mortars wouldn't wait on our exhaustion and general lack of hygiene. When he noticed that one of our officers (a very good one, by the way) wasn't out digging with his men, Gunny found him and gently suggested that said officer check out the creativity in the fortifications that his Marines were building. It worked—the man went outside and, seeing firsthand how hard his men were working, he picked up a shovel and dug alongside them.

Just a few weeks later, Gunny found me rushing about our primitive base, deeply engaged in the apparently crucial task of finding some wooden legs for a makeshift map table we were building. It felt good to be running around, accomplishing discrete tasks. Unfortunately, these tasks were not at all central to accomplishing any useful mission. They were minutiae that I was using as an excuse to avoid doing work that only I could do. After observing my well-intentioned but misdirected exertions for a bit, Gunny pulled me aside and gently advised me that perhaps my time was better spent studying the map, as opposed to building the map table. It was a small thing, but it made a big difference.

However, Gunny Jaugan's masterpiece, in my mind, came on May 16, 2004, when he found me crying in a dirty bathroom in Iraq after I'd lost my first Marine to hostile fire. It had been a terrible day. We were conducting counter-mortar patrols in the middle of a hostile city when we stopped at a school to check on the pace of its rebuilding. After about fifteen minutes spent checking the construction's progress, we concluded the trip by handing out soccer balls and pencils to the schoolchildren, who had formed an anxious circle around our vehicles, their hands outstretched, frantically grasping at whatever we could give them. Once everything was distributed, we began climbing into our vehicles. The children were crowded together on the sidewalk, watching us go.

Just as I climbed in the lead vehicle, insurgents fired a rocket at us from a cluster of buildings to our south. It missed my men but impacted squarely in the middle of the knot of schoolchildren. They simply exploded. Bodies and body parts scattered across the sidewalk and street. We chased off the attackers and began collecting the dead and wounded. We called for an ambulance and secured the perimeter of the school while our naval corpsmen went to work, administering first aid to those still living.

We waited at the school for another twenty minutes or so, and as the time ticked past I was certain that we would be attacked again. As the ambulance pulled up, the expected attack came. This time the rocket impacted a light pole near one of my Marines. The resulting shrapnel sheared both of his legs off at the knees.

We packed the severed limbs in ice and loaded him into the back of a Humvee. The docs jumped up with him into the truck bed and went furiously to work, applying IVs to replace the blood loss and tourniquets to stop the bleeding. Half of the platoon went with them on an immediate medical evacuation while the other half went with me to pursue our attackers. It was fruitless—they had disappeared into the middle of the heavily populated city.

Several hours later, the platoon had reconstituted in a police compound in the middle of the city's downtown. I pulled the men together and gave a talk—I don't remember much about it—about how we could not afford to react in anger and revenge at the loss of our man and how we had to persevere with honor regardless of how we felt. Then I left the platoon to find a place to cry my eyes out alone. Somehow Gunny was there at the back of the room while I gave my talk, and somehow Gunny was the only person to notice later that I'd disappeared. Somehow he found me, in the middle of a filthy foreign bathroom, the kind with no toilets, just holes in the ground, and human excrement lying everywhere. Gunny didn't say anything for a while. He just put his arms around me and held me, and it was awkward, with all of our combat gear on. After I stopped sobbing, Gunny quietly told me that I would be okay. Then he told me that though one of my men was gone, the rest were still there and they still needed a leader. I needed to get back out with them and do my job, because they were hurting as bad as I was, or worse. So I did what I always did when it was Gunny who spoke—I did exactly as he told me to do.

Gunny Jaugan was a far cry from the smartest Marine in our company. Technically, I outranked him by several levels. But no matter what the circumstances, Gunny somehow always knew the right thing to do and the best way to get it done. I would take one Gunnery Sergeant Jaugan over a hundred of the best and brightest strategic planning majors.

Too often, we recognize intellect divorced from action. In a modern, celebrity-oriented culture, leaders of all stripes are lionized for their intelligence, for their charisma, or sometimes simply for their cultural ubiquity—rather than for their moral choices. In the last twenty years, numerous leaders have been excused from the normal rules of behavior because they were deemed so smart that normal rules did not apply to them. In 1995 Enron was named by *Fortune* magazine as the most innovative company in America, a title it kept for the next five years. In 2001, *Worth* magazine named that company's leader, Jeff Skilling, as America's second-best CEO. However, that very same year, Enron failed to supply a cash flow statement and a balance sheet after announcing earnings. For most companies, that would be considered a serious red flag, and perhaps a fatal error. But because Skilling and Enron's intellectual capital was viewed as so superior, most observers excused the delay. Seven months later, Enron filed for bankruptcy.

From Bernie Madoff—whose deceptively smooth stream of year-on-year earnings masked a deeper Ponzi scheme—to Eliot Spitzer—the crusading attorney general (and eventually governor of New York) whose war on corporate evil masked routine dalliances with prostitutes—our recent history is awash in examples of brilliant leaders granted undeserved grace. Too often we suspend disbelief and ignore reality because we place blind faith in superior intelligence. Thus we accept as rational the irrational—for example, the belief that home loans made to individuals with no proven income will certainly be repaid—because people with intimidating intellects have asked us to do so. We want so badly to believe that some experts, those people with proven intelligence, divine the overall operation of the system that we place tremendous unfounded trust in them.

THE THREE CHARACTERISTICS OF TRUE WISDOM

No matter how smart we are, we can never understand the overall operation of life's train system. Intelligence and wisdom are two very different things, and a leader can be said to possess the latter only if they exhibit a consistent pattern of discerning the morally correct thing to do and then taking action to ensure that that is, in fact, done. Leaders will make mistakes, and their designs will be frustrated by time and chance, but a leader who has wisdom is a leader who demonstrates consistency in decisions and actions. Such a leader recognizes that a single deliberately immoral act, the proverbial fly in the ointment, can jeopardize a lifetime spent building credibility.

True wisdom has very little to do with higher intelligence or better education. Indeed, this virtue is something different altogether. Wisdom is, rather, simply *the ability to discern the best and highest goal in any situation and the ability to choose the best and surest means of attaining it*. Put another way, wisdom is the practical side of moral goodness. It is not so much a virtue of intellect as it is of decision-making. It has everything to do with action, and it is nothing if decoupled from day-to-day choices.

So, how can we begin to discern if we, or others, possess this virtue? To start, there are three characteristics that mark wisdom in a leader. First off, a wise leader understands where their sphere of control begins and ends. One of the single greatest sources of frustration in life is the inability to orchestrate events as we desire. Too often, we believe that circumstances and outcomes are under our control when in fact they are not. A Fortune 500 CEO, for example, has been shown to have as little as a 5 percent effect on the performance of their company in any given year. Oftentimes, we believe that we have a good handle on what tomorrow will bring and what fruit our efforts will bear over the long haul. We envision the optimum result of our work and believe that our work will therefore bring about that optimum result.

For many, these results play themselves out as career success, a well-functioning family, and overall physical and mental health. Our best efforts at work lead to promotion, flourishing company performance, and healthy individual paychecks. Our relationship with our spouse goes smoothly (whether we work at it or not), and our children are generally obedient and enjoy success in school and in life. Each checkup at the doctor produces a clean bill of health. We can fall asleep at night secure in the knowledge that tomorrow will bring more of the same. We are in control.

Unfortunately, reality says otherwise. Economic catastrophes outside of anyone's control can destroy the best-run businesses and disrupt the best-laid life plans. Poor leaders in the workplace can fail to recognize, or can be threatened by, our own talents and efforts. Our hard work may not result in promotion and recognition but rather in marginalization and persecution. Our children have their own free will, and may make choices that hurt them and us even if we are the best parents in the world. Our spouses may also make poor choices, or their mental or physical health may degrade suddenly and rapidly. The doctor may detect a suspicious lump somewhere in our aging bodies and turn our entire lives upside down. What was a fight to thrive can become, in a heartbeat, a fight to survive.

Time and chance happen to us all. To paraphrase a famous verse: "The race is not always to the swift, nor the battle to the warrior, nor favor to men of intelligence, nor riches to those with discernment." A wise leader recognizes that they are no exception to this rule. They do not try to control the uncontrollable. They do not believe that they can map the future. They realize that they cannot orchestrate circumstances to ensure comfort and predictability, much as they might like. Their work and family may turn out much differently than they had expected. But to be wise means to accept life's inherent unpredictability. Wise leaders accept their own inability to bring about the outcomes they desire.

The first characteristic of a wise servant leader is *recognition of, and submission to, their own limits of control.* Reinhold Niebuhr's famous Serenity Prayer sums up this concept as well as any:

> *God, grant me the serenity to accept the things I cannot change;*
> *Courage to change the things I can;*
> *And the wisdom to know the difference.*

The second characteristic goes hand in hand with the first. Having accepted the limits of their control, *a leader should live in the present and try their best to enjoy it thoroughly.* The first step toward doing this is to regard each day as a gift rather than a given—no easy thing to do, or else we would all do it naturally. Having come from a combat environment, it helps me to remind myself of all the long rows of white headstones at Arlington National Cemetery. My fellow soldiers lie there. Some of them I knew, but most of them are anonymous. All of them, however, no longer have the present.

Their mourning parents would love one more day with their buried sons or daughters. Their wives and husbands would love one more day with their spouses. Their children would love one more day with their fathers and mothers buried beneath the earth. Those who have lost their loved ones know the value of one more day and the precious gift that time truly is. However, those of us who still have time tend to take it for granted, diminishing its value and our own joy in receiving it.

Each day is indeed worthy. As we have seen throughout this book, time is the only resource that can never be recovered once it is gone. We can replace money, friends, and even love if we lose it. But yesterday can never be pulled forward, because we have lost yesterday, which makes today infinitely precious. A leader seeking wisdom recognizes this and keeps it at the forefront of his or her mind. By believing that today is a gift, we truly set the stage to take joy from the days that follow.

In combat, for me, waking up each morning, far from my family and knowing that in half an hour I would have to walk down the middle of a road looking for bombs, was no easy thing. I cannot say that I took much joy from days spent fighting my fellow man. Many of us face situations as bad or worse than mine: angry leaders at work, abusive spouses at home, illness, injury, depression, or a whole host of other things that make each day physically and emotionally painful. The time that we have been given may be time that is far from easy.

But wisdom does not mean ignoring the pain that present circumstances may bring. Rather, wisdom means acknowledging that simply having life is a good thing and that continued time means continued hope, for without time, there is no moving forward. Ultimately, this acknowledgment translates into a focus on the present and an increased joy in the day that we have at hand. As we work toward greater wisdom, we will find it in the present moment, the present day.

Having acknowledged their limits and recognized the value of each day, *a wise leader seeks the ability to work hard at whatever it is that each day has set before them and the grace to enjoy the work as they do it.* They seek to do their best in the realm that is theirs and then rest when their work is done. They recognize that the fact that they have work means that they also have time, the most precious of gifts. Still, one might ask, even if we recognize the gift of time, why would we attempt to take pleasure in filling that time with something that is fundamentally difficult, as is implied by the very word *work*?

It's actually quite simple: a wise leader works hard and tries to enjoy doing so because 1) it makes the most of the time that they have and 2) if they can persist, they become better at everything they get their hands on. Professor K. Anders Ericsson at Florida State University published a landmark paper in 1993 focusing on sports, music, and chess—professions where performance is fairly easy to measure over time. In his work, Ericsson and his colleagues argued that for exceptional performers to hit their zenith, they required a minimum of ten years of deliberate practice, defined here as practice that has a concrete goal and that makes consistent adjustments based on feedback. This rule held constant across violinists, chess masters, and football players, implying that innate ability has less to do with success than does hard work done toward a specific goal. Several international chess grand masters, for example, have been measured with IQs in the 90s. An average score for the general population is 100.

In his book *Outliers,* Malcolm Gladwell argues essentially the same thing, only he frames it in a different way: to be truly excellent, one needs 10,000 hours of practice regardless of the time frame. The Beatles, for example, achieved more than 10,000 hours of live performance in just four years in Hamburg. While still in high school in 1968, Bill Gates gained access to a local computer, and over the next several years he managed to log more than 10,000 hours of programming time. According to

Gladwell, the main reason that the world's richest man and the Fab Four succeeded above and beyond their peers was that they had the discipline — and a significant amount of good fortune and luck—to focus on practicing a task for the time required to become true masters. They worked deliberately and they worked hard, and their hard work paid off.

Most of us will never become software impresarios or iconic musicians (nor may we want to), but we can still focus on deliberate practice in our day-to-day environments. The key to engaging in deliberate practice is to approach our work with a new goal: rather than simply doing our jobs, we aim to become better at them and to make changes that make the jobs themselves better. When amateur singers take a singing lesson, they relax and experience it as fun, for they have no real goal. When professionals take the same lesson, they have just the opposite reaction: they increase concentration and focus on improving performance. The same activity approached with two different mindsets yields two different results.

Research shows that those who approach work with the mentality of making it better process information more deeply and retain it longer, which in turn allows them to quickly build accurate mental models of their world. We become better able to understand events around us, and we adapt rapidly to changing environments. What is more, we are more likely to experience success beyond that of our peers. Best of all, we are more likely to enjoy what we are doing. We get better at our work and make the work better as we go.

No matter what our walk of life, we can all make ourselves better by applying our best efforts to the task at hand. Parents can study their children to help them raise the next generation more successfully. Those of us in the working world can focus on improving something, either daily or over time, to make our daily worlds at work just a little bit better. Neighbors can make their neighborhood just a bit more inviting or just a bit more beautiful. Friends can try to improve their friendships and spouses can try to improve their marriages. Putting forth our best effort with the deliberate aim of improving what we do and how we do it will inevitably make us better as people and as leaders.

Thus the third mark of wisdom is hard work at that which is under our control, and rest from that which is not. A wise leader recognizes that continued time on earth imputes a responsibility to use that time well. We cannot always control our futures, but we can control the effort that we put toward the daily tasks that we have in front of us. By giving our all, we make the most of the day we have been given. By refusing to worry about the future or future events outside of our control, wisdom helps us apply ourselves to the areas in which we can truly make an impact. What is more, wisdom allows us the perspective to realize that hard work is not simply a necessary response to continued time on earth; it is also a gift that helps make our lives better and us better at our lives. No matter where we are and no matter where we work, we can all aspire to make the most of our time, to "fill the unforgiving minute with sixty seconds' worth of distance run." Those of us who work with a purpose and sustain it over time will have achieved the third characteristic of wisdom.

As we attain wisdom in increasing measures, not only will we make better decisions at each twist and turn on the road that is life, but we will also find that we take greater pleasure in each stage of the journey. With more wisdom comes greater joy—a happiness independent of circumstances. Wisdom helps us narrow our focus to the things that are truly within our control rather than the things that are well outside of it, and wisdom helps us to increasingly recognize the difference between the two. As we become better able to distinguish that which we can affect from that which we cannot, we will find that our enjoyment of our present circumstances increases. Furthermore, as we begin to recognize that merely having present circumstances is a gift rather than a given, we become happier by just having the day that is at hand. Focusing on what we can control and giving thanks for what we have—as opposed to worrying about things out of our control and wishing that we had more—will inevitably increase our satisfaction regarding exactly where we are.

As our joy increases, so will our consistency. When we recognize the reality of the present and rest content at each day's end, we are better able to stay focused on what matters rather than becoming distracted by what does not. Our emotional state will be more stable over time and our decisions will be less influenced by it. What is more, our decisions will better hang together—we will be more holistic in our choices and trade-offs. What we decide to do will be increasingly grounded in reality and increasingly focused on the items within our sphere of control rather than influenced by emotion and scattered across things over which we have no influence. As we attain greater wisdom, we will find that our actions and our attitude become more consistent.

REFLECTION

A wise leader is one who recognizes the limits of their control. They realize that as life progresses, our understanding of the why behind things may not progress. They see that they are more like the automobile driver than the train dispatcher. So they seek to make the best decisions they can as each set of circumstances presents itself, and know full well that they may never be able to predict—or even understand—the outcome of those decisions. They adjust their preconceptions to fit current facts rather than vice versa, and they seek to recognize the world as it truly is, not as they wish it to be. They realize that they have a duty to choose the morally correct action rather than the easy one or the one guaranteed to bring wealth or comfort. They work hard and with a purpose at the things that truly matter, seeking to make themselves better as they work. They take joy in the day at hand, knowing that each day is a gift, not a given. They make the most of what life throws at them and are not overwhelmed by events.

Reflection Steps

Attaining the virtue of wisdom defies any simple, prescriptive recipe. There is no easy way to seamlessly marry up understanding and action, but there are several steps we can take to help ourselves. They begin with regular reflection and end with realigning our expectations with life's realities. If we want to increase in wisdom, then the following five steps are the best place to start:

1. *Realize that wisdom is not omniscience.*
   We will never fully understand all of life's events and the purpose behind their occurrence, and we should not expect to. We should not, therefore, be frustrated that as we grow in knowledge and experience we do not necessarily grow in our understanding of why things happen (particularly bad things).

2. *Reflect on the fact that wisdom finds its fullest expression in action.*
   Wisdom is ultimately a practical virtue, and its goal is to choose the best means to the best ends. As we increase in wisdom, then, we will make better choices as difficult situations confront us, even if we do not fully understand the future that those choices imply. Better education and higher intelligence are not necessarily related to this virtue, nor are they necessary for its attainment— popular culture preconceptions to the contrary. What is necessary is the willingness to make decisions that are morally correct and practically attainable.

3. *Realign our preconceptions to fit facts, quickly.*
   If wisdom is dependent on the right choices in the right circumstances, then we must be able to diagnose the reality of our circumstances quickly and accurately. Unfortunately, every human being has a natural propensity to bend facts to fit theory—to believe what they want to rather than what they should. Humility helps us avoid this fallacy. If we want to be wise, we must be willing to question ourselves and willing to accept questions, and criticism, from others.

4. *Resign ourselves to the limits of our control.*
   Time and chance happen to even the smartest, hardest-working, and most visionary of us. We are lucky if we can get through today with our plans intact. Controlling tomorrow is a more difficult and

less achievable task, which isn't to say that we should not plan for the future. It is simply to say that oftentimes the future is unplannable. A wise leader recognizes and accepts this fact. We conserve our energy to affect the things that make a difference rather than worry about the things we cannot control.

5. *Rejoice in the day at hand and work hard at each day's tasks.*
A wise leader understands that each day is not a given; it is a gift, one that could very well have been granted to someone else. As we increase in wisdom, we become increasingly thankful for this gift and for the time we have at hand. We also recognize that our right response to the gift of time is to do our best with all of our time by working hard at the tasks we have in front of us. The more we perform these tasks with the attitude of making them, and us, better, the better they, and we, will become.

In many ways, wisdom is the virtue that synthesizes all of the others and helps transform them into the best possible actions. If we know our mission and can be disciplined and brave as we seek after it, if we can be humble and kind as we try to take others with us, and if we can give our best at each task simply because our best is worth doing, then we are likely to make the right decisions at each fork on life's road. We are much more likely to be able to choose the best means to attain the best ends, to transform morality into action.

However, if we achieve all of the other virtues but fail to synthesize them into wisdom, our ability to lead well will be significantly impaired. Wisdom enables us to make the hard choices easily and gives us peace as we do so. Wisdom allows us to see the purpose and meaning in each day and to take joy in the days at hand. Without wisdom, and the perspective on life's events that the virtue brings, we find ourselves trapped in an unending odyssey of frustration as we seek knowledge and control of a life that was never ours to begin with.

If we pursue wisdom, we can attain it. If we do not, we must resign ourselves to days that are far harder than they need to be.

SUMMARY

- Wisdom is neither omniscience nor prescience. Many people believe that the virtue of wisdom is one that allows us to know the meaning behind life's current events and the outcome of life's future ones, but nothing could be further from the truth.
- True wisdom is the ability to discern the best and highest goal in any situation and the ability to choose the best and surest means of attaining it. Put another way, wisdom is the practical side of moral goodness. Wisdom has everything to do with action, and it means making the best choices possible as each different situation in life presents itself.
- Wisdom is founded on humility, because humility helps us to see ourselves as we truly are. When we cannot see ourselves accurately, we cannot clearly see the choices that life presents us. When this is the case, we are highly likely to make poor decisions. Most of us are more likely to change facts to fit our own predetermined theories than we are to change our own predetermined theories to fit facts.
- Intelligence and wisdom are two very different things, and smart, well-educated leaders are often leaders who fail most spectacularly. For a leader to be wise, they must demonstrate consistency in decisions and actions. A wise leader is one who regularly discerns the morally correct thing to do and then takes action to ensure that it is in fact done.
- A wise leader has three characteristics. First, they understand where their sphere of control begins and ends. They recognize that time and chance happen to all humanity and that events are rarely as they would orchestrate them. Second, having accepted the limits of their control, a wise leader lives in the present and enjoys it thoroughly. Third, a wise leader seeks the ability to work hard at whatever it is that each day has set before them, and the grace to enjoy the work as they do it.
- Wisdom enables not only good decisions but also greater pleasure in life's journeys. With more wisdom comes greater joy—happiness independent of circumstances—and as joy increases, so does consistency. When a leader recognizes the reality of the present and rests content at

each day's end, they are better able to stay focused on what matters rather than become distracted by what does not.

• Wisdom enables us to make hard choices, gives us peace, allows us to see meaning in our days, and gives us joy in the days that are at hand. If we pursue this virtue, we can and will find it.

CHAPTER 8

VIRTUE AND THE SERVANT-LEADER

All Marine officers must pass through Quantico, Virginia, at the onset of their training. In this respect, the Marines are unusual—the other branches of the armed forces have several different locations where new leaders are minted, whereas the Marines have just the one. No matter what their education or prior service experience, everyone who hopes to be a Marine officer must endure the Quantico-based screening process of Officer Candidate School. Everyone who passes that process must then endure six more months of basic training. Buried deep in the woods of rural Virginia, the small base of Quantico is the starting point for every single Marine officer.

It is Quantico that puts civilians through the training and refining process that transforms them into Marine officers. It is here that they learn the fundamentals of military life, the discipline of the rank structure, and the etiquette unique to America's armed forces. It is here that new officers are taught the basic skills that will keep people alive in combat. Most important, it is at Quantico that all future leaders learn the culture of the Marine Corps, a culture founded on the servant-leader mentality that is expected of everyone who wears the uniform.

The primary way that the Corps imparts its culture is by teaching new leaders the virtues of the old ones through stories, case studies, and examples. Quantico is steeped in history—you cannot walk through Camp Barrett, the area that houses the Basic School, without literally bumping into the legends of the Marines. Buildings are named for past leaders who embodied the key virtues of the Corps. O'Bannon Hall, for example, is named after Presley O'Bannon, the Marine who led a bayonet charge against heavily armed Barbary pirates in one of America's first foreign engagements. No space goes wasted—in typical military fashion, even the Hawkins bar—affectionately referred to as "The Hawk"—tells the story of William D. Hawkins, a leader who ignored his own chest wound and led his men from the front as they assaulted Japanese pillboxes on Tarawa in World War II.

Among all of these tributes to the past, though, there is one monument that stands apart. In front of the Basic School headquarters building stands a nine-foot-high statue of a Marine in combat. He wears grimy fatigues with the sleeves rolled up, and ammunition pouches dot his chest. He stands erect, with his right leg slightly bent, preparing to charge forward. His combat helmet is tipped back from his head as he looks back over his left shoulder. His right arm is outstretched, with his rifle held straight out, pointing to where he is heading. He looks backward with his left arm shoulder high, the forearm up and crooked, beckoning to those behind him. If the statue could speak, there is no doubt what he would be saying. It is the motto of the officer corps, the creed that inspires them to lead from the front, to embrace whatever danger, difficulty, or horrors lie ahead for their team. It is the creed that charges them to lead by example, to persevere through adversity, to keep going when all hope seems lost. That statue speaks mutely the two simple, powerful words that sum up the leadership philosophy of one of the world's greatest fighting forces:

Follow Me.

Unlike many heroic statues, this one is not a product of the sculptor's imagination. It is actually pulled from real life. The man leading from the front is Colonel William Leftwich, a man who embodied the servant-leadership model throughout the course of his career. In his first tour in Vietnam, Colonel Leftwich served as an adviser to the Vietnamese Marine Brigade. In this capacity, Leftwich was awarded a Navy Cross for personally leading a charge against enemy hilltop positions and then rescuing a wounded comrade under heavy fire. Ignoring the machine gun wounds in his back, cheek, and nose, Colonel Leftwich delayed his own evacuation in order to continue to take care of those under his command. The statue of Leftwich charging forward while looking backward is inspired by the events of that day.

Leftwich's story does not end there, however. After spending nearly three hundred days in the field in Vietnam, he returned to the United States to teach others at the Basic School. Three years later, though, Colonel Leftwich was back in Vietnam, this time as commanding officer of the First Reconnaissance Battalion. In this role, the Colonel could have easily chosen to spend the majority of his time safely with rear-echelon troops. After all, his duty was to coordinate the actions of his on-the-ground commanders, not to lead them personally. And as a reconnaissance unit, many of Leftwich's teams were often sent deep behind enemy lines, exposing them to more danger, more often, than regular combat troops.

Nevertheless, Leftwich continued his tradition of leading from the front. Whenever one of his teams got into deep trouble and called for an emergency extract, Leftwich personally accompanied the extract unit, riding in the same helicopters that would pick up his men, often under heavy fire. On November 18, 1970, Leftwich had just finished supervising the evacuation of one of his teams that had taken heavy casualties when his helicopter crashed into the side of a mountain, killing all aboard. His final moments on earth were spent in the same way that his life in leadership had been lived—taking care of those under his charge, sacrificing himself to try to spare them.

This is the man whose statue stands as the mute embodiment of leadership for all new Marine officers. It is this "Follow Me," self-sacrificial spirit that the Marines hold up as the ideal, as the archetype that all should follow. There is no other way of leading, no other model that is viewed as acceptable. There is no philosophy that competes with "Follow Me."

There is only the one statue.

WHY THEY FIGHT

How can there be such clear alignment across such a large organization? To put it simply, it is because the Corps has learned over three hundred years of combat history that only the servant-leadership model works under fire. Servant-leadership is the only form of leadership that inspires people to keep going through the most difficult times, when they have nothing to look forward to other than wounds or death. Unlike almost nowhere else in life, in combat the job of a leader is to ask their teams to do something that they know—and their teams know—might very well get them all killed. In our time in combat, we took it a step further, executing missions that we believed would *certainly* get us killed. Before one such outing, I sat through a briefing in which intelligence officers pointed out to us that when we left the next morning (at two o'clock), we should expect to fight for the next forty-eight to seventy-two hours straight, and that we should expect that at least a third of us would come back wounded. I took this information straight to my men as soon as the briefing was over. Just six hours later, all forty of us were leaving the patrol base. Not a single man quit.

Another standing mission that we had to endure once every four days was to sweep the main road through our city clear of bombs. To do this, we had to walk down the middle of the street, looking for the infernal devices with our naked eyes. Because they were well camouflaged, in most cases we never found them until we were less than ten feet away, well within killing distance. Yet every fourth morning, every one of my men geared up and walked down that highway.

In the heat of battle, I have watched eighteen-year-olds charge straight into the teeth of enemy machine gun positions, knowing full well that they will likely not survive the encounter. I have watched four-man teams fight desperate rearguard actions. I have watched twelve-man squads deliberately expose themselves to enemy ambushes in order to set them off. In all of these cases, one of the most likely outcomes of executing the mission was wounds and death.

Clearly, the military is exceptionally hierarchical, with strict discipline throughout all ranks. Some argue that that is why people can execute in these harsh and demanding environments—that they are so conditioned to obeying orders and submitting to authority that the idea of disobedience is totally foreign to them. This is not true. Military members are not robots. Independent thought and rapid innovation are encouraged, especially in the chaotic conditions that prevail on the front lines. Yet even if the misconception were correct, discipline and hierarchy alone cannot explain why someone would obey orders when they have absolutely nothing to gain and only their own lives to lose. Even the most conditioned of people will balk at dying for no reason other than their instructions call for it. No, there is something greater at work than hierarchy and discipline, and that something is the servant-leadership model, a clear leadership philosophy that the entire organization embraces and upholds.

VIRTUE AND THE SERVANT-LEADER

For all of its effectiveness, the servant-leadership model is extremely hard to sustain over time. The only way to achieve it consistently is to lay it on top of the virtues we have outlined, virtues that we patiently and intentionally develop throughout the course of our lives. Without virtue, no matter how well-intentioned we are and no matter how badly we want to serve our teams, we will be unable to maintain servant-leadership. It is almost impossible to keep constant in support of a mission and to continually subordinate our own self-interest unless we develop the character traits that give us a compelling reason to do so. Without the servant-leadership model layered on top of virtue, virtue is less effective.

But without virtue as our foundation, servant-leadership is impossible. For us to be true servant-leaders, each of our seven character traits is necessary if we hope to effectively practice the servant-leader model in our own lives.

Mission

The model begins with the mission. The first pillar of servant-leadership is the ability to place our organization's cause above our own personal welfare. Making and sustaining this commitment over time is no easy feat, and if we are not already accustomed to the idea of submission to mission, then it will be nearly impossible for us to even take the first steps toward servant-leadership. However, if we have a clearly defined mission in our own lives and if we are clearly committed to serving it, then integrating the mission of an organization into our personal leadership model becomes much easier.

As we saw earlier, every possible definition of the very word *mission* implies service to something outside ourselves. Thus, in the process of building and defining our personal missions, we inevitably commit to the concept of service and submission. Indeed, a well-built mission answers the fundamental question that underpins whatever it is that we find worth doing: what is it in our lives that we would give our lives for? Nelson Mandela sacrificed nearly two decades of jail time in service to the mission of freedom and equality for all people in his country. Winston Churchill gave up his political career in his quest to oppose Nazi Germany. Both of these men were effective leaders before their missions were crystallized, but they ascended to the highest pinnacles of leadership only after their fully understood missions had been put fully into play.

As it did for these famous leaders, constructing, understanding, and committing to our own personal mission lays the foundation for the idea of service more broadly. What is more, as we pursue our personal missions over time, we train ourselves to place mission above self-interest. This training translates across contexts and across organizations, making us more effective at assimilating, understanding, and serving different missions in different contexts. The more we prepare ourselves to serve in any context, the better we will be at serving in every context.

A personal mission also prepares us to take care of our teams before we take care of ourselves. At the heart of any good personal mission is the acceptance of our own mortality and the bone-deep understanding that our time on earth is limited. If we have limited time, then we must make the most of the time that we have by making the most of each day we are given. And the best way to make the most of the days that we are given is to make the biggest positive impact we can on the lives of others every single day. Thus the idea of a personal mission prepares us not only to serve our broader organization over the course of time but also to serve our teams on a day-in, day-out basis.

Moreover, one of the key principles of servant-leadership is the ability, and willingness, to model what is expected of our teams. If we do not understand what it is that informs and drives us as people and as leaders, then how can we possibly expect our teams to do the same? How can we convince them of the importance of an overarching mission if we have none in our own lives? How can we make an effective transition from one context to another, each of which may have different contextual missions, if we do not have constancy in our own lives? A leader must take great pains to understand their team's shared mission, to educate their team on the importance of the mission, to communicate that mission constantly, and to live it daily themselves.

Thus mission is the foundation underpinning the entire servant-leader edifice. Without a broad, well-understood personal mission, we will be ill-accustomed to the idea of sacrifice and submission, whether that be for the well-being of our organization or the well-being of our teams. With it, we train ourselves for service and we model what we expect in those whom we lead. We understand the crucial importance of impacting lives in a positive way, every single day, and we sacrifice our own well-being to do so. We live lives that matter because we put our own well-being behind that which truly matters—the service of mission and the service of others.

Humility

The next pillar of the servant-leader model is the application of humility. Fundamentally, humility helps us to see ourselves and reality in the truest possible light, not the one that's the most flattering. Too often, though, leaders lionize themselves for nothing more than the fact that they have assumed leadership. They believe that the position makes the person, and they fail to realize that after assuming the position, they are still the same flawed people as they were the day before they took on their new mantle.

This inability to see ourselves in the truest possible light is a tremendous impediment to servant-leadership, for it prevents us from seeing our teams as valuable sources of advice and insight. What is more, it blinds us to the simple fact that to be successful in accomplishing the mission, we will need our teams to be an integral part of the effort. It keeps us from acknowledging that we will need our people to keep us balanced and in check. We will need them to point out our flaws, weaknesses, and mistaken decisions.

If we do not realize the worth of a good team in supporting a flawed leader, then how can we approach our people with the mindset that we must serve them? How can we possibly view serving our people as a valuable use of our time if we don't believe that we need help from our people? If we do not expect our teams to help take care of us—because we need the help—then how can we possibly view a key portion of our role as maximizing their worth as team members? And how can we put their own welfare ahead of ours, consistently, if we do not believe that their welfare is a necessary component to our success?

What is more, humility provides a necessary temper for mission. Mission gives us purpose and a driving force outside ourselves, a reason to sacrifice for a higher cause. Humility, however, gives us boundaries on our sacrifices, sacrifices that are likely to include both ourselves and others. Humility helps us catch ourselves when we are reaching unethical extremes, or throwing our team to the wolves needlessly. In my opinion, the hardest question in the Marine Corps was "Which takes priority, the mission or the Marines?" Given our mission set, the sacrifices required of our teams was not always time or treasure—many times it was their lives.

The standard answer to the hardest question was "Mission first, Marines always," and the implied meaning behind this answer is that no one should be sacrificed unnecessarily—that when the mission does not require sacrifice, then the job of a leader is to take care of their teams, period. Humility ensures that leadership can answer truthfully: "Mission first, team always." It is the virtue that reigns in the needless pursuit of mission, the one that allows us to see ourselves as we really are. Humility allows us to accept advice and correction from others around us so that we are less likely to go off course and more likely to course-correct quickly when we inevitably make the wrong decisions. Humility prevents us from destroying our teams in pursuit of a goal, and permits us to serve them with the first fruits of our time and effort because we realize how much we need them in return.

The servant-leader realizes that they have warts and that the more they surround themselves with people willing to point those out and prevent them from transferring those flaws to others, the more likely everyone is to succeed. Humility is the virtue that convinces us of our need for others, because we know how much we fall short ourselves. And when we know that we need others, we know that we need to take care of them.

Excellence

A clear mission inspires servant-leadership, humility guides it, and excellence sustains it. Mission is the spark, the passion, that inspires us to pursue the servant-leader model, but it is excellence that keeps that pursuit going, day in and day out, when the daily grind threatens to extinguish the embers of inspiration. Thus excellence is the next pillar of the servant-leader model. Without it, we would find it impossible to continue to lead by serving others. The inevitable failures in life will extinguish the servant-leader mentality and leave us self-focused and self-absorbed.

Why does excellence sustain servant-leadership? First off, it allows us to persevere by giving us an achievable goal every day. In our context, excellence is an input, not an output. It is our best effort every day in response to the gift that is each day. We do not have to be masters or produce masterpieces in our professions to be excellent. We simply have to do our best with the gifts that we have. And if we can do this, then we find that each day brings us an achievable mission—to do our best in that day.

That simple accomplishment produces perseverance, for it allows us a daily sense of achievement. Without at least some light at the end of the tunnel, we will find it impossible to sustain our commitment to our teams and to our mission no matter how strong, tough, or disciplined we are. We can only keep sacrificing face for so long before we either see some results or decide to give up on our current course and choose a new one. However, if we know that we can achieve a worthy goal every day, it makes it much easier to keep going through the difficult times. Small wins are necessary to keep hope alive, and hope is necessary if we want to keep serving.

Combined, perseverance and hope allow us to serve our teams by maintaining a positive attitude and by promoting a stewardship, not an ownership, ideal. When we believe that each day is a gift, then it is much easier for us to place our gifts in the service of others. It is much easier for us to believe that our excellent, best efforts are best used in service to someone else because we ourselves are fortunate to even have a day in which to use them. Hope, in its turn, helps us to inspire our teams. We serve them by showing them a positive attitude, one that results from the belief that today will be better than tomorrow because today we and they have given the best that we have.

Excellence also produces contentment, a satisfaction with life's journey rather than its outcomes. And contentment allows us to serve our teams by maintaining our composure and radiating optimism regardless of the circumstances. We remain steadfast, constant in pursuit of our goals, with choices and trade-offs that are clear and consistent. Our teams know what is important to us, because they see us hew to it day in and day out. Our integrity helps them to maintain their integrity. They realize exactly what they need to pursue and why they need to pursue it. They remain on course because we remain on course, and they remain inspired because we persevere regardless of the circumstances—hopeful, optimistic, and content.

Kindness

If excellence helps our teams to do their best every day, then kindness helps them to be their best every day. Kindness is the next piece of the servant-leader puzzle, for kindness is the virtue that helps keep a leader attuned to the needs of others. Kindness builds a servant-leader's emotional antennae. Without this virtue, it is difficult for a leader to even recognize the needs of their teams, let alone sacrifice to meet those needs. However, the antennae are not enough. They are merely the instruments that help us determine that there is a need for action. Once we realize that our teams have a need that we can meet, we have to close the loop by acting. And for kindness to be kindness, that act must contain some element of sacrifice and some element of grace. Otherwise it is simply a transaction—giving someone exactly what they have earned at no cost to ourselves.

In addition to helping us identify when to give of ourselves, kindness helps sustain the servant ethic by training us to give above and beyond what is earned or deserved. Of all the virtues, kindness is the one that focuses explicitly on training a leader to identify opportunities to go above and beyond basic remuneration and into the realm of grace. It is the one virtue that teaches us both to identify needs and to give disproportionately to meet them. Humility helps lay the groundwork for both of these things by helping us stay focused on the most accurate view of ourselves and our teams, but only kindness translates this focus into tangible action prompted by recognized need. Kindness helps us give without ceasing.

This giving of ourselves has life-altering effects on our teams. It makes them feel valued as individuals, for who they are and not simply for what they can do. It shows them that someone is willing to pay a price for them, which makes them much more willing to pay a price for others. Without kindness, people become jaded and halfhearted. After all, why would we go above and beyond the minimum for someone else when no one goes above and beyond the minimum for us? However, the deliberate sacrifice implied by kindness convinces a team that their leader truly cares about them and transitions a team from acting out of a fear of loss to acting out of a love of gain, from giving just enough to giving their all. Thus kindness builds loyalty, cohesion, and risk-taking among a team and helps them to give their very best every day. Operating in this manner removes limits from our teams and pulls the best out of people.

Furthermore, kindness increases trust, speeding decision-making and efficiency across an organization. Without kindness, we would easily lose the human dimension—and the human costs—of leadership in the quest for our best efforts in service of the best mission. When we as leaders embrace kindness, we find that, like excellence, we embrace an achievable goal every day. In this case, however, that goal is externally focused—an impact on the lives of others—whereas with excellence the goal is internally focused—satisfaction in having given our best.

Like excellence, kindness reinforces our sense of purpose, because we receive daily positive reinforcement, this time from others rather than from ourselves. We see people improving their lives, people responding as our care for them produces results. Seeing tangible goals met in the lives of others helps rejuvenate us and reinforces our sense of purpose, creating a virtuous circle of self-sustaining behavior. Thus kindness complements excellence. One fuels us internally, and the other fuels us externally. Together these virtues remind a leader that their servant model is worth pursuing and that it can be sustained over time, no matter how hard it is and how much it demands of them.

Discipline

Even though at first glance discipline may seem counterintuitive to a philosophy that calls a leader to serve others, the reality is that this virtue is absolutely imperative if we hope to maintain a servant-leadership model in our own lives. If excellence helps give the servant-leader model the energy to keep going, discipline helps give it the daily direction to stay on course. If kindness helps keep us attuned to human emotions and the mutable human side of leadership, then discipline helps keep us in line with immutable ethical and executional standards. As we faithfully pursue our missions, one of the most important ways to serve our teams and to keep our missions (and our lives) on track is to faithfully adhere to a demanding set of ethical and executional standards.

Too often leaders lose sight of this basic truth and use the weight of their responsibilities to justify a double standard: a tight set of rules for their teams, and a very loose set of rules for themselves. Teams cannot long survive under these conditions. They will quickly lose their cohesion, their effectiveness, and perhaps even their morality. However, a disciplined leader serves their team by eliminating any and all double standards, starting with themselves. They adhere to the exact same ethical and executional rules as does everyone else around them. They avoid the small lies, have the hard conversations, and keep their promises. They ask nothing of their teams that they would not be willing to do themselves. They set an example and in so doing give their people daily reassurance that standards mean something.

This consistency builds into the servant-leader model in several ways. First off, it keeps a leader close to the lives of their team by forcing them to experience the same set of rules on a regular basis. With this virtue in place, the detachment of the ivory tower disappears and is replaced by messier day-to-day reality. Second, it forces a leader to practice making the right moral decisions in all of the small areas so that when tested in the large ones they will pass with flying colors. If a leader fails the critically important moral tests that inevitably come with the job, then they will destroy their team. No group can long withstand the pressures of doing the wrong thing for long, and a moral façade inevitably crumbles to reveal the corruption beneath. An undisciplined leader who does not obey and enforce demanding ethical standards ultimately condemns their teams to murder their own consciences.

Third, discipline serves a team by bringing meaning to their good acts. If a leader cannot bring themselves to punish behavior that falls outside of ethics and common norms, then no one's good acts have meaning because no one's bad acts are punished. A true servant-leader is one who does not shirk the responsibility of doing the hard thing when standards are violated. Rather than dispirit a team, knowable, enforceable rules actually raise morale in the long term. They keep chaos at bay and help a team perform their functions efficiently. Not only does this keep them pulling in the same direction, but it also helps them feel good about what they accomplished and worked for at each day's end. A leader who maintains standards thus serves their team, making their work worthwhile, effective, and ultimately enjoyable.

Finally, the virtue of discipline enhances the servant-leader model by continuing to build our personal integrity and credibility. Our teams see that we are consistent in the large as well as the small. We model for them what we expect in the day-to-day decisions in addition to the life-changing ones. We stay close to the reality that they are experiencing and do not distance ourselves from expectations that are difficult or demanding. Thus we maintain the credibility to speak with authority and the humility necessary to serve our teams daily. We not only keep ourselves immersed in their worlds but also demonstrate for them that their worlds are ours and that the right standards can be maintained, that the rules and good work mean something, and that no matter what the circumstances are, they can trust that they, and we, are acting ethically.

Courage

In the servant-leader model, courage is the necessary companion to the other virtues, for it is the virtue that empowers the others. Without courage, the servant-leader model will falter because at some point in time all of us are going to be faced with a stark choice: persevere in our mission—keep doing what we believe is right with the best of our abilities—and risk severe consequences *or* compromise our mission and our ethics—give something less than our best or perhaps quit entirely—and avoid any unpleasant consequences. Sooner or later, we as leaders will have to consciously risk our reputations, our careers, and perhaps even our lives to uphold our mission and take care of our people. Without courage to help us make the hard choices, we will make the easy ones. Either our missions or our teams—and possibly both—will fall victims to cowardice.

In many ways, courage is the natural companion to discipline. In fact, in a manner of speaking, courage jump-starts this virtue. If discipline allows us to uphold ethical and executional standards day in and day out, then courage helps us take the plunge initially. Courage helps us to grit our teeth and determine that we will maintain what is right, that we will hold the line, regardless of the consequences. And when those consequences come, courage is the virtue that helps us maintain and enforce the ethical and executional standards that we profess to believe. It is the virtue that helps us do the right thing in the face of persecution and pain.

But the reach of courage extends far beyond discipline. Physical courage gives us instant credibility, credibility that excellence and discipline help us maintain over time. Physical courage proves that we have integrity because we demonstrate with our own lives that we are prepared to make tangible, visible sacrifices to uphold what we believe. Courage is the best way for a servant-leader to answer the key questions, "Do you really believe what you say you believe?" and "Do you really mean what you say?" It is the surest rebuttal to the assertion that we will quit the hard servant-leader model as soon as that model runs into hard times.

However, we will not always have the chance to put our lives on the line to demonstrate our beliefs. Still, we will all have the opportunity to put our livelihoods on the line, and it is here that moral courage pairs with physical courage to enhance credibility. Moral courage demands that we identify our key ethical principles in advance of difficult ethical tests. It asks us to be prepared for negative outcomes, to be willing to bear responsibility for failure and to admit mistakes. It helps us determine our missions, steel ourselves to accept them, and to accept failure, counsel, and correction along the way.

Courage keeps the servant-leader whole. It ensures that their commitment to their teams and their missions stays firm through the best and the worst of times. It enables leaders to make difficult decisions and it proves that they mean what they say. It shows that they understand the difficult circumstances that their teams endure and shows that they are willing to endure those same circumstances alongside their team members. It keeps the other virtues intact when life gets hard and the mission becomes painful. It keeps a leader faithful.

Wisdom

Combined, all of our other virtues produce wisdom, and it is wisdom that caps off the model. Our six other virtues give us a mission to pursue, the stamina to pursue it, and the principles to keep it on track. These virtues help us see ourselves and our teams as we and they truly are. They help us understand the reason why we need to take care of others before taking care of ourselves, and they help us make personal sacrifices to further our missions and the well-being of others. They help us maintain the model through difficult and demanding periods, when it would be much easier, and less personally costly, to simply give up. They help keep our integrity, our wholeness between words and deeds, intact. Wisdom builds on all these things and takes them to the next level.

First off, wisdom allows us to serve our teams by putting ourselves and them into life's proper context. It allows us to recognize events clearly and to apply the proper mental model to the current situation. Without the ability to recognize the truth of our circumstances and quickly adapt to it, we cannot serve our teams well no matter how reflective and emotionally attuned we are. Our teams may be mission-oriented, productive, disciplined, and personally fulfilled, but if we are marching them off the edge of a cliff because we cannot see reality for what it is, then we have ultimately failed to lead them. For example, we may create the best work environment possible in pursuit of the most noble mission around, but if we are driving our institution toward bankruptcy, then we are doing our teams a great disservice.

Second, wisdom allows us to serve our teams by keeping them grounded in reality. We and they can only control so much. Life and life's events always have a vote in the results of our best efforts, and often those results are not the ones that we had planned. Wisdom allows us to realize the limits of our control and to translate those limits to our teams. It is what keeps them from deep disappointment, or outright quitting, when the results of their hard work and best efforts fall short of the goal. It is what keeps them motivated when the reality of life disrupts their carefully laid plans. Conversely, wisdom keeps our teams working hard at the things that they do control, knowing that these are the only areas in which they can make a difference and knowing that these are the things that they *should* be working on. Wisdom serves our teams by keeping them both balanced and focused because we ourselves are both balanced and focused.

Finally, wisdom allows us to translate to our teams the gifts that really matter—the joy inherent in another day of life, the benefit of hard work, the knowledge that work done well and intentionally makes us better at the work that we do. Wisdom helps us teach our teams that every day with life and every day with health is an unalloyed blessing, no matter how difficult the circumstances. What is more, wisdom allows us the perspective to realize that hard work is not simply a necessary response to continued time on earth; it is also a gift that helps make our lives better and us better at our lives. Wisdom puts life with all of its ups and downs in the proper perspective for our teams. Wisdom serves them by giving them a sense of meaning, belonging, and worth.

Like anything else worth doing, there is no shortcut to servant-leadership, no easy way to sustain this model over time. The only way to consistently apply this model to our teams and to our lives is to intentionally build our own character over the course of time. If we can do so, if we can pursue the virtues outlined in this book and pour them into our own lives, then we will find that the self-sacrifice required in servant-leadership comes more easily as the days, weeks, months, and years pass. What is more, we will find that we become the type of person that people want to follow, and, more important, the type of person that people want to become. Ultimately, that is what truly matters in life—the impact that we leave on the lives of others, the positive effect that we have on those whom we touch. If we can pursue character, and if we can lead by serving others, then we will find that no matter where life takes us and no matter where we end up, we can rest assured knowing that we made a difference, that our lives had meaning, that the world was just a little bit better for having had us in it.

And at the end of our days, that knowledge will be the greatest reward that we can hope for. Nothing else compares.

APPENDIX

Practical Application

During the Korean War, U.S. forces flying the F-86 fighter jet consistently outperformed their North Korean opponents flying the MiG-85, a Russian plane that was superior to the U.S. one in nearly every way—faster speed, better maneuverability, more armament, etc. However, there was one key difference between the two planes. The MiG-85 had a small, closed-in cockpit that gave its pilot a limited field of view. The F-86, by contrast, had a large, bubble-like cockpit that sat high up on the nose of the plane, giving its pilots a nearly 360-degree view of the surrounding airspace. Despite their plane's technical inferiority, the F-86 pilots usually prevailed in aerial dogfights because they were usually able to spot their opponents first. As a result, the American pilots began processing information necessary to make decisions well before their counterparts did.

American pilot and military strategist John Boyd noticed this phenomenon and from it derived a famous iterative theory of decision-making, called the OODA loop. Short for Observe, Orient, Decide, Act, this theory postulates that leaders who excel are ones who can most rapidly repeat an iterative decision-making cycle. They observe the phenomena around them, put their observations into context through analysis and synthesis, make decisions, and act on those decisions. Then they immediately begin to repeat the process. These leaders do not sit static in a single course of action; rather, they constantly observe and re-assess their environment, making course corrections as they observe the results of their actions. The better the leader, the faster they progress through this cycle.

As it is with strategic decision-making, so it is with the pursuit of virtue. To build our character, we need a series of steps that gives us a practical model to work our way through. In this model, we iterate through a defined series of steps, described as follows:

1. Reflect on ourselves.
2. Check into reality.
3. Set measurable goals.
4. Develop a cadence of accountability.

These steps build a character-creation cycle similar to Boyd's famous decision-making loop. Throughout this book, we have focused on the first step, reflection: asking ourselves hard questions to provoke thought. Now we will turn to the next three steps, starting by checking into reality.

CHECK INTO REALITY

The first step to helping determine the values that we are really pursuing—as opposed to the ones we hope we are pursuing—is to track where we spend three of our most precious resources: our time, our money, and our energy. This exercise helps us determine our actual missions—and to determine whether there is a breakdown between desire and reality—by showing us exactly where, and for what, we are willing to pay a tangible price. But without recording the hard facts, we risk falling victim to self-deception. We are much more prone to make up items that fit what we want to be rather than facing facts that reveal who we truly are.

Time

The first step to applying our character-building model is to track, for one month, exactly where we spend our assets, starting with our time. At the end of each day, we can write down where we spent our hours and minutes, using two-hour or four-hour blocks. *One important note: if this exercise is to be effective, it* must *be done every day. Otherwise, we will forget, and when we forget, we will guess, and when we guess, we will almost always be far too easy on ourselves.* It is not onerous: after the first week of practice, this exercise takes roughly five to ten minutes to complete every day.

As we think about how we break down our journal into categories, the following five buckets can be useful guides (or you can create your own—the key is to not overcomplicate the analysis with too many categories).

1. Work (including work done at home)
2. Family (family meals, outings, vacations, etc.)
3. Leisure
4. Community (church, volunteer work, time with friends and neighbors, etc.)
5. Maintenance (exercise, home repair, reading for personal improvement, etc.)

The key questions that this exercise answers are 1) what percent of our time are we actually spending in each area and 2) does this align with what we say we value? As we look at the numbers, are there any areas of clear imbalance with our values—for example, are we spending 85 percent of our waking hours at work but saying that we value our families more than our work? Are we saying that we care about our friends but spending virtually no time connecting with them each month?

Energy

In addition to spending the right hours in the right places, we need to expend the right energy in the right places. Energy is a fundamental unit of life and is routinely measured in everything from our home heating bills to the thruster lift on NASA space shuttles. For most of us, though, measuring the amount of energy we personally expend in the different areas of our lives is no easy thing, but we have to try. The fact of the matter is that we can spend significant time engaged in an area, but if we are not applying energy to what we are doing, then we are probably wasting our time.

Unfortunately, there is no clear measure—like hours or minutes—that we can use to help us analyze where we give the majority of our precious energy. However, there are a few principles that can help us. First off, we need to determine if we are actually engaged in an activity—that is, pursuing it in a focused and deliberate manner—while we are spending time in it. For example, we could be at home, physically alongside our children but mentally distant while we check our email on our cell phones. We are with our families but not engaged with them because we are giving them almost no energy. Conversely, we may be spending a significant amount of energy in an area without spending much "formal" time in it. For example, we might be at home with our children, wrestling on the ground with them while the outside world disappears for the twenty minutes before they go to bed.

Second, we can determine how tired we feel after spending time in any major area of our life. Are we exhausted after a day at work? An afternoon with our children? A dinner with our spouse? A late-night party that we helped plan? If we are pouring our energy into a particular area of our lives, it is highly likely that we will feel tired in its aftermath.

Finally, we can ask ourselves how deliberately we approach the various areas of our lives. For example, if we approach our family with a significant amount of forethought and planning—building a values statement, outlining questions to ask our children at dinner, constructing a date-night routine with our spouse, etc.—then we are probably spending a good amount of energy on our families even if we are not spending a large amount of time with them. Conversely, if we are spending significant time at home and doing nothing, just watching television, then we are probably not spending much energy on our families.

With these principles in mind, we can correlate our energy expenditure with that of our time. I recommend that we rank, on a scale of 1 to 5 (5 being significant energy, 1 being very little energy expended), the amount of energy we spend in each of our buckets, every day. At the end of the month, we can average our daily rankings to arrive at an overall total for the energy expended in each key area of time. If the time chart gives us quantity, then the energy chart gives us quality. In a perfect world, we would be putting significant amounts of quality time toward the areas we say we value most.

This exercise is likely to reveal that we do not live in a perfect world.

Money

In the same way that we track our time and energy, we can track our money. The principles of daily recording over the course of a month apply in this area just as they do in the above two. We can use the following buckets as a simple framework (or make one of our own using one of the thousands of financial planning books and tools available).

1. Fixed living expenses (house and car payments, student loans or tuition payments, credit card payments, etc.). These are the payments that you have to make but that are very hard to change in the short run.
2. Variable living expenses (groceries, gas, diapers, cell phone bill, etc.). These are the payments that you have to make but that can be changed, though not eliminated, relatively easily in the short run.
3. Entertainment expenses (meals out, movie rentals, etc.).
4. Consumption expenses. Anything bought that is nice but not *necessary* (new clothes, electronics, etc.).

5. Charity/giving.
6. Savings.

Analyzing our money outflows helps answer the same question as does analyzing our time: are we aligning our resources with our values? Wherever we log the majority of our hours and our energy will tell us what we serve with our time. Wherever we log the majority of our income dollars will tell us what we serve with our money.

As we look at the results, we are likely to find that there are some clear mismatches between what we want to believe we value and what our resources say we actually value. We may find that the missions that we pursue in reality are very different from the ones that we pursue in theory, and that what we want to pursue excellently are things that we pursue halfheartedly. If that is indeed the case, then we have taken the first step toward deliberately building our character: determining where we need to course-correct to get ourselves back on mission.

Virtue-Specific Tracking

Once we have built an overall picture of where we are investing our resources, we can move down to tracking some virtues more granularly, outlined as follows:

1. Humility: document every time in the course of a week that we publicly admit a mistake or ask for constructive criticism. Track the total times over the course of a month.
2. Courage: identify every time in the course of a week that we have an opportunity to disagree with an authority on a matter of principle or judgment. Distinguish between the times we actually spoke up and the times when we sat silent.
3. Kindness: separate our kind acts into two categories: large and small. Large ones are those that demand significant sacrifice of one of our resources, and they indicate the *range* of our virtue—that is, the extent to which we are willing to sacrifice to be kind to some-

one else. Small acts, by contrast, reveal the *frequency* of our kindness—that is, the routine by which we sacrifice. Put another way, large acts demonstrate the depth of our kindness while small acts demonstrate its breadth. Record each act in each of these two buckets every day for a month, and see how often we truly sacrifice to be kind to another.

4. Discipline: For one month, track every easy promise that we make shortly after we make it. We can use our cell phones, a notebook, or anything else that we carry with us both at work *and* at home. The home context is as important as the work one—too often we damage ourselves in this area by taking it for granted, and failure to apply discipline in this area inevitably bleeds over into others. At the end of the month, look at how many commitments we make, and how many we keep.

Doing all of the above exercises in the course of a single month may be a bit much, so we will want to first focus on tracking the virtues where we have the least clear insight into ourselves. No matter what we think we are or what we hope to be, checking our reality by gathering the facts will firmly ground us in where we are today, and where we need the most significant improvement.

SET MEASURABLE GOALS

Once we have gathered the data that tells us where we are currently investing our resources and where we are currently practicing (or not practicing) specific virtues, we can move on to the next phase of the cycle: setting measurable goals. Now that we know where we are, we can decide where we want to improve, and by how much. We should start with the same categories that we used to check into reality: time, energy, and money.

As we look at the five buckets of time outlined above, we need to ask ourselves which ones are the most important ones for us to do well in—

practical considerations aside. It helps to rank these buckets in order of priority. Next, we can look at the hours per week we spend in each bucket and set a target for each bucket, by week and by month, that roughly aligns with what we say we value. For example, if we say that our family is our number-one value, then we should probably be aiming to spend more time per week with our families than we do, say, exercising.

There is no right answer to how many hours — or what percentage of our time — we need to allocate to each bucket based on our values. And we very well may not get the balance right the first time. The important thing is the process of deliberately assessing where we spend our single most valuable resource and creating specific targets for where we *want* to spend our single most valuable resource. If you are at all like me, without a plan for time allocation you will probably spend your time indiscriminately, which generally means that you will allocate your time to whichever crisis is greatest.

Energy works the same way, although with energy it is a bit harder to set clearly measurable goals. I recommend simply using the metrics of high, medium, and low to determine the amount of energy we want to allocate to each of our buckets. For example, we may always want to be high energy in our community bucket, so we should expect that community events should generally leave us tired. We may want our leisure events to be low energy, so we might avoid taking up mountain climbing as a hobby.

With money, we are looking for opportunities to match our spending habits with our values. Do we say that we value community, for example, yet give no money to charities, or buy relatively few gifts for friends? Do we find that we are spending less money on family events than we are on trinkets for ourselves? As with time, there is no magic answer as to how much money should be spent in each category. The important thing is again the process of goal setting, of deliberately aligning our money out-flows with what we think is important.

Once we have set targets for our overall resource expenditure, we need to drill down to the virtues of humility, courage, kindness, and discipline and set specific goals for each of these. With humility, we can decide how many pieces of constructive criticism we solicit and receive per month. With courage, we can identify how many times we actually demonstrated moral courage when presented the opportunity to do so and set a goal of 100 percent of the time. With kindness, we can set a target for how many times per month we want to sacrifice our resources to meet the needs of another.

Setting measurable goals is a critical step in the cycle, but the resulting numbers are less important than the process of completing the step. It is this step that transforms reflection and facts into action. Taking what we have learned about ourselves, our lives, and our resources and setting specific targets for each forces us to start aligning who we are now with who we want to become. It brings clarity to what we are doing now and focus to what we want to do in the future. And it sets the stage for the next step—after all, if we do not have any goal, how can anyone hold us accountable?

DEVELOP A CADENCE OF ACCOUNTABILITY

Accountability, the final step before the cycle repeats itself, is what keeps us persevering toward the goals that we set. Put another way, setting measurable goals lays out the path for us, but developing accountability is what keeps us moving down that path. It is much easier to say what we are going to do than it is to actually go out and do it. Setting goals is the right start, but setting goals and achieving them—or even trying to achieve them—are two very different things. Typically we need to be prodded and encouraged along the way. A routine of accountability does just that.

Start with Ourselves . . .

To begin, we need to apply accountability to our own lives. We can start by identifying those people who tell us hard truths about ourselves. We need to find people who are not afraid to tell us things we do not want to hear because they have a genuine desire to make us better. Once we have found them, we need to construct an informal network of advisers from among these people. This concept is nothing particularly new. Indeed, the idea of a "personal board of directors" has come in vogue recently, especially given the number of leaders who have run their organizations, and themselves, blindly over a cliff. Self-help literature is full of ideas on how to surround oneself with highly qualified people who can help you to see what you yourself cannot. Many, myself included, think that this idea is exactly the sort of thing that friends—to use the old-fashioned word for "personal board of directors"—do for each other.

Unfortunately, the concept of authentic friendship and community seems to be dying, choked by an increasingly inauthentic, interconnected world that allows us ever more ways to carefully manage our image. And while the idea of constructive criticism often sounds attractive in theory, in practice it can be quite painful to subject ourselves to repeated exposure to our own faults and failings. It feels much better to ignore or explain away our weaknesses. In some cases, we may well accept feedback, but only in certain "safe" categories, like those involving business decisions or childhood education choices. The areas where we most need exposure are often the ones we most want to keep hidden. We are worried about what will happen if other people get to know the real us.

Still, no matter how hard we compartmentalize, our character is formed from actions across the entire spectrum of life. Expecting honest, transformative advice without exposing our true selves to others is a fool's hope. For example, hoping for good parenting advice when you are unwilling to reveal the state of your marriage is like asking a doctor to diagnose a heart condition when you are only willing to discuss your ankle pains. If we want effective advisers, and effective friends, then we must enter these relationships with full transparency and open up all areas of our lives to them.

Once we have the right friends and the right mindset, we need to set the right routine. Meeting with our friends and advisers is no different than anything else we want to do well at. If we want to do it well, we must do it often. Individual needs will vary according to individual circumstances, but I recommend meeting at least twice monthly with trusted friends. Once a routine is set, we must stick to it. Three missed meetings become a trend, and once we establish a trend, then we tell ourselves and our friends that we do not really care. After all, we never just "have" the time for anything in life. Rather, we *make* the time for what we find important.

... Move to Our Teams ...

In Chapter 2, we got a glimpse of the institutional accountability and learning process that the military has instilled: the after-action report. In the same way that the military applies this process to all of its teams, we can do the same to all of ours. To do so, we need to take our teams through an after-action review after any major event or project. This process is something very different from the typical end-of-year or semiannual review, as it focuses on an entire team rather than an individual and a specific event or project rather than a predetermined time period.

One helpful technique to get us started is to get the entire team to jointly build or review the event or project timeline, looking for key decision points, outcomes, and mistakes. The results of this piece of the exercise are very insightful. Just like in a firefight, it is rare that any single individual has a full view of all the decisions that led up to major actions and all of the consequences—intended or unintended—that resulted. It never fails that a team member will have seen or noticed or decided something of crucial importance that the rest of the team will have missed.

After the timeline is constructed, we need to understand what we did poorly *and* what we did well. Too often we focus only on the former—fear of loss is more powerful than love of gain, after all. We often ignore the latter, assuming that good work will happen of its own accord and that it will somehow be spread across our teams through osmosis, or perhaps telepathy. So as we move through the after-action process we need to solicit from each team member what they thought was bad and what they thought was good. We also need to ask ourselves the hard question:

did we accomplish what we set out to, and, if not, did we accomplish less or did we accomplish more?

It is as important to know and propagate our strengths and best practices as it is to shore up our weaknesses. We can spend a lot of time and effort reacting, closing one barn door after another, or we can spend our time creating, building better barns from the get-go. Understanding what our teams did poorly accomplishes the former. Understanding what our teams did well—and replicating that as widely as possible across organizations—does the latter. What is more, it raises morale.

Moreover, as leaders we often forget to celebrate success. It is easy to take positive outcomes for granted—just another something that comes with the job. However, it seems that we never hesitate to come down harshly when major mistakes are made. The tendency to ignore the good yet treat the bad with extreme seriousness can lead to a tremendously unbalanced and beaten-down organization. I once worked for a company where senior leadership—myself included—spent almost no time and energy thanking people for their hard work after we successfully completed complex projects. However, we spent two hours every other week grilling frontline employees about manufacturing jobs that had gone awry.

Thus, implementing the after-action process with our teams helps keep us accountable to learn from our mistakes and to celebrate our successes. The process can take different forms in different contexts, but it is something that can be done in any environment. For example, in one of my first jobs, every Monday we had a team meeting that began with the question "What went well last week?" The very next question: "What went poorly?" Some weeks we had little to say, as everything was status quo. Other times we spent more than an hour discussing failures and successes. In many cases, I was surprised by what my team had to say. As often as not, our discussions revolved around how well we had functioned as a team or how poorly we had supported one another. Over time, team trends became readily apparent, for better and for worse. In other cases, issues in the broader competitive or business landscape were identified early, as different team members pointed out the same issues cropping up in their own separate spheres. As a result, we were able to spot local market trends relatively quickly and begin to plan our responses appropriately.

There are many ways to make the after-action process relevant to our context. We can do it at work with our teams, and we can do it around the dinner table at night by asking each child to list one thing that went well in their week and one that went badly and then exploring the results together. We can do it with our spouses by asking them the same question once the children go to bed. We can do it with our friends after a major social event, or (less pleasantly) a major confrontation. Wherever two or more are engaged in an enterprise together, the after-action process can keep teams accountable for adhering to a clear set of standards.

. . . And Finish by Building Our Own Code of Conduct

Thus far, our routine of accountability has focused on helping us achieve a set of specific, narrow goals. While they are the right place to begin, these narrow goals are not complete in and of themselves. Life's trials often have a way of surprising us in unplanned ways. At some point in time, we will find ourselves immersed in circumstances that we never imagined, facing a set of tests or decisions for which our immediate targets are irrelevant. In these cases, the question arises—now that we are in uncharted territory, what, exactly, can we be held accountable to? Is there anything tangible enough to help us navigate specific decisions but broad enough to be applicable to nearly any context?

The answer is yes. To help us set a standard of accountability that does not change with circumstances, we can establish our own personal Code of Conduct. Though it takes time and reflection, fortunately there is no need to reinvent the wheel to do this. We can model our own code after that of the military. To do so, we need to keep it short and break out the following three components:

1. Who we are and what we stand for, broadly speaking.
2. The things that we believe we must do.
3. The things that we believe we must not do.

Fortunately, the first component stems directly from our overarching mission. For example, the first element of my own code might be "*I am a Christian and a Campbell, a husband and a father. My role on earth is to glorify my Creator, honor my family name, love my wife, and raise my children well.*" Writing things down helps throw them in sharp relief—a code that begins with "*My goal in life is to make as much money as possible as quickly as possible*" somehow doesn't seem that appealing when stacked up against "*I am an American, fighting for freedom . . .*" Even if our first point is aspirational—what we want our life to be about rather than what it actually is about—it is still worth crafting, because crafting it will help us focus on bringing our actions into line with our aspirations.

Next, we need to identify, in broad brushstrokes, the few things that we must do during the difficult periods in our lives. For example, we could write that we will always take responsibility for our actions and those of our team, or that we will be generous to others no matter what our circumstances. It may seem clichéd to write down such simple things, but in trying circumstances the simplest things become complex and the easiest things become difficult. I have had days where just getting out of bed felt like a monumental task. Those days will come again, and when they do, I hope that I have something to refer to that can help ground me in how I should respond.

In addition to identifying the few things that we will do during difficult periods, we need to spell out with equal clarity the things we will not do under any circumstances. In the military's Code of Conduct, there are specific prohibitions for our soldiers: "I will never surrender . . . I will not accept special favors . . . I will give no information . . . I will make no disloyal statements." Knowing in advance what we want to avoid at all costs is extremely helpful if we want to say and do the right thing when the pressure is on. To guide ourselves, we can reflect on the ways in which we have struggled during times of both difficulty and leisure. For me, my failures include avoiding responsibility for mistakes, telling lies and half-truths, and envying those more successful or prosperous than I am as I walk through painful periods of life. If we know our most likely worst-case reactions to life's most probable worst-case circumstances, we can best guard against our own predicted weaknesses by writing down what, exactly, we will not do no matter how weak we are feeling or how much we are struggling.

In combat, I was issued a laminated version of the Code of Conduct. I carried it on me at all times in my right sleeve pocket. I do the same now, only I carry my personal Code of Conduct in my wallet, as my civilian uniform has far fewer pockets than my military one. When I am struggling, I pull out my code and read it and try to remind myself of what really matters. I try to remind myself of what I am ultimately accountable to, and why I took the time to spell it out. I remind myself of what I truly value—those things that I identified when I had a clear head, outside of the pressure of the immediate moment.

REPEAT

The character cycle is not a linear process. There is no end-state we can reach and declare victory at, no time at which we can announce that we have finally arrived at our long-sought destination. No, the character cycle is just that, and as long as we want to grow, we must move through it again and again. Some tools, like the Code of Conduct, will survive multiple cycles. Others, like our goals for each virtue, may last only one.

What is most important, though, is not how well we define each step but the rapidity with which we move through the process. As time passes, circumstances change, and we grow, we will need to reflect, analyze, set different goals, and establish different rhythms of accountability. The best leaders are the ones who move through this cycle the most quickly, the ones who constantly reinvent themselves based on new growth and new challenges. They are never content to rest. They are always learning more about themselves and the world around them and then transforming that learning into action.

———

So, the bad news about building character is that our work is never complete. The good news about building character is that our work is always necessary, and it is always worthwhile.

And the best news of all is that we can all do it. We can all make ourselves into the best possible versions of ourselves if we just take the time and make the effort. No matter what our circumstances, we can all rest secure knowing that character is not a lofty ideal that is incompatible with real-world living. It something that is very real and well within our reach.

All that we need to do is give our best efforts, every day.

ACKNOWLEDGMENTS

As with most things that work out in my life, I must begin by thanking my wife, without question my better half. Her wisdom, courage, and strength have supported our entire family through the best and worst of times. She has served as my moral compass, my counselor, my confidante, my best friend, and, yes, my first editor throughout this entire process. I could not ask for a better woman with whom to face life, and with whom to raise three daughters to be the best leaders they can become.

I must also thank my dear friend and agent, Eve Bridburg. First of all, I still cannot believe that someone with her talent and her wisdom ever took on a complete unknown like me. Second, throughout this entire process—from idea, to editing, to marketing and onward—she has served as an incredible source of advice and insight. I am fortunate that I get to write in concert with a woman of her caliber. I could not ask for a better agent and supporter. Most important, however, I could not ask for a better friend, and it is her friendship that I value most of all.

My editor, Will Murphy, also deserves praise for taking the work of a complete amateur—that would be me—and making it professional. Anything good in this book is a direct result of his wisdom, oversight, and editorial guidance. Any failures and shortcomings in this book are due solely to my own shortcomings. His assistant, Mika Kasuga, has also done an excellent job keeping me in line and on time.

My amazing parents, Donovan Jr. and Polly, have been true models of the servant-leader principle throughout my life. One of the reasons that the servant-leadership model that the Corps taught me seemed somewhat familiar was that my parents had been following it their entire lives. Growing up, I was privileged to watch my father sacrifice greatly for his family and for causes he knew to be right. No matter what hardship he faced, he never complained. My mother has been equally staunch, and equally generous with her time, teaching, and, yes, discipline.

Finally, I am deeply grateful to God for allowing me to be born to such parents and to be born in a country that afforded me the opportunity for health and education. I have now been made keenly aware of the fact that many in this world are born with none of the above. I am also deeply grateful that I was brought back from war alive and unharmed when so many others were not. Like most gifts, I did not deserve this one, and I can only hope that my life moving forward will fully honor the Giver of life.

ABOUT THE AUTHOR

DONOVAN CAMPBELL is a management and technology consultant and the bestselling author of *Joker One: A Marine Platoon's Story of Courage, Leadership, and Brotherhood*. He graduated from Princeton University and Harvard Business School, finished first in his class at the Marines' basic officer course, and served three combat deployments. He was awarded the Combat Action Ribbon, the Defense Meritorious Service Medal, and a Bronze Star with Valor for his time in Iraq and Afghanistan. After his combat tours he returned to Dallas, where he is now a consultant with Credera, a rapidly growing management and technology consulting company. He has lectured at Harvard Business School, the Air Force Academy, PepsiCo, and the Barbara Bush Celebration of Reading. He lives in Dallas with his wife and daughters.

Donovan Campbell is available for select readings and lectures. To inquire about a possible appearance, please contact the Random House Speakers Bureau at 212-572-2013 or rhspeakers@random house.com.